Metalinguistic
Development

Metalinguistic Development

Jean Émile Gombert

UNIVERSITY OF CHICAGO PRESS
CHICAGO

The University of Chicago Press, Chicago 60637
Harvester Wheatsheaf, Hertfordshire, England

Translation copyright © 1992 Harvester Wheatsheaf

ISBN: 0–226–30208–3 (cloth); 0–226–30209–1 (paper)

Originally published as *Le Développement Métalinguistique* © 1990
Presses Universitaires de France

This book is printed on acid-free paper

Library of Congress Cataloging-in-Publication Data

Gombert, Jean Emile.
  [Développement métalinguistique. English]
  Metalinguistic development / Jean Emile Gombert.
    p.   cm.
  Translation of: Le développement métalinguistique.
  Includes bibliographical references and index.
  1. Language awareness in children. 2. Metalanguage.
  3. Language acquisition.
I. Title.
P118.3.G6 1992
401'.93—dc20   91–41761
                                                       CIP

Contents

Preface

This work owes much to those people who, sometimes without knowing it, have influenced its author. It was Michel Moscato who once convinced him of the necessity for the experimental study of psychological phenomena. Pierre Gréco was, and remains, the scientific mind to whom the author is most indebted. Michel Fayol is today the theorist of cognitive development, the militant scientist and the research colleague who inspires, motivates and participates in his everyday work.

The first version of a text is often inelegant, imprecise and sometimes incorrect, and the final version of this work owes much to the readers of the initial manuscript who, by rights, should be considered as the co-authors of the finished product. Hervé Abdi, Michel Fayol, Marcel Frochot, Henri Lehalle, Daniel Zagar and, above all, Jean-Pierre Bellier may all lay claim to this status.

Finally, the driving force behind this research was often to be found outside the laboratory, and even outside the discipline. Jacqueline, André, Marie-Claire, Sophie, Franck and Charles-Edouard Gombert have all had a part to play in producing the finished document.

Pierre Gréco had agreed to write the preface to this volume. Illness prevented him. Like all those who knew him, he inspired in me an unwavering fascination and a profound admiration. It was he who supervised my thesis and his loss leaves me a scientific orphan. This book is dedicated to his memory.

Chapter 1

General considerations

Defining the term 'metalinguistics'

It is one thing to find an adequate way of treating the comprehension and production of language. It is quite another to succeed in adopting a reflexive attitude with regard to language objects and their manipulation. It is to this second task that a recently developed psycholinguistic tradition has given the name 'metalinguistics'.

The neologism 'metalinguistics' emerged only a short time ago. Between 1950 and 1960, linguists used this term to designate activities associated with *metalanguage*, a language composed of the entirety of words forming linguistic terminology (for example, syntax, semantics, phoneme, lexeme . . . as well as terms in more current usage, such as word, sentence, letter, etc.). In a more general sense, the word metalanguage is used to refer to the language, whether natural or formalized (as in logic), which is itself used to speak of a language. More precisely, as Benveniste (1974) emphasizes, this word refers to a language whose *sole* function is to describe a language. Thus the language itself must constitute the sole sphere of application for the entire vocabulary of the metalanguage.

The functional perspective which concentrates on the workings of language as used by real speakers has lent a particular importance to this level of language, in which the signifiers of language become the signified, and has accorded it a new status in the activity of language speakers.

In 1963 Jakobson divided the functions of language into principal functions and secondary functions. The principal functions are those which directly concern the three principal participants in situations of communication, namely the speaker, the addressee and that to which the message refers. He thus describes three principal functions: the *expressive function* (or emotive function), which concerns the speaker's involvement in what he or she says; the *connotative function*, which deals with the part of the message which is intended to influence the partner; and finally the *representative function* (or denotative function), which is centred on the referents of the message and thus on the content rather than on the speech act. The secondary functions, for their part, consist of: the *phatic function*, which is seen at work when language no longer serves to communicate a message but principally to maintain contact between two interlocutors (for example, the conversations of lovers or the exchange of polite formulae . . .); the *ludic and poetic function*, which corresponds to a playing on language (for example, plays on words as well as any poetic manipulation of language); and finally the *metalinguistic function*, which is concerned with the activity of speaking about words, the linguistic activity which takes language itself as its object.

In its linguistic sense, which has developed from Jakobson's ideas, metalinguistics is concerned with linguistic activity which focuses on language. Or again, as Benveniste (1974) writes, the metalinguistic ability refers to 'the possibility of raising ourselves above language, of abstracting ourselves from it, of contemplating it, whilst making use of it in our reasonings and our observations'. From this viewpoint, metalinguistics is limited by its dependence on the ability of language to refer to itself. But if this ability lies at the basis of metalinguistic activity, then it also implies, from the psychological viewpoint which we have adopted, a cognitive effort which goes far beyond the boundaries of strictly linguistic activity (if indeed this latter can, in isolation, possess any psychological reality). In the text which follows we shall go so far as to defend the idea that the reflexive use of language does not necessarily imply that the cognitive activity of the subject is metalinguistic in character.

Psycholinguistic conceptions

In his analysis of the subject, Chaudron (1983) characterized metalinguistic activities by the fact that they treat language as an object. And Content (1985) points out that this is an object whose properties can be studied by subjects who, in turn, are able to enjoy intuitive insights into it, construct hypotheses about it or acquire knowledge of it. Here we have an initial psycholinguistic definition which is accorded a differing significance by the increasingly numerous studies conducted within the subject field. At its most basic, it is the attention of the locutor that differentiates metalanguage from natural language for the psycholinguist. However, this is the point at which consensus ends. In fact, depending on one's chosen author, the emphasis shifts between the declarative aspect of metalinguistic awareness, its procedural aspect, or a balance between the two.

One group of authors defines the field of metalinguistics as the subject's *knowledge* of the characteristics and functioning of language (C. Chomsky, 1979; Downing, 1979) or, from a more functionalist perspective, of its structure, its functioning and its usage (Bredart and Rondal, 1982). Within this perspective, Read (1978) correlates the primary linguistic ability of knowing something and the metalinguistic capacity of knowing that one knows it. Here the primary criterion is provided by subjects' *awareness* of their declarative knowledge of language. To this same tradition, which insists that language is an *object of thought*, but is more intent on situating metalinguistic functioning in the activity of the subject (or more influenced by the Piagetian tradition), belong the definitions which describe metalinguistic activity in terms of *reflection* on language, its nature and its functions (Pratt and Grieve, 1984*b*; Van Kleeck, 1982). This idea is sometimes distinguished from the narrow linguistic conception by the insistence on the notion that this reflection does not bear solely on the rules of a particular language but on language activity in its entirety (Boutet *et al.*, 1983). For her part, Kolinsky (1986) not only defines metalinguistic ability as the awareness of language as an object, but also insists that this object has a particular structure. This insistence is important for the attempt to study the specific nature of metalinguistic functioning with reference to other reflective activities concerning other products or other cognitive processes (see the section devoted to metacognition below).

Other authors, viewing the question from a different perspective, attempt to characterize metalinguistic activity as a part of the treatment of language, whether this is in terms of production or comprehension. From this point of view, metalinguistic activity is characterized by an *intentional monitoring* which the subject applies to the processes of attention and selection which are at work in language processing (Cazden, 1976; Hakes, 1980). Cazden (1976) points out that the ability to use language, like any other behavioural ability, normally requires no particular cognitive effort, and that this process functions effectively without conscious control. However, there are times when certain aspects of language itself become the principal object of attention. Referring to the retrieval of vocabulary, Cazden provides the example of stopping to search for a word. This type of activity demands a metalinguistic awareness which is defined as 'the ability to make language forms opaque and attend to them in and for themselves' (p. 603). With this formulation, which excludes neither the aspect of 'awareness of language' nor the aspect of control, the author evokes individuals' ability to distance themselves from the normal usage of language, and thus to shift their attention from the transmitted contents to the properties of language used to transmit them.

In the same way, other authors propose (either explicitly or implicitly) definitions which encompass both declarative and procedural aspects without appearing to consider that these are two distinct instances of metalinguistic activity. This is particularly true of the Australian team headed by Tunmer (Pratt *et al.*, 1984; Tunmer and Bowey, 1984; Tunmer and Herriman, 1984), which speaks simultaneously of reflection on and manipulation of the structural characteristics of language and control of the mental mechanisms implied in the processing of language. As Kolinsky (1986) points out, it would be better to separate these two instances, and indeed this is what is done explicitly by Martlew (1983) and, above all, by Bialystok (Bialystok, 1986*b*; Bialystok and Ryan, 1985*a*, *b*).

For Bialystok, metalinguistic activities include, on the one hand, the analytical activities concerned with linguistic knowledge which are performed by the subject and, on the other, the activities which control linguistic processes, controls which presuppose the selection and coordination of information within a context of temporal constraints. Bialystok postulates a relative independence between these two 'cognitive dimensions' of metalinguistic ability. The analysis of knowledge is necessary whenever the situation in which linguistic processing occurs is devoid of the extralinguistic contextual signs which generally make unreflected production or comprehension possible. Conscious cognitive control intervenes whenever the situation requires an objective consideration of the formal aspects of language at the expense of its meaning. Arguing against this in her commentary on the Bialystok model, Menyuk (1985) asserts that these two dimensions are not independent and that the former capacity necessarily precedes the latter, since awareness of the structural characteristics of a language is a prerequisite for their intentional application by subjects in their own language-processing activities ('we cannot use knowledge which we do not have': p. 256).

Linguistic usage and psycholinguistic usage

Whichever definition we decide to adopt, the psycholinguistic meaning of the term 'metalinguistic' is thus broader than that which linguists give to the concept. Linguistically speaking, metalinguistics covers everything which has to do with metalanguage. In other words, the linguist identifies the 'metalinguistic' by examining verbal productions in order to find those linguistic features which indicate the existence of self-referential processes (the use of language to refer to itself). Psychologists, in contrast, analyze the behaviour (verbal or otherwise) of the subject to discover elements which permit them to infer cognitive processes of conscious management (reflection on or intentional control over) of the language objects, either as objects *per se* or in terms of the use to which they are put.

This terminological distinction is not superfluous. In effect, what some consider to fall within the sphere of the metalinguistic will not necessarily do so for others. Thus the ability to adapt a verbal message to the different parameters of the context of emission (see the chapter on metapragmatic development below) will be metalinguistic for the psychologist, provided that the adaptation is performed voluntarily by the subject. However, if this adaptation is not accompanied by some identifiable mark of self-reference, linguists will avoid such a categorization, with only the most functionalist amongst them emphasizing the metacommunicative character of this ability (metacommunication then refers solely to the nonverbal aspects of communication: see the section below describing this concept). In contrast, the comments made by young children about their own language, which for the linguist are unambiguously metalinguistic productions, do not necessarily point to a metalinguistic ability from the psychologist's point of view. For this to be the case, it is first necessary to establish the conscious, reflective nature of the cognitive activity determining the production.

At this point in our summary it is necessary to refute a contradiction which is apparent only but is the source of much fruitless argument. The linguist's exclusive object of study is language. From this viewpoint, it is the *metalinguistic utterance* which is capable of providing an object of study for the discipline, and the extralinguistic factors which intervene in the production of this utterance can be considered only as secondary. In contrast, some of these factors constitute the focus of attention for psychologists. For them, the only legitimate way to qualify a *linguistic production* is by reference to the psychological factors (and particularly the cognitive factors) which determined it. The psychologist speaks of metalinguistic *awareness*, *ability*, *behaviour* and *attitudes*, and there is no reason why the corresponding productions should admit of the same classifications that are used by the linguist, who understands such productions as utterances. If they are to complement one another, it is best that these two fields of study and the points of view which they imply are accorded their own separate delimitations.

Metacognition

Following the ideas of Flavell (1976, 1978, 1981; Flavell and Wellman, 1977), a large number of authors have considered that metalinguistic capacities form an integral part of the general heading 'metacognition'.

In 1976 Flavell provided the following definition of metacognition:

> Metacognition refers to one's knowledge concerning one's own cognitive processes and products or anything related to them, e.g. the learning-relevant properties of information or data. For example, I am engaging in metacognition (metamemory, metalearning, meta-attention, metalanguage, or whatever) if I notice that I am having more trouble learning A than B; if it strikes me that I should double-check C before accepting it as a fact; if it occurs to me that I had better scrutinize each and every alternative in any multiple-choice type task situation before deciding which is the best one; if I sense that I had better make a note of D because I may forget it. ... Metacognition refers, among other things, to the active monitoring and consequent regulation and orchestration of these processes in relation to the cognitive objects or data on which they bear, usually in the service of some concrete goal or objective. (p. 232)

In short, metacognition refers to all knowledge which has as its object, or regulates any aspect of, any cognitive task. It is what Flavell (1981) describes in the concise formulation 'cognition about cognition' (p. 37). In fact, as Reynolds and Wade (1986) emphasize, even if the term 'metacognition' is relatively new, the concept is far from being so. Thus these authors quote Vygotsky who, in 1934, described the development of what we now call meta-attention and metamemory:

> Attention, previously involuntary, becomes voluntary and increasingly dependent on the child's own thinking: mechanical memory changes to logical memory guided by meaning, and can now be deliberately used by the child. One might say that both attention and memory become 'logical' and voluntary, since control of a function is the counterpart of one's consciousness of it. (Vygotsky, 1934/1962, p. 90)

In contrast to what has been said with reference to the definitions of the term 'metalinguistic', all are agreed that metacognition embraces the introspective awareness of cognitive states and their operations as well as individuals' ability to control and plan their own thought processes and their products.

As far as the introspective aspect of metacognition is concerned, it is possible to draw a parallel with what Piaget termed *operational knowledge*, which is characterized by subjects' ability to transform their own knowledge to conform to the requirements of the task with which they are confronted. Indeed, this is the path followed by Bialystok and Ryan (1985*b*) when dealing with this aspect of metalinguistic ability. The question which then arises is: 'is the concept of metacognition of any real use (even if this is only instrumental), or is it simply a change of terminology without any heuristic import?' The relevance of such a question is underlined by the model put forward by Kitchener (1983). This author bases her argument on the idea that the mechanisms of metacognitive control described in the literature are most often applied to very simple tasks and are inadequate for the successful comprehension of problems whose outcome is probabilistic (this is the case in the majority of cognitive problems with which adults are confronted in their everyday lives). For this reason, she postulates that from adolescence onwards there exist high-level control processes (at the 'meta-metacognitive' level) which allow us to resolve those problems which have an indeterminate outcome. She classes these meta-metacognitive processes under the term 'epistemic cognition'. The course from primary knowledge to metacognition (which appears later) to *epistemic cognition* encapsulates the whole of the Piagetian developmental model. However, this does not appear to be a question of simple redundancy. In fact – recalling the terminology which was fashionable in Geneva in the 1970s – the metacognitive approach may be thought of as a 'procedural' operationalization of Piaget's 'structural' model. This approach is capable of greatly enhancing the heuristic significance of the Piagetian model and seems to us to be better described by the classification 'neo-Piagetian' than other approaches in terms of information processing and the limitations of working memory (however, these two approaches are not mutually exclusive and are, indeed, frequently complementary). Moreover, the scope of metacognition is more restricted than that of cognition, whose development has been studied by Piaget. It is limited to the process of 'reflection' and by no means extends to the totality of cognitive processes at work in the processing of information.

Apart from metalinguistic ability, the most frequently cited 'meta-abilities' are: *metalearning*, which refers to the knowledge and control of the learning processes; *meta-attention*, which describes the ability to pay attention voluntarily; *social metacognition*, which designates knowledge of the cognitive processes at work in other people, along with their behavioural implications; and finally *metamemory*, which shares with the metalinguistic the distinction of being the most frequently cited and studied of the 'meta-abilities'.

At the most general level, metamemory corresponds to the ability to control one's own memory (Schneider, 1985) and thus constitutes the conceptual link between memory and intelligence (A. L. Brown, 1978). In some ways this ability is the prototype of the metacognitive ability in that it is easy to distinguish here, as Flavell (who has been using the term since 1970) has done, between the aspect of declarative knowledge of the factors which affect individual mnemonic performances – Wellman and Johnson (1979) add the understanding of the verbs 'to remember' and 'to forget' – and the procedural aspect involved in the voluntary effort to add to or retrieve from memory (see, for example, Flavell, 1981).

If, as has been indicated above, the majority of authors consider that metalinguistic abilities form part of the general heading 'metacognition', this position is certainly not a unanimous one. In fact this conception, which implies the primacy of the metacognitive over the metalinguistic, is opposed by that of Gleitman *et al.* (1972), which sees a total separation between the two fields, which are simply linked by a number of underlying skills, themselves dependent on the general development of consciousness. A third point of view, represented by E. V. Clark (1978), postulates both differences and intersections between metalinguistic and metacognitive abilities. Finally, taking Piaget's model as a starting point, Van Kleeck (1982) attempts to reconcile the last two points of view. For her, metalinguistic abilities on the one hand, and metacognitive abilities on the other, are both dependent on cognitive development. They should thus be distinguished as specific abilities which may overlap when realized by subjects as new areas of competence. Even if this debate remains marginal, it is important for the psycholinguist to situate metalinguistic abilities as clearly as possible in relation to other cognitive abilities.

At the beginning of this section we recalled Flavell's (1981) definition of metacognition: 'cognition about cognition'. What, then, is the nature of the other meta-abilities: is metalearning 'learning about learning'; is meta-attention 'attention to attention'; is metamemory 'memory of memory'? Certainly not! The most suitable general characterizations are: cognition about learning; cognition about attention; cognition about memory. In the same way – and here we encounter the difference in viewpoint between linguists and psycholinguists – metalinguistic activity refers not to language about language but to cognition about language, and is a fully fledged member of the set of metacognitive activities. However, the cognitive products on which metalinguistic reflection in part bears (language objects) manifest peculiarities which invest this subfield of metacognition with completely original characteristics. They are the symbolic objects which are, nevertheless, easily perceived and are probably more frequently (quantitatively speaking) manipulated by the child than any other. Their importance for the general development of thought – and, more specifically, for metacognitive development – could thus be crucial.

Metaprocesses, epiprocesses

The exposition above demonstrates the existence of a relative consensus that metalinguistic activities (as well as the other metacognitive activities) can be deemed to acquire their metalinguistic status only if they are consciously performed by the subject and if, because of this, their emergence supposes that the child is in possession of a capacity for reflection and intentional self-monitoring. This does not imply that cognitive activity in the young child is not monitored before the appearance of this capacity. Indeed, Karmiloff-Smith (1983) goes so far as to write that metaprocesses are 'an essential component of acquisition, which continuously function at all levels of development, and do not merely occur as a late epiphenomenon' (pp. 35–6). In fact, Karmiloff-Smith uses the term metaprocess to cover a broad scope of meaning which leads her to distinguish between 'unconscious meta-processes' and others (later ones) which are accessible to the consciousness and can be verbally reported (Karmiloff-Smith, 1986, 1987). This classification within a wide category which includes the totality of processes 'which operate on the internal representations themselves' (Karmiloff-Smith, 1983, p. 36), whether they are conscious or not, finds an echo in Kolinsky's (1986) account of metalinguistic activity which, following Hakes (1980), distinguishes between early episodic metalinguistic behaviour and later metalinguistic behaviour which can be induced by external stimulation. In the same way, the definition of 'metalinguistics' given by Levelt et al. (1978) includes both the phenomena which they themselves situate at the limits of consciousness (such as the spontaneous self-repairs performed by the young child) and other phenomena which are clearly the result of real, explicit reflection on language. It is the admission of so large a definition that has led a number of authors to postulate the existence of early metalinguistic activity before the age of $4\frac{1}{2}$ to 5, some indeed putting this as early as the age of 2 (see below).

In fact, it seems as if the same word is used to designate phenomena whose similarity is due to an observational bias. In 1984, Gilliéron wrote: 'All awareness is necessarily "meta" from the point of view of the observer. It bears not on the real but on the intelligibility of the real.' The relevant psychological description cannot be made in the abstract. It requires that researchers and theorists widen their focus to the point where they can embrace the significance of behavioural acts in the cognitive context of the subjects who perform them. Following Bredart and Rondal (1982), Chaudron (1983) and Kolinsky (1986), we are of the opinion that it is necessary to distinguish between the skills observed in spontaneous behaviour on the one hand and, on the other, the abilities which are based on systematically represented knowledge and can be intentionally applied. More than a difference of degree, this is a qualitative difference in cognitive activity itself which seems to us to delimit these two groups of behaviour. For reasons of terminological clarity, therefore, it is necessary to avoid designating the two groups by the same name.

A satisfactory manner of indicating this distinction clearly might be the systematic use of the expression 'metalinguistic skill' to designate linguistic knowledge applied more or less automatically without reflection or deliberate decision on the part of the subject. The expression 'metalinguistic ability' would then be reserved for situations where this intentional, reflective character is established (for a discussion of the distinction between 'skills' and 'abilities', see Ammon, 1981). However, quite apart from the fact that these expressions do not easily admit of adjectival usage, we are obliged to note that in the past they have been used without distinction in the literature to refer to both concepts (even if a number of authors do appear to make an implicit distinction). While attempting to respect this distinction, we are thus forced to search elsewhere for our terminological differentiation.

In 1968 the French linguist Antoine Culioli wrote:

Language is an activity which itself supposes a perpetual epilinguistic activity (defined as 'unconscious metalinguistic activity'), as well as a relationship between a model (*competence*, that is to say, the appropriation and acquired mastery of a system of rules operating on units) and its realization (*performance*) which provides us with phonic or graphic records, or *texts*. (p. 108)

The concept of *epilinguistics* has enjoyed very little success and has never spread beyond the frontiers of the French-speaking world (with the exception of the brief usage made of it, with a different meaning, by Karmiloff-Smith, both a French- and English-speaking author, in 1979*a*). Nevertheless, the term has been used by a number of French-speaking linguists and psycholinguists, and seems perfectly adequate for the class of phenomena which we want to describe. *We shall employ the term 'epilinguistic' to designate the 'unconscious metalinguistic activities', supposing by definition that a reflective, intentional character is inherent in metalinguistic activity in the strict sense of the term* (just as before – Gombert, 1987; Gombert and Fayol, 1988 – we shall differentiate more generally between *epiprocesses* and *metaprocesses*). For Culioli, these epilinguistic activities are implicated in all language behaviour and thus represent the implicit self-reference which is automatically present in all linguistic production. This conception is inherent in the linguistic meaning legitimately assigned to the term 'metalinguistic' by Culioli. The semantic slippage which occurs in the psycholinguist's use of this term thus logically recurs in the use of the term 'epilinguistic'. We shall therefore reserve the term 'epilinguistic' for the designation of behaviour which is related to metalinguistic behaviour but whose unconscious nature appears to be established.

If we call epiprocesses those 'unconscious metaprocesses' which govern epilinguistic behaviour, it could easily be agreed that they are at work in all linguistic behaviour whose control level lies beyond the initial, purely associative, response that often constitutes the child's first deictic utterances, vocal games, greetings, or ritual usages (see, for example, Nelson, 1974). However, epilinguistic behaviour is the only kind of behaviour in which the action of epiprocesses is manifest in the behaviour itself.

Insisting on the criterion of the reflective and intentional character of metalinguistic behaviour allows us to differentiate clearly between the concept of *metalinguistic competence* and Noam Chomsky's concept of *linguistic competence*. In fact, the latter concept refers to the speaker's unconscious knowledge of the set of rules which determine the grammaticality of sentences. This is what Chomsky (1965) called *tacit knowledge*. Under no circumstances does linguistic competence require that individuals should be able to give an explicit account of the rules they follow while speaking or listening. In other words, *linguistic intuition* does not form part of the field of metalinguistics. As far as the 'epilinguistic' is concerned, the restriction and displacement which we have applied suffice to differentiate it from the concepts of generative grammar.

It is becoming clear that one of the major problems faced by the psycholinguist who is interested in metalinguistic development is that of demonstrating the conscious character of mental activity. Traditionally, the subject's ability to provide an explicit verbal statement of the determining factors of his or her own behaviour has been seen as proof of consciousness. Unfortunately, this introspective approach is not always satisfactory. Indeed, even if on an initial analysis we can qualify as 'conscious' those cognitive processes which can be explained by the subject (and again, the possibility of reconstructing a plausible explanation *a posteriori* cannot be excluded), it is clear that the failure to explain does not necessarily imply lack of consciousness. E. V. Clark (1978) indicates that this is all the more true when one turns to the case of young children, from whom it is difficult to expect a clear commentary on a language which they have only just begun to acquire. However, as Kolinsky (1986) recalls in a reference to Piaget (1974*a*, *b*), the fact that verbalization is not a sufficiently sensitive criterion to establish consciousness does not imply that it has no role to play in metalinguistic development. In particular, the Piagetian theory which states that attempts to verbalize an action may help the subject to accede to a higher level of consciousness could be extended to cover linguistic actions.

If lack of consciousness is difficult – or, indeed, impossible – to establish in connection with spontaneous behaviour, it remains possible to demonstrate its likelihood in experimental situations. To do this it is necessary to show that the adapted behaviour observed in the resolution of metalinguistic tasks (for example, a task of grammatical correction) does not differ from the behaviour caused by similar nonmetalinguistic tasks or tasks which demand conscious control but where the expected effect is the opposite of that predicted for the first task (for example, a task which requires the verbatim repetition of ungrammatical sentences; see below). A second approach – which, though promising, causes problems that are difficult to resolve when young children are the objects of study – might be the analysis of subjects' response times. Here, however, there is a risk of confusion between control and consciousness.

Metalanguage, metacommunication and metapragmatic abilities

The degree of formalism in the varying situations of language treatment is not irrelevant to the question of whether, for the resolution of a set linguistic problem, a truly metalinguistic functioning rather than simply an epilinguistic one is required. For example, Bialystok and Ryan (1985*a*, *b*) suggest that conversations taking place within natural contexts require little explicit knowledge of language and little intentional control, since the interlocutors' attention is focused on meaning. On the other hand, tasks of the reading and writing kind would require a higher level of metalinguistic activity. The authors explain this difference by using the distinction between *metacommunicative* tasks and *metalinguistic* tasks, where metacommunicative control, in which the subject's attention is focused on the communicative intention, is cognitively less costly and less complex – and therefore obtained at an earlier age – than metalinguistic control, which demands the ability to focus attention on formal aspects.

For Flavell (1977, 1978, 1981), *metacommunication* refers to the subject's awareness of the factors which are at work in any behaviour involved in communicative activity, whether verbal or nonverbal, and, in particular, awareness of the factors connected with interacting individuals, those connected with the task to be accomplished and those linked with the strategy of the speaker. Van Kleeck (1984) proposes a slightly different definition. This author suggests that metacommunication refers solely to the nonverbal aspects of situations of verbal communication, and that it is thereby distinguished from metalinguistic reflection about language itself. Thus metacommunicative activity would simultaneously refer to the flow of conversation and the extralinguistic context in which a particular production has to be interpreted (exchanges of looks, postures, imitation, contact, interpersonal distance, intonation, dress, etc.). Seen from this perspective, 'the metacommunicative' would no longer be able to overlap 'the metalinguistic'.

The debate concerning whether an overlap between these two fields exists or not does not directly concern us here. In fact, the question whether metalinguistics forms a part of metacommunication or not will not, in the first instance, affect the analysis of metalinguistic behaviour but rather that of metacommunicative behaviour, and we do not intend to deal with this latter analysis here. However, it is important to distinguish between metacommunicative behaviour and *metapragmatic* behaviour, which will be the object of a later chapter of this book.

For Bates (1976), metapragmatic awareness corresponds to the subject's conscious awareness of the social rules of language (words and expressions which are suitable for use in any particular situation, ways of speaking, ways of conducting a conversation, etc.) as they are reflected in his or her own explicit comments. Referring to this definition, Van Kleeck (1984) excludes metapragmatic behaviour from the field of metalinguistics, just as she excludes the metacommunicative, by arguing that metapragmatic activity bears on the social use of language, not on language itself. This standpoint is not shared by Hickmann (1983), who defines the metapragmatic ability as 'a particular metalinguistic ability, namely the ability to represent, organize and regulate the use of speech itself' (p. 21).

If we accept that metalinguistic activity covers the totality of activities which suppose a reflection on and/or intentional control over language, then metapragmatic activities seem to us to correspond naturally to those metalinguistic activities which bear on the pragmatic aspects of language – aspects which, according to Bates herself, cover the entire set of 'indexical rules that link a linguistic form to a given context' (1976, p. 3). We shall therefore adopt Hickmann's stance, in view of the fact that it seems difficult to exclude metapragmatics from metalinguistics without also excluding pragmatics from the language of linguistics, an undertaking which would run counter to the development of the discipline. Whereas a linguist might take the risk, any psycholinguist who adopted such a position would risk drastically reducing his or her field of research.

As far as metacommunication is concerned, the necessity of limiting the overlaps between concepts has led us to adopt Van Kleeck's position.

However, we continue to suggest that awareness of the nonverbal aspects of situations of verbal communication is independent of the linguistic characteristics of the speech used, and thus corresponds to an awareness of the factors at work in all communicative activity, whether verbal or not. Here we encounter another terminological slippage of linguistic meaning, with linguists – following Watzlawick *et al.* (1967) – generally using the concept in a restrictive manner to refer to the illocutionary acts which arise in a particular exchange (see Caffi, 1984).

Conclusion

With reference to the use of certain Piagetian concepts, our mentor Pierre Gréco (1980) wrote:

> We can term whatever we want 'scheme' or 'operation', provided that the chosen definition allows us to observe the observable without too much subtlety or hypocrisy. (p. 633)

This appears to be an invitation to come to some firm decision about the seemingly unavoidable polysemy of the concepts presented in this introductory chapter. Therefore, throughout the text which follows, the following definitions will apply:

Metacognition: a field covering: (1) introspective, conscious knowledge possessed by particular individuals about their own cognitive states or processes; (2) the ability of these individuals intentionally to monitor and plan their own cognitive processes with the aim of realizing a deliberate goal or objective.

Metaprocesses: cognitive processes which are accessible to the consciousness involved in metacognition.

Metalanguage or metalinguistic activities (different from 'metalanguage' in its linguistic meaning; see above): subfield of metacognition concerned with language and its use – in other words comprising: (1) activities of reflection on language and its use; (2) subjects' ability intentionally to monitor and plan their own methods of linguistic processing (in both comprehension and production). These activities and abilities may concern any aspect of language, whether phonological (in which case we speak of *metaphonological activities*), syntactic (*metasyntactic activities*), semantic (*metasemantic activities*) or pragmatic (*metapragmatic activities*).

Epilinguistic activities: behaviour manifested from an early age which is related to metalinguistic behaviour but is not (and has never been – see Chapter 8) consciously monitored by the subject. Such activities in the subject's behaviour are, in fact, explicit manifestations of a functional awareness of the rules of the organization or use of language.

Epiprocesses: processes which are inaccessible to consciousness, are manifested in epilinguistic activities (and, more generally, in *epicognitive* activities) and participate in the management, regulation and monitoring of linguistic processing (or other complex tasks).

This division of metalinguistic activity into a number of specific activities is somewhat artificial. The psychologist would doubtlessly prefer a classification which pays more attention to the specificities and levels of complexity of the cognitive processes implied by different instances of metalinguistic behaviour. Although such a classification may remain a desirable long-term aim, it seems to us to be premature. Moreover, each of the subfields cited above groups together studies which are related to one another, whilst the subfields themselves remain separate. This imperative, which is by nature pedagogic, will lead us to use the different levels of linguistic analysis mentioned above as a framework for our exposition. The chapters which follow will thus deal in succession with metaphonological development, metasyntactic development, metasemantic development and metapragmatic development. Broadening our perspectives, we shall then devote a chapter to textual metalinguistic development, a subject generally ignored in the literature, followed by a chapter dealing with the specificities of the manipulation of the written language. Finally, we shall attempt a synthesis of metalinguistic development before returning briefly, at the conclusion of our discussion, to the concept of 'consciousness' which is central to the entire work.

Chapter 2

Metaphonological development

Introduction

The meaning of the term *metaphonology* here is different from that given by Boysson-Bardies *et al.* (1984) or Oller *et al.* (1985), who use the term to qualify the parameters which play a role in establishing phonology – in other words, those which specify linguistic sounds in relation to other sounds. As a specific metalinguistic ability, *the metaphonological ability corresponds to that of identifying the phonological components in linguistic units and intentionally manipulating them* (this is what is generally called 'phonological awareness' in the English-speaking tradition). This field of study is, without doubt, the most homogeneous of those addressed in this volume (for detailed reviews of the question, see Content, 1984, 1985; Morais *et al.*, 1987*a*; Nesdale *et al.*, 1984). In particular, Paul Bertelson's Brussels team, whose work is frequently cited, has spent several years developing a uniquely rich collection of research.

Following other authors, Content (1985) suggests a clear distinction between the ability to analyze speech explicitly into its phonological components and the unconscious and automatic processes of analysis by which language is habitually perceived and understood. It is one thing to identify linguistic behaviour which supposes the ability to extract and take into account phonological units of varying size, but it is quite another to apprehend a word as an object and to realize that it is made up of isolatable segments, namely syllables and phonemes. It is the manifestation and development of this latter ability that we shall concentrate on here.

The first part of this chapter will review the available data on the early skills of distinguishing linguistic sounds – skills which constitute a prerequisite not only for later metaphonological abilities but also for the comprehension of language. The emergence of metaphonological awareness will then be studied in the light of experiments devoted to the child's identification and counting of syllables and phonemes. The implementation of metaphonological control will be illustrated by the study of phonological manipulation, in particular by the interplay of analytical and synthetic tasks. In approaching this subject, our discussion cannot remain on a purely theoretical level. In fact, a valuable body of literature has been devoted to the study of the relationship between metaphonological ability and the performance of children learning to read, and this will provide the subject of the last part of this chapter. We shall then conclude with a summary and tentative synthesis of the reported data.

Early discrimination of linguistic sounds

An ever-increasing number of studies have unambiguously established that from their very first months, even their first days, babies are capable of distinguishing between very small differences in linguistic sounds (for an overview of this question, see Bertoncini, 1984).

For the most part, these studies use the experimental paradigm of habituation. In other words, they are concerned with the infant's response when confronted by a new stimulus, after a period of habituation to another stimulus. If a baby one month old or more is repeatedly presented with a sound (for example, /ba/, /ba/, /ba/, . . .), it will initially respond to the novelty (for example, by a slowing of the heartbeat or an increase in non-nutritive sucking), then, as the repetition continues, the level of response will diminish. If another sound (for example, /pa/) is then introduced into the repetition, a sudden increase in the level of response can be observed (Eimas *et al.*, 1971). This reappearance of the response to novelty points to the functional discrimination between the two sounds. If the baby had not perceived the difference between the two sounds, the curve of habituation would have continued to decrease (or remained constant if the initial level of response had already returned to the baseline, i.e. the normal level in the absence of stimulus). Similar results were obtained for the sounds /ba/ and /ga/, /ba/ and /ma/, /bi/ and /di/ or /si/, and for vowels. In fact, most of the phonetic contrasts seem to be distinguished as effectively by a baby as by an adult. In particular, as Bertoncini and Mehler (1981) have demonstrated, variations of phonemic features are better perceived in syllables (for example, /tap/ versus /pat/) than in nonsyllabic clusters of phonemes (for example, /tsp/ versus /pts/). Mehler (1986) has further shown that from five days old the newborn baby can distinguish its mother tongue from another language.

Given that the auditory system is functional several weeks before birth, these results could be linked in part to the auditory experience of the foetus during the intrauterine period. This has been suggested by the results obtained by DeCasper and Spence (1986) which demonstrate, by using non-nutritive sucking as an operant response, that newborn babies can distinguish a story read aloud every day by their mothers during the last six weeks of pregnancy from a formally similar story. In the same way, babies are capable of distinguishing the voice of their mothers, but not their fathers, from other voices (DeCasper and Prescott, 1984). These data are developed by Streeter (1976), whose results show that while there are some sounds which can be differentiated by all babies, there are others which can be distinguished only by those babies who have been confronted by examples of these sounds in the language they have listened to. These data are confirmed by studies showing that infants can discriminate between phonetic oppositions absent from the language of their family circle (see Lasky *et al.*, 1975). This would suggest the existence of a processing mechanism capable of functioning without prior exposure to the oppositions of sound under consideration. It is this which led Eimas (1985) to hypothesize the existence of an innate mechanism for the perception of language. This author thinks that the child, during the course of its development, would have retained, and in all probability refined, those perceptive abilities which correspond to the phonetic distinctions of its mother tongue, but would have lost the ability to detect the distinctions which do not exist in that language. This is why, for example, the Japanese cannot discriminate between the phonemes /r/ and /l/, which form an important opposition in other languages such as English or French (Miyawaki *et al.*, 1975).

While the innateness of certain general properties of the auditory system is indisputable, the same cannot be said for the existence of specific innate mechanisms for the perception of speech (Jusczyk, 1981). Working in a completely different sphere, Pisacreta *et al.* (1986) have demonstrated, by means of an operant-conditioning method, that pigeons can discriminate between certain words of spoken English. Other studies have demonstrated the existence of abilities for phoneme discrimination and categorization in the rhesus monkey and the chinchilla (see Kuhl, 1987*a*, *b*). Of course, no one is attempting to affirm that specific mechanisms for the perception of language exist in animals. In fact, as Bertoncini points out (1984, p. 43) in a study of the baby's perception of speech, 'many of the results can be explained as an acoustic processing of the characteristics contained within the signal, without it being necessary to postulate a distinct mode of perception'.

As Nesdale *et al.* have pointed out (1984), it is important to distinguish clearly between the early-acquired discrimination of sounds (be they linguistic or not) and the awareness of phonemes (this awareness being, by its very nature, metaphonological). The former is manifested at an earlier age than the latter and is, in all probability, automatic and involuntary in character both in the child and in the adult (to be convinced of this phenomenon in the adult, one need only attempt not to distinguish between /ba/ and /pa/).

Wallach *et al.* (1977) compare two groups of 5-to-6-year-old children, the first from a socially disadvantaged background and the second from a middle-class background. In a first test the children listened to a list of referents whose names were phonologically different only in the initial phoneme – for example, 'jail' and 'whale' – and had to select each of the objects from a picture. In a second test the names of all the referents were phonologically very different – for example, 'man' and 'house'. In this test the children had to pick out the representations of only those objects which began with a certain sound (for example, /m/). The first test simply involved discriminatory skills, while the second required conscious identification of a phoneme. The results show that while all the children, whatever their social background, were successful in the first test, only 50 per cent of the children in the socially disadvantaged group were successful in the second, whereas almost all the children in the other group were successful.

Beyond considerations of the effects of favourability of background, these results show that there is no direct relationship between the discrimination of linguistic sounds and the ability to distinguish phonemes. While the former is evidently a prerequisite for the latter, it does not on its own provide sufficient conditions for the latter to occur. In other words, the functional discrimination between two linguistic sounds does not imply conscious identification of the phonological difference between these sounds. These two types of language perception should therefore be clearly differentiated in the behaviour provoked by the tasks involved in any experiment designed for the study of metaphonological development.

Metaphonological identification

Differentiation between linguistic and nonlinguistic sounds

During a series of experiments, to which we shall refer frequently, C. L. Smith and Tager-Flusberg (1982) study the ability of children aged 3–5 to differentiate between 'speech sounds' and other sounds (for example, clicks and snores). In an initial training phase the subjects are individually presented with a collection of sounds, some of which are syllables while the rest consist of a variety of noises. The child has to decide whether each sound belongs to their language or not, with the examiner correcting any errors while the test progresses. Immediately after this training phase, an identical experimental phase (but without corrective feedback) begins. The levels of success attained (63 per cent in 3-to-4-year-olds and 67 per cent in 4-to-5-year-olds) are significantly greater than that of random choice (50 per cent. At P = 0.01, the limits of confidence are in the 40 per cent to 60 per cent range). Moreover, 22 per cent of 3-to-4-year-olds and 28 per cent of

4-to-5-year-olds gave at least nine correct answers out of the ten required. The authors use these results to support the theory of the existence of early-acquired metaphonological abilities. While there can be no doubt of the effectiveness of the observed performances, it is, nevertheless, doubtful whether they point conclusively to any reflection on language. What would be the result of a similar test using only nonlinguistic sounds (for example, one in which the subject has to differentiate between animal noises and other nonlinguistic sounds)? The most probable hypothesis is that similar success levels would be attained, thus invalidating the authors' interpretation but allowing for an interpretation in terms of the ability to discriminate and categorize sound stimuli. The existence of metaphonological awareness can be proved only by conscious discriminations performed within the phonological system of natural language.

Syllabic identification

Most of the works dealing with the conscious identification of syllables focus on the child's early-acquired identification of rhymes. This item of linguistic behaviour, which is common in everyday experience and reported in a large number of studies, does not lend itself easily to interpretation and generalization. Thus Nesdale *et al.* (1984) report Kate, aged 3, saying, 'Can I have a bit of cheese please? – cheese please – that's a rhyme.'

Lenel and Cantor (1981) used a forced-choice technique to examine the ability of children aged 4–7 years to identify rhymes. For example, each child was asked to choose which of the two words 'chair' and 'flag' rhymes with 'pear'. In the experimental phase which followed six attempts with corrective feedback, the level of success was 77 per cent in 4-to-5-year-olds, 83 per cent in 5-to-6-year-olds and 87 per cent in 6-to-7-year-olds. Using a similar technique, Smith and Tager-Flusberg (1982) obtained a corresponding result in 4-to-5-year-olds (79 per cent) and a 67 per cent success level in 3-to-4-year-olds. These authors further report that from the age of 3 onwards, 28 per cent of their subjects gave at least nine correct answers out of ten.

As several authors have stressed (see Content, 1985), it is becoming increasingly clear that success in this type of test does not require the specific identification of a syllable, and that it could perhaps be explained by the simple use of overall similarities between the words presented.

Moreover, Content *et al.* (1986c) show that there is no correlation between performance in tests of the ability to recognize rhymes and performance in other metaphonological tests, and that this is as true of 'normal' 6-to-7-year-old children as it is of 6-to-9-year-old dyslexic children, illiterate adults and adults who have learned to read in adolescence.

In fact, the only experiment which can be related to a metaphonological discrimination of syllables seems to be that performed by Liberman (1973;

Liberman *et al.*, 1974) which required children of 5, 6 and 7 to repeat multisyllabic words and then to tap once on the table for each syllable in the word. The experimental phase, which comprised 42 attempts, followed a training phase consisting of 12 attempts. In both phases the children were provided with explicit corrections of their mistakes. Taking six consecutive correct answers as a criterion for success, the success rate was 46 per cent in 5-year-olds, 48 per cent in 6-year-olds and 90 per cent in 7-year-olds. The mean number of attempts needed for success in the test was 25.7 in 5-year-olds, 12.1 in 6-year-olds and 9.8 in 7-year-olds. Finally, the percentage success rates over the first six attempts were 7 per cent, 16 per cent and 50 per cent respectively.

Identification of phonemes

Difficulty in identification increases considerably when we pass from the syllable, considered by numerous authors to be the natural unit for the segmentation of speech (see, for example, Mehler, 1981), to the phoneme, whose identification entails the deconstruction of this natural unit.

In parallel with the above-mentioned tests of the ability to count syllables, Liberman (1973; Liberman *et al.*, 1974) applied the same method to the study of children's ability to discriminate consciously between phonemes. Thus subjects aged 5, 6 and 7 had to repeat a syllable or a monosyllabic word, then tap the table once for each phoneme (1–3). Here again, during the training phase of 12 attempts and the experimental phase of 42 attempts, errors were explicitly corrected by the experimenter. The success criterion of six consecutive correct answers gave success levels of nought in 5-year-olds, 17 per cent in 6-year-olds and 70 per cent in 7-year-olds. No child in any age group succeeded in the first six attempts, and the average number of attempts required to succeed was 26 in both the 6-year-old and 7-year-old age groups. Hakes (1980), who faithfully reproduced Liberman's experiment with children aged 4–9, obtained slightly better success rates: 10 per cent in 4-to-5-year-olds, 30 per cent in 5-to-6-year-olds, 85 per cent in 6-to-7-year-olds, 95 per cent in 7-to-8-year-olds and 100 per cent in 8-to-9-year-olds. Of course, apart from age, an important factor in differentiating these groups is the effect on the older children of encountering writing through learning to read. It is possible that a process of visualization of the presented syllable enables these older children simply to count the number of letters of which it is composed. There is thus a risk of confusion between phoneme and letter.

This last analysis is validated by the results of Tunmer and Nesdale (1982) who repeated Liberman's test but with half the test items containing phonemes which, in the written language, are represented by two letters (for example 'book', which is composed of three phonemes but four letters). When the test items contained no such digraph, these authors obtained a 70 per cent success rate in 7-year-olds, in confirmation of Liberman's results. In contrast, only 35 per cent of the subjects in this age group were successful in a test using both types of test item, and were therefore the only subjects to manifest an ability to identify phonemes.

Thus the simple task of counting phonemes seems to be possible only at a relatively late age. Things become more complicated when the task is extended beyond simply counting to actually identifying the individual phonemes in a given syllable. Calfee *et al.* (1973) asked subjects aged 6–17 to arrange colour cubes to reflect the arrangement of phonemes in syllables which were presented orally. In the first test the subjects were asked to listen to various sequences of the phonemes /i/ and /p/ (/pi/, /ip/, /pip/ . . .) and then to arrange the colour cubes to represent the positions of the phonemes. In a second test, more complex syllables were presented orally to the subjects, who were simultaneously shown corresponding arrangements of cubes. The subjects then had to create other syllables using the same phonemes (for example: 'here is /ips/, now you show me /psi/'). In such a test – in which, besides showing their metaphonological awareness, the subjects also had to manipulate an arbitrary relationship between a colour and a specific phoneme – it was not until the turn of the 8-year-olds that there was a majority of correct answers, and even one-third of the 12-year-old subjects failed.

The metaphonological ability to identify phonemes is thus late to develop. Furthermore, it does not always correspond to the ability displayed by a literate adult. Thus Treiman (1985) demonstrates that while children of 5 to 8 years of age can make coherent phonetic judgements, their judgements are different from those of adults. For the children, 'chill' begins with /t/ and 'Jill' with /d/. Such judgements testify to a certain independence of the alphabetic system, and are often reflected in the spelling of these children when they begin to write.

Metaphonological control

In 1962 Weir recorded the following sequence from the speech of her $2\frac{1}{2}$-year-old son: 'Berries, not barries. Berries, not barries. Berries, not barries'. A child of 4 observed by Gleitman *et al.* (1972) asked its mother: 'Mommy, is it an A-dult or a NUH-dult?' Carlson and Anisfeld (1969) describe how Richard, at the age of 2 years and 5 months, could deliberately manipulate phonemes – for example, by substituting one phoneme for another in songs. To the tune of 'The bear went over the mountain' he would sing: 'Da de de doder da doundin'; to the tune of 'I've been workin' on the railroad' he would sing: 'I pin purkin' on a pail poad'. Shortly afterwards he was capable of giving rhymes on request. The 3-year-old daughter of Slobin (1978) was capable of segmenting a word of her own invention ('hokadin') into syllables ('hoke-a-din'). Scollon (1976) reports the case of a child of 1½ repeating a word several times while changing its pronunciation to emulate that of an adult. Finally, Bredart and Rondal (1982) show how, from the age of 2½, children are capable of phonetic self-repair, although these authors also point out that children of that age remain incapable of giving the slightest explanation of the repair process.

While these utterances undeniably constitute phonological manipulations, there is nothing to show that this is not just a case of the simple manipulation of sounds comparable to other manipulations of a nonlinguistic nature. This is suggested by Carlson and Anisfeld (1969) who, on the basis of their observations, believe that there is a distinction operating in the young child between the meaningful language used for communicating with others and another language denuded of this communicative function. Here again it is only by recourse to controlled situations that the metaphonological ability of children can be distinguished from their early-acquired functional skills.

The intentional manipulation of syllables

Curiously, while most authors consider the syllable to be a particularly important unit of language processing, very little work has been done to investigate the child's ability to manipulate syllables intentionally. Most of the data have been concerned with the spontaneous production of rhymes, though most authors agree that these word games do not necessitate any deliberate manipulation of the syllable (see, for example, Hakes, 1982; Kamhi, 1987).

To our knowledge, only the study carried out by Rosner and Simon (1971) includes instructions referring specifically to syllables in subtests of an 'Auditory Analysis Test', whose validity they attempt to demonstrate using a sample of children aged 6 to 12. A word was presented orally to the subjects, who had to repeat it once, then repeat it a second time, but with one syllable missing. This could be the final syllable, as in 'birth(day)', where the remaining segment should be rendered as 'birth' (a meaningful segment in its own right), or the first syllable, as in '(car)pet', where the segment to be restored is 'pet' (again, a meaningful segment), or indeed a medial syllable. In contrast to the two initial subtests, in which only the above-mentioned types of words were presented to the subjects, the final test comprised ten items, of which half required a nonmeaningful word as the correct answer – for example, 'auto(mo)bile' renders 'autobile' – and the other half required a meaningful word as the correct answer – for example, 're(pro)duce' yields 'reduce'. Unfortunately, the authors did not study the meaningfulness of the required segment as a factor. However, as we shall see in Chapter 4, Costermans and Giurgea (1988) demonstrate that this factor has a role to play up until the age of 6. In fact, wherever possible the young child shows a tendency to segment words in such a way that at least one of the isolated elements is meaningful (for example: auto-mobile).

When asked to omit the final syllable, thus repeating the first syllable ('birth'), 80 per cent of the 6-year-olds and all the 7-to-12-year-olds were successful. However, in the corresponding task requiring the final syllable to be repeated ('pet'), only half the 6-year-olds and three-quarters of the 7-year-olds were successful, and it was only at the age of 9 that virtually all the children gave the correct response. We note here how much easier it is to delete the final segment of a word than the first. This phenomenon is also encountered in connection with phonemic segmentation. In this regard we might also emphasize that while the repetition of the final segment requires the omission of the initial element, the repetition of the initial segment merely requires an interrupted repetition of the original word. Such a repetition requires little metaphonological control on the part of the subject (Morais *et al.*, 1987*a*, produce a similar argument to explain the greater success rate encountered in the reproduction of initial phonemes than in that of final phonemes in tests of phonemic segmentation). Nevertheless, it would be interesting to know how well even younger subjects would fare when confronted with these tests.

Research carried out by Fox and Routh (1975) provides only scanty information on this point. After a training period, the authors presented bisyllabic words to children aged 3 to 7, asking them to repeat 'just a little bit'. If a subject repeated the whole word, he or she would be given clearer instructions and asked to try again. Not surprisingly, a 60 per cent success rate was obtained by the 3-year-olds and maximum performance emerged from the age of 4 onwards. Whether such a task of freely repeating a single sound from the two which make up the sound stimulus can be said to be truly metaphonological in nature seems extremely doubtful.

The deletion of a medial syllable, however, requires a high degree of conscious control. First, the word must be analyzed in order to extract the syllable from it. Then it must be synthesized in order to recompose the remaining syllables. In the study carried out by Rosner and Simon, all the 6-year-old subjects failed in this test, and only a minority of subjects in the other age groups were successful: 14 per cent of 7-year-olds, 25 per cent of 8-year-olds, 29 per cent of 9-year-olds, 33 per cent of 10-year-olds, 38 per cent of 11-year-olds and 45 per cent of 12-year-olds. This task is thus shown to be even more difficult than the equivalent tasks performed on phonemes (see below). It is true that the removal of a phoneme – for example, 'de(s)k' – results in a syllable with a sound akin to that of the original word, whereas the removal of a syllable effects a much greater change in the sound pattern.

The most reliable subtest for determining the metaphonological manipulation of the syllabic unit would therefore seem to be the task of removing the initial syllable of a word, and this task is carried out successfully by a considerable proportion of children aged 6 and over. If – as a number of authors assert – the syllable, which is easy to isolate acoustically, is more readily apprehended by the child than the phoneme, then success in tasks involving this latter unit should be found to occur rather later.

The intentional manipulation of phonemes

Fox and Routh (1975) use the same experimental paradigm for phonemic segmentation as they do for syllabic segmentation (see above). Children (from socially privileged backgrounds) were presented with syllables composed of two or three phonemes and then asked to repeat 'just a little bit of what I say'. The resulting success levels in the extraction of phonemes were 28 per cent of 3-year-olds, 70 per cent of 4-year-olds, 86 per cent of 5-year-olds and 93 per cent of 6- and 7-year-olds.

It should be noted that in cases where the subject produced insufficient segmentation (by repeating a block of two phonemes for the triphonemic syllables) the tester continued to ask for additional segmentation. Moreover, in two tests immediately preceding this test, the subjects had already been asked to segment sentences into words and then words into syllables using the same procedure. Even if these tasks had not been specifically designed as training tasks by the authors, it is nevertheless the case that they could have influenced the levels of performance in the test for phonemic segmentation. Indeed, the results obtained by Zhurova (1973) show that in order for 3-to-4-year-old children to isolate the initial phoneme of a word (in this case the child's first name), the experimenter had to accentuate this phoneme, repeating it several times before pronouncing the whole word. This same author showed that it was not until age 5–6 that half the children were able to isolate the first phoneme of their first names without prior help.

Other early successes have been identified by Goldstein (1976). This author asked subjects to isolate the components of monosyllabic words comprising two or three phonemes by pronouncing each of the segments (for example, 'tuh-ee' for 'tea'). The experiment extended over four sessions, the two experimental sessions following two sessions in which the subjects were taught to break down bisyllabic and then trisyllabic words into syllables. Furthermore, before making the attempts which supplied the results for analysis, the children were asked to re-create words which had been fragmented into their constituent phonemes (for example, 'tuh-ee'). These words constituted half of those which the children were asked to segment. The author obtained levels of success varying between 17 per cent and 46 per cent in 4-year-olds. As Nesdale et al. believe (1984), it is highly probable that these results were heavily biased towards success by the training procedure employed, and therefore that they cannot, on their own, establish the existence of any degree of metaphonological ability in young children.

The method most frequently used for studying children's capacity for phonemic segmentation consists of presenting them with words or syllables which they are then asked to repeat with one of the phonemes omitted. This method was used by Bruce in 1964 with children aged 5 to 7½, who were presented with words like '(h)ill' (the remaining segment being a meaningful word, 'ill') or 'lo(s)t' (the remaining segment being a meaningful word, 'lot'). Classifying the subjects on the basis of their mental ages, Bruce found that no 5-year-olds, 6 per cent of 6-year-olds and 29 per cent of 7-year-olds were successful. The author interpreted these findings to affirm that the phonemic analysis of words cannot be performed by children below the mental age of 7. Fox and Routh (1975) stress that this type of task is particularly difficult, especially in the case of 'lo(s)t', where the phoneme to be removed is in neither initial nor final position. As we have already seen in the discussion of syllabic analysis, in such a case the subject has first to analyze the word to extract the phoneme and then synthesize it to combine the remaining phonemes.

In their 'Auditory Analysis Test', cited earlier in connection with the manipulation of syllables, Rosner and Simon (1971) attempted to control the task difficulty factor. Like Bruce, they asked the children to remove a phoneme from a word and then say the new word they had produced. However, these authors used the following distinctions in their analysis of the results: removal of a final consonant – for example, 'bel(t)' – gave a success rate of only 20 per cent in 6-year-olds but over three-quarters in 7-year-olds and almost all subjects of 9 or over; removal of an initial consonant – for example, '(l)end' – began with a poor success rate in 6-year-olds (7 per cent) which, however, rose to 70 per cent in 7-year-olds and almost 90 per cent in 8-year-olds and older; removal of the initial consonant in words beginning with a double consonant – for example, '(s)mile' – gave the same level of success for 6-year-olds as in the preceding case, but produced below 50 per cent success in 7- and 8-year-olds and below 75 per cent in subjects aged 12 or under; the removal of a medial consonant – for example, 's(k)in' – produced no success in the 6-year-olds, and success rates of 23 per cent in 7-year-olds, 34 per cent in 8-year-olds, 53 per cent in 9-year-olds, 57 per cent in 10-year-olds, 62 per cent in 11-year-olds and 45 per cent in 12-year-olds. Depending on the difficulty of analysis required, the age at which most of the subjects could give the correct answer could thus vary between 7 and 12.

If the subjects' attention is focused not on the removal of a phoneme – as in the experiments of Bruce or Rosner and Simon – but on the remaining segment, success is obtained earlier. Thus Calfee (1977) set the following exercise: 'If I say *greet*, you should say *eat*, if I say *ties*, you should say *eyes*' ... and obtained a success rate of 70 per cent among 6-year-olds. However, this procedure actually consists of asking the subjects to identify a word within a word, which does not seem, *a priori*, to require any real capacity for phonemic analysis.

A final series of studies shows that while the performances of 5-to-6-year-olds in tasks of phonemic segmentation are poor, they can be considerably improved by a short session of teaching. After a prior training period, Content *et al.* (1986*a*) asked children aged 4–5 and 5–6 to remove the initial consonant from pseudo-words (words with no meaning) of the form consonant-vowel-consonant, so that the children repeated the syllable vowel-final consonant. The success rate was very low (10 per cent) in the 5-to-6-year-olds and zero in the 4-year-olds. The children from each age group were then divided into two subgroups. The control group continued with the same task. The experimental group did the same, but in addition were given explicit corrections of any mistakes after each answer. After fifteen attempts, while the children in both control groups and those in the experimental group of 4-to-5-year-olds had made no progress, those in the experimental group of 5-to-6-year-olds had achieved levels of success approaching 50 per cent. Children of 5–6 would thus appear to be able to benefit from a learning process which fails to have any effect on their juniors. Nevertheless, these results raise two questions: how stable is this degree of progress? (What would be the result, for example, if the test were repeated by the same children a week later?); could this progress be reemployed by the children in a similar task (for example, the removal of the final consonant of the triplet)?

Another experiment conducted by Content *et al.* (1982) goes some way towards answering our first question. This study shows not only that after four half-hour sessions of games involving the identification, isolation and manipulation of a number of phonemes, most children aged 5–6 are able to perform formal tasks of removing the initial phoneme in pseudo-words, but also that this ability is still present six months later. As far as any generalization of this learning is concerned, the subsequent study conducted by Content *et al.* (1986*a*) is partially devoted to this.

The children aged 4–5 who had participated (without success) in the first test then took part in a second test, which was a French adaptation of the technique used by Fox and Routh (1975) ('say just a little bit . . .'). Only the subject's first response was retained, and the children were not asked to segment the product of their first response further. For this test a control group was used comprising children of the same age who had not taken part in the first test. The syllables or syllable clusters to be segmented were of the consonant-vowel-consonant type (CVC) or the consonant-vowel-consonant-vowel-consonant (CVCVC) type. The average percentages of answers effectively corresponding to a segment of the item presented were, for CVCVC and CVC items respectively, 80 per cent and 68 per cent in the experimental group and 63 per cent and 64 per cent in the control group. Unlike Fox and Routh, these authors concentrated on establishing a typology in these responses. For the CVCVC items there was no difference between the two groups. No child spontaneously extracted an isolated phoneme, and in nearly three-quarters of cases the initial syllable was the segment retained.

In contrast, the two groups differed in the responses they provided for the CVC. In the control group 98 per cent of subjects retained an initial segment (86 per cent the syllable CV, 12 per cent the first consonant), whereas in the experimental group 36 per cent of subjects did not retain an initial segment, 25 per cent removing the initial consonant in accordance with the different method which they had employed in the first experiment (11 per cent removed both consonants, retaining the medial vowel). There thus appears to be a transfer from the first experiment (although it is not performed successfully at this age) to the second, although this transfer runs counter to the general tendency to be able to reproduce the initial part of a pseudo-word more easily than the final part (this tendency has been confirmed elsewhere by the authors in a third experiment).

While the metaphonological nature of the skills demonstrated in tests of the type set by Fox and Routh has not been established, they undeniably possess an epiphonological character. When exposed to external constraints, this epiphonological behaviour seems to be modified to enable the subject to exert a greater degree of control. This control can be considered as the procedural counterpart to the growth of awareness which characterizes the progressive accession to true metalinguistic functioning.

Evidence thus exists for the ability to perform tasks of phonemic analysis successfully from the age of 5–6 onwards. The full importance of this will be realized when we take account of the data reported in the next subsection. These data will identify the links between metaphonological abilities and learning to read.

The establishment of metaphonological abilities and learning to read

Metaphonological behaviour as a consequence of learning to read

Certain authors have suggested that the metaphonological ability involved in phonemic analysis could be a simple consequence of learning to read. Alegria and Morais (1979) asked first-grade and second-grade pupils either to add a certain phoneme to the beginning of a word, or to remove the initial phoneme. In first grade, at the beginning of the school year, the percentages of success were 16 per cent (addition) and 26 per cent (removal) respectively. In mid-year they were 34 per cent and 64 per cent, and at the start of second grade they were 74 per cent and 79 per cent. Two groups were used, composed in such a way that the age distribution in one group at the time of the first test would be the same as the age distribution of the other group at the time of the second test. Thus performance in this type of test does seem to be sensitive to the effect of schooling and, probably, more specifically to the effect of learning to read, which confirms the results of several studies already cited. This point of view is reinforced by the results of Morais *et al.* (1979), who conducted a similar test on two groups of adults, one group of whom were illiterate, the other group comprising adults who were from the same social background but had gained literacy either as adolescents or as adults. While the first group attained only a 19 per cent success level, 72 per cent of the second group took part in the test successfully.

Read *et al.* (1986) obtained similar results with two groups of Chinese adults. One group had learned to read after 1949, the year when an alphabetic writing system was introduced in China for teaching purposes, while the other, older group had learned only the traditional logographic characters. In tasks of segment analysis (removing or adding an initial phoneme), while their juniors had a success rate of 83 per cent, the subjects of this latter group enjoyed only 21 per cent success, a performance comparable with that of the group of illiterate adults. Furthermore, even those adults who had learned alphabetic writing but could no longer use it were successful in tasks of segmentation.

Likewise, from an interlanguage perspective, Mann (1986) shows how American first-year primary-school children are capable of counting syllables and phonemes, whereas Japanese children at the same academic level are capable only of counting syllables. This difference is attributed to the fact that Japanese is a syllabic language and the Japanese pupils therefore had no experience of alphabetical transcription. However, this difference is not found in 10-year-olds after four years of elementary education, a result which seems to contradict those obtained from the group of illiterate adults and those observed in China. Morais *et al.* (1987*a*) invalidate this contradiction by stressing that the ability to read Japanese (more precisely Kana) to a certain degree of sophistication requires an awareness of diacritical marks, and that this awareness necessitates an intrasyllabic analysis comparable to phonemic analysis.

Finally, Patel and Soper (1987) conducted tasks of segmentation with Indian children who were learning to read and write in Gujarati, a 'syllabo-alphabetic' language in which vowels and consonants have graphemic correspondents but which combine, in writing, in a nonsequential way into spatially isolated syllabic units. The results showed success rates in syllabic segmentation of 76 per cent in 7-to-8-year-olds (second year of learning to read) and 95 per cent in 8-to-9-year-olds. However, only 42 per cent of 7-to-8 and 8-to-9-year-olds and 65 per cent of 9-to-10-year-olds were successful in tasks of phonemic segmentation. Even in the case of 'super-morphemes', the possibility of establishing correspondences which are syllabo-graphemic rather than phonemo-graphemic thus seems to permit the apprentice reader to ignore the minimal phonological unit.

Taken as a whole, what emerges from these studies is that it is not learning to read in general but learning to read in an alphabetical language which is linked to metaphonological ability. Besides the numerous studies conducted in English and French, the same results have been obtained in Serbo-Croat, Swedish, Spanish and Italian.

The results provided by Alegria *et al.* (1982) also help to confirm the effect of learning to read. These authors show that, from the very start of learning to read, clear differences emerge depending on the method used. In tasks of phoneme swapping, children learning to read by a whole-word method have a much lower success rate (15 per cent) than those being taught by a phonic method (58 per cent). In contrast, no difference appears between these groups in tasks of syllable swapping or in tasks requiring the immediate recall of verbal items presented visually. Similar results had already been obtained by Bruce (1964), who suggested that this difference disappears after a few years.

Nevertheless, Alegria *et al.* (cited by Morais, 1987*b* and Morais *et al.*, 1987*a*) found that within a population of first-year primary-school pupils learning to read by a whole-word method, only 13 per cent showed clear progress between the beginning and end of the year in a task of removing initial consonants, while the rest of the class failed in this task no matter when it took place. The most interesting finding of this study is that only those pupils who had made progress in the segmentation task were able, by the end of the year, to read words they had not encountered before. This finding may be compared with the results obtained by Jorm *et al.* (1984), which show that those pupils who are the most adept at tasks of reading nonmeaningful words at the end of their first year of learning to read are better readers than the others a year or two later.

Results comparing good and bad readers confirm those cited above. Morais *et al.* (1984) found that dyslexic children aged 6–9 were just as able as normal readers to remove the initial note of a series of four notes on a xylophone. However, their performance was clearly poorer in a task of segmenting words or pseudo-words into phonemes (an average 13 per cent success rate compared to 60 per cent in the normal readers), while there was little difference in the results obtained by the two groups in a task of syllabic segmentation. Using the same method, the authors also obtained similar results when comparing, as in their study of 1979, a group of illiterate adults and a group of adults who had learned to read late (Morais *et al.*, 1986). This suggests that it is indeed metaphonological ability, not the general ability to perform segment analyses, that is linked to the ability to read.

These results confirm those of Fox and Routh (1980), who found a similar correlation between phonemic analysis and reading difficulties. Finally, Tornéus (1984), also working with normal and dyslexic children (at the end of their first year of primary school), demonstrates that performances in reading (and spelling) are linked more to metaphonological abilities than to the level of linguistic and cognitive development.

In contrast, Simpson and Byrne (1987), comparing normal adult readers and poor adult readers, found no difference in a task of syllable pairing. The subjects had to choose the two syllables which sounded the most alike out of a set of three. Pairings based on a common initial phoneme (for example, *biss – burn*) were made in 60 per cent of cases in both groups of subjects, as against 30 per cent of pairings based on an overall similarity of syllables (for example, *biss* /bɪs/ – *deez* /dɪz/) and 10 per cent of 'abnormal' pairings (*deez – burn*). Although the cognitive burden imposed by such a task is not very clear, the results suggest that links between metaphonological ability and reading performance should be studied in less general terms than they have been hitherto if we wish to determine which factors are truly relevant. In particular, Morais (1987*b*) suggests that reading and writing require not only phonological awareness, but also that this should become automatic. It may be that certain bad readers possess phonological awareness, but that this has not been automated.

Metaphonological ability as a precondition for learning to read

The results cited above do not, however, imply that reading is the causal factor for metaphonological ability. Morais himself (Morais *et al.*, 1979) – who, as we have seen, points out the effects of learning to read on metaphonological ability – believes that if this ability is a consequence of learning to read, then that is precisely because it constitutes a prerequisite for it. If it is generally the case that awareness of the units of speech does not develop before the age of 6, then that is principally because before this age there is no necessity for this kind of awareness.

> Since the learning of the alphabetic system necessitates the analysis of words, it constitutes a privileged circumstance for the development of this analysis. Seen from this perspective, the critical factor most likely to influence learning success would not so much be the fact of being aware of phonetic units as the ability to become so. (For a detailed argument, see Content, 1984, pp. 562–3; cf. also Morais, 1987*a*.)

In fact, it would then be the metacognitive abilities necessary for the appearance of behaviour of phonological analysis which would constitute a prerequisite for learning to read. The fact that metaphonological behaviour and the first stages of reading have frequently been seen to emerge together suggests that they both constitute the actualization of the same abilities, and that improvement in one area would be paralleled by improvement in the other.

Thus Ehri *et al.* (1987) demonstrate that if children aged 5–6 are given simple instructions for the spelling of words, their performances improve as much in a task of reading a series of words as at the level of phonetic segmentation.

The point of view which holds that metaphonological ability can be considered as a simple consequence of learning to read thus seems excessively simplistic. A small – but not negligible – proportion of children (and adults) who have not yet learned to read do achieve success in tasks of phonemic analysis. Moreover, there are some fifteen studies which seem to indicate that the metaphonological ability to perform segmentation is a good predictor of subsequent performance when learning to read (see Tunmer and Nesdale, 1985). Furthermore, Share *et al.* (1984) found that out of thirty-nine types of task given to children just starting primary school, the tasks of phonemic segmentation provided the most accurate prediction of these children's reading performance two years later. Even if this ability is not necessary for learning to read, it does at least seem to be a facilitating factor.

Moreover, certain features of metaphonological activity coincide at the start of learning to read. Thus the results of a certain number of studies (see Treiman and Baron, 1981) show that when reading monosyllabic words or pseudo-words, learner-readers make fewer mistakes with initial consonants (easier to isolate) than with final consonants.

One study, conducted by Mann and Liberman (1984), has revealed a significant correlation (0.40) between 5-to-6-year-olds' ability to segment syllables and their reading performances a year later. This result seems to contradict others given by Mann (1984), which show no relationship between the ability of children of that age in tasks of syllable inversion and their later performance in reading. In contrast, the study cited above demonstrated the existence of such a link (a correlation of 0.75) between the early ability to invert phonemes and the reading level after one year of learning. These results confirm those reported by Lundberg *et al.* in 1980. Furthermore, in a longitudinal study conducted with 400 children over a period of three years, Bradley and Bryant (1985) found significant correlations (0.50 and greater) between the scores of children aged 4–6 in tasks of categorizing words on the basis of a common phoneme – for example, find the odd one out in the following list: 'cot', 'hut', 'man' and 'fit' – and the results of two tests of reading levels carried out three years later. Finally, Stanovich *et al.* (1984) show similar correlations between reading performance and results obtained a year earlier in tasks of phoneme identification, segmentation and categorization, but no such correlation between reading performance and the identification and production of rhymes.

These different results are probably less contradictory than they may at first appear. It is important to look at the type of reading performance studied by the different researchers. Thus Maclean *et al.* (1987) show that the early-acquired ability to detect rhymes and alliterations (and we have shown that it is doubtful whether this necessitates any real metaphonological ability) has a significant correlation with later performances in tasks of reading words, but not with performances in tasks of recognizing letters of the alphabet.

Moreover, as Content points out (Content *et al.*, 1986*b*), it would appear that the ability to perform explicit phonemic analysis and the ability to identify grapho-phonological correspondence, to which it would appear to be linked, probably play a much more important role in the acquisition of reading (for deciphering new words) than in the recognition of words by the experienced reader.

Thus Campbell and Butterworth (1985) report the case of an educated woman with phonological processing difficulties, probably of neurological origin, whose performance in reading and writing was above average, but who was incapable of reading or writing nonmeaningful words, judging rhymes, or pairing homophones.

Lack of metaphonological ability thus seems to cause more trouble for someone learning to read than it does for someone who can already read. This agrees with the results obtained by Stuart-Hamilton (1986), who suggests that phonological awareness enables young readers to make better use of graphemic clues. Nevertheless, should this problem occur at the beginning of the process of acquisition, it can obliterate the rest of the learning process.

Kochnower *et al.* (1983) demonstrate that 10-year-old children who are poor readers sharing the same reading level as 'advanced' 8-year-olds spend longer than the latter on deciphering words in a list or deciphering nonmeaningful words. The authors believe that these children have difficulty using the sounds of the letters in the process of recoding words. These results are related to those – already cited – obtained by Jorm *et al.* (1984), which demonstrate that those children who are most skilled in tasks of reading nonmeaningful words at the end of their first year of learning are better readers than their contemporaries one and two years later.

As Bertelson points out (1986), these data reveal the limitations of approaches which attempt to construct hypotheses of development from material drawn from theories which relate to adult functioning. Nevertheless, Siegel and Ryan (1988) show that, *whatever the age of the reader*, there is a strong link between the ability to read nonmeaningful words and accuracy, speed, *and also comprehension*, in reading exercises.

While the link between the ability for phonemic analysis and reading performance seems to be well established, the same is not true of simpler phonological analyses. Thus while Bradley and Bryant (1978), experimenting with groups similar to those used by Kochnower *et al.*, found that the older poor readers performed less well in tasks of identifying alliterations and rhymes than their juniors who were good at reading, Katz (1986) found the opposite. Katz demonstrates that in 8-to-9-year-old children there is no difference between the performances of good and bad readers in tasks of judging rhymes. In fact, we can agree with Bryant and Goswami (1987) that the ability to detect rhymes can facilitate the reading of new words which rhyme with words already known to the reader (the authors give the example of a child who can already read 'beak' reading a new word, 'peak'). In order for this to be possible, however, it is indispensable for the child to be able to distinguish between the letters 'p' and 'b' and to make them correspond to their phonemes /p/ and /b/, an ability which seems to be linked to the awareness of phonemes. The ability to detect rhymes, therefore, is helpful in learning to read only for children with an awareness of the phonemic unit – in other words, if it is accompanied by true metaphonological competence (which perhaps also implies it).

From the results collected here, it would seem that, as Perfetti *et al.* (1987) deduce from a longitudinal study of 82 first-year primary-school pupils, learning to read and phonological awareness develop in interaction with each other. On the one hand, phonological awareness seems to facilitate learning to read; while on the other hand, progress in reading seems to facilitate the ability to divide the spoken word into segments.

However, we would be well advised to be cautious about the scope of this analysis. Whatever overall validity it might possess, it nevertheless appears inadequate as an explanation for the sum of individual cases.

For example, Cossu and Marshall (1990) report the case of a 9-year-old hyperlexic child (verbal IQ = 53; nonverbal IQ = 50) who, although performing well in tasks of reading and writing words and logatomes (nonmeaningful words), obtained scores of zero in metaphonological tasks (production and comprehension of rhymes, removal of phonemes, counting of phonemes by tapping on the table). This result (which should have been analyzed earlier, as Morais *et al.*, 1987*b*, have emphasized) seems to point to the independence in this subject of the two abilities which were considered above to be linked.

It is thus apparent that thorough understanding of the relationship between phonemic analysis and learning to read (and the possible compensations when normal learning processes are suppressed) requires additional research. The neuropsychological clinic would provide fertile ground for such an examination.

Early metaphonological training and its effect on learning to read

It is important to emphasize that it appears that the establishment of the facilitating factor which metaphonological awareness constitutes can be actively assisted. Using their 1975 method, Fox and Routh (1984) set tests of phonemic segmentation to children of 6, and were able to identify two groups, those who performed segmentation and those who failed in the exercise. The latter, more numerous group was divided into three. One of the subgroups was given no special training. The children in the second subgroup were taught to form segments (identification of initial and final phonemes in triphonemic words). The children in the third subgroup were given more extensive training comprising not only segmentation but also tasks of breaking down and reconstructing monosyllabic words differing by only a single phoneme (for example, 'man', 'fan', 'fat', 'mat'). All the children then participated in sessions of learning to read. The authors found that the children in group 1 (the 'segmenters' of the pre-test) were able to learn more easily than those who had not been able to form segments and had received no training – a result of no great interest, as these two groups were serving as control groups. The most interesting result was that the children who had been taught simple segmentation were no better able to learn than those who had received no teaching. (Bradley and Bryant, 1983 and Olofsson and Lundberg, 1985, obtained similar results, but Scheerer-Neumann, 1981, found that segmentation training had a facilitating effect on 8-to-9-year-old poor German readers.) In contrast, those children who had been taught more extensive phoneme manipulation attained performances comparable to those who had been able to form segments in the pre-test. These results confirm the findings of other authors which all indicate, in varying degrees, a positive effect of metaphonological training on learning to read.

The findings of Fox and Routh throw new light on certain earlier interpretations. In fact, it would seem that what facilitates learning to read is not the simple ability to form segments but a wider metaphonological ability of which segmentation is only a part. This is the type of ability which is probably possessed by those children who are predicted to be good readers, even though it is possible to identify such children by means of a simple segmentation test.

These results do not contradict the hypothesis proposed by Wagner and Torgesen (1987) on the basis of a detailed analysis of the results available in the literature. For them, the metaphonological ability reflected by the possibility of phoneme manipulation would be necessary for the acquisition of reading skills. On the other hand, the ability to perform phonemic segmentation would be a simple consequence of being taught to read. They propose to put this hypothesis to the test in the future. While the first part of the hypothesis seems legitimate, the same cannot be said of the second, since a prerequisite for the ability to perform phoneme permutation seems to be the ability to isolate phonemes.

According to the hypothesis of Morais *et al.* (1979), it would appear that learning to read in an alphabetic language necessitates the activation of a 'metaphonological competence' which is already present but, in most cases, not previously invoked. Activation of this competence before learning to read would in itself have a facilitating effect on the latter and could be stimulated only by the use of sufficiently complex tasks of deliberate phoneme manipulation. Such complexity is provided by manipulation exercises, but not always by the type of exercise classed as 'segmentation tasks'.

While the collection of studies reported here seems to demonstrate the importance of grapho-phonological correspondence in learning to read, there is nothing to suggest that a complementary approach (not an alternative one) based on meaning, which we do not intend to discuss here, does not play an equally important role. On this subject, Fox and Routh (1984) insist on the importance of distinguishing between pre-lexical phonemic decoding and post-lexical recoding of meaningful units, and Barron (1986) argues that these two types of process cannot be mutually independent. This position is compatible with that defended by Downing (see, for example, Downing and Fijalkow, 1984).

Nevertheless, the fact remains that the results currently available validate the position of Content (1984) who, like Williams (1980), believes it is useful to employ phonetic analysis exercises in the teaching of reading. Such exercises could also be used as an effective 'early learning programme' at pre-school level. On the other hand, Morais *et al.* (1987*a*), who defend the same viewpoint, justifiably argue that while these exercises can be useful, they are by no means indispensable, since the capacity for phonetic analysis develops perfectly well during the process of learning to read. Furthermore, they warn against the risk of segregation which might result from the application of psychometrics to the capacity for phonemic segmentation. They argue that:

> The introduction, in preschool education, of activities that require the child first to pay attention to the phonology of his language and then to analyse his utterances into smaller and smaller constituents may help the potential backward reader when he is later faced with the task of learning to read.

Conclusion

Observation and research have revealed two types of phonological manipulation in the child, and these manifest themselves at different ages.

Epiphonological behaviour

Very early, even before the age of 3, the child can actively experiment, in speech games, with the morpho-phonological characteristics of language. This activity soon leads to the ability to produce rhymes, sometimes even on request, and then a little later to the ability to recognize rhymes in artificial contexts. At the same age the child is capable of distinguishing between a linguistic sound and a nonlinguistic sound. These early-acquired processes do not seem to require the child to possess either a reflective attitude towards the phonological composition of language or any awareness of manipulating the constituent elements of meaningful segments in the speech chain. It is again at an early age, between 3 and 5, that the first processes of segmentation appear. Here again, however, these appear to be more a manipulation of items of sound than a deconstruction of symbolic objects. Indeed, such segmentations are obtained either from open-ended tasks (like that given by Fox and Routh [1975] which required the child simply to reproduce 'just a little bit' of an item) or from tasks requiring the removal of the final syllable of a word. This latter task simply requires subjects to interrupt their repetition of the word.

We consider that these are manifestations of an epiphonological order based more on intuition than on any real reflection. Children's experience of their linguistic environment gives them an unconscious awareness of certain aspects of the system of language sounds which tacitly enables them to organize phonological segments (according to Read, 1971, into categories which might be definable in terms of articulatory features).

Adultomorphism on the part of the observer can lead to the child being credited with the possession of the same cognitive processes which underlie the observer's own isomorphic behaviour, and thereby to the child's linguistic behaviour being categorized as metaphonological when it is actually based on other processes. Nevertheless, as we shall be arguing in Chapter 8, these epiphonological processes are probably indispensable to the emergence (when it becomes necessary) of later metaphonological activity. This is consequent initially on the growth of a conscious awareness of – and then on the possibility of deliberately controlling – the activities of metaphonological manipulation which were functionally effective at an early age.

Metaphonological behaviour

In 1978 Golinkoff pointed out that 'recognizing the presence or absence of a unit should be easier than adding or deleting the element itself. Performing a deletion and recombining the remaining elements should be easier than performing the deletion and replacing the deleted element with another element' (p. 26). The data presented throughout this chapter confirm this analysis.

First of all, there seems to be an interval between the manifestation of metaphonological awareness and that of deliberate control of the means of processing the phonological components of language. Thus the ability to count phonemes (6–7 years of age) seems to emerge slightly earlier than the ability to perform phoneme segmentation on request. Once segmentation is possible, the removal of the initial or final phoneme of a word, performed at approximately 7 years of age, is clearly earlier than the removal of the medial phoneme which is achieved by only a quarter of children of this age and still by only half of 9-year-olds. The removal of an initial syllable – performed by the majority of children at around 6–7, but also by a non-negligible proportion of much younger children – is very much earlier than the removal of the medial syllable, which still causes problems for 12-year-olds. Certainly, earlier successes have been recorded, but these are generally in tasks in which a meaningful item is produced from an original item which is also meaningful. In other words, these are tasks which can be described in terms of a test for the recognition of one word within the sound configuration of another. Curiously, the effect of the significance of the source and target items has never been systematically studied (although Morais, 1987*a*, points to the attention paid to the semantic factor in a study currently being conducted by Content *et al.*).

The ability to perform phonemic analysis presupposes the ability to pay attention to the formal properties of language without taking account of meaning, and herein lies, no doubt, an explanation for its late appearance. Nevertheless, Morais (1987*b*) points out that this explanation is insufficient on its own. In fact, this same precondition seems to apply to the ability to analyze syllables, which is realized earlier. This leads Morais to postulate that phonemic control requires the ability to ignore the unity of the articulatory act. Be that as it may, the study of the factors at work in phonemic control is still very much in its infancy. In particular, current research into children's ability to segment syllables into 'onset/rime' segments (Wise *et al.*, 1990) would seem to provide a fruitful approach to this topic.

The appearance of the first metaphonological behaviour can be stimulated from the age of 5 by simple training sessions, which need not necessarily rely on explicit teaching of the phonological characteristics concerned, or of the procedure best used to perform correct segmentation. This observation led Content (1984, 1985) to defend the idea that, from the age of 5–6, most children possess the abilities necessary for the appearance of this metaphonological behaviour. In fact, this behaviour seems to be able to emerge as soon as the corresponding epiphonological functioning has become well established. It then appears either as a result of deliberately stimulated activities of phonological manipulation or, more generally, at the age of 6–7 with the emergence of such activities of manipulation through learning to read and write in an alphabetical language.

Generally speaking, epiphonological skills would appear to be the prerequisite for the implementation of a metaphonological ability. The pragmatic constraints, for their part, would be the condition for its actualization, and the awareness of phonological characteristics would be necessary for their deliberate manipulation during langue processing. The variable difficulty of the metaphonological tasks used by individual researchers would account for the horizontal *décalages* observed within this actualization.

Chapter 3

Metasyntactic development

Introduction

Analyzing the results of numerous studies, Markman (1981) emphasizes that although children use the syntax of their language correctly in their spontaneous productions, they frequently fail at tasks which require explicit analysis and conscious awareness of the structure of the language. In other words, the *linguistic competence* of generative grammar, which refers to the tacit knowledge of the grammar of the language, does not imply metasyntactic awareness. *Metasyntactic competence refers to the ability to reason consciously about the syntactic aspects of language, and to exercise intentional control over the application of grammatical rules.* Here, too, it will be possible to distinguish between a declarative aspect and a procedural aspect in the metasyntactic knowledge manifested by the subject.

Conscious knowledge of syntax is manifested in metalinguistic speech which focuses on the grammaticality of sentences.

Taking and developing an example used by Dubois (1968), the sentence 'The boy sleeps the soup' is *ungrammatical* because the verb 'to sleep' is intransitive and cannot, therefore, be associated with a direct object (except in highly specialized applications such as 'sleep the sleep of the just'). In contrast, the sentence 'The boy reads the soup' does not transgress any rule of grammar. It is *anomalous*. However, Chomsky (1965) considers that such cases demonstrate a violation of the rules of lexical selection which impairs the grammaticality of the sentence. In itself, the sentence 'The boy eats the soup with a hammer' is perfectly grammatical in the same way as 'The boy loves the soup'. High-level metasyntactic awareness should lead us to reject the first sentence for grammatical reasons (not because of any incompatibility between soup and sleep) and the second for reasons of bad lexical selection (not for reasons of plausibility), just as it should lead us to recognize the grammaticality of the third (even if pragmatic references cause us to judge it unacceptable) and of the fourth (even if it contradicts our everyday experience).

There is a risk here of confusing the *judgement of grammaticality* and the *judgement of acceptability*, and it is this risk which provides the key to the debate about the appearance of metasyntactic knowledge presented in an early subsection.

Metasyntactic control, which is the subject of the next subsection, is at work in subjects' intentional decisions to apply particular rules of grammar in the elaboration of their own verbal messages. Unfortunately, the literature contains no data directly associated with the emergence of such processes in the speech-planning of the child. Therefore, in order to study the emergence of syntactic control, we shall turn to the syntactic repairs which children address to their own productions (*self-repairs*) or to those of others (*other-repairs*). In conclusion, we shall devote a subsection to an attempted synthesis of the reported data.

Metasyntactic judgements

Even if they are not always able to agree among themselves and are frequently unable to explain the determining factors in their own responses, most educated adults are able to judge both the grammaticality and the semantic acceptability of spoken sentences (Gleitman and Gleitman, 1970). Similar results are found in the judgement of written sentences (Vetter *et al.*, 1979). A growing number of studies have concentrated on the emergence of this ability in children. These studies have provided results which have sometimes led to divergent interpretations.

Judgements concerning utterances

Gleitman *et al.* (1972) asked three small girls aged $2\frac{1}{2}$ to say whether the imperative phrases presented to them were 'good' or 'silly'. The task is presented as 'a game in which mothers and children play together'. At first, just the mother and the experimenter take part in the game. Then the child is asked to join in. The sentences are spoken by the mother. There are four types of sentence to judge:

1. Correct imperatives, for example, 'Bring me the ball';
2. Imperatives in telegraphic form: 'Bring ball';
3. Inverted imperatives: 'Ball me the bring';
4. Inverted imperatives in telegraphic form: 'Ball bring'.

The three subjects judged the well-formed sentences to be 'good' more frequently than if they had given random answers (the subjects achieving 92 per cent, 80 per cent and 80 per cent respectively, whereas random response would give a 'good' response rate of 50 per cent). The telegraphic sentences elicited the response 'good' in 100 per cent, 82 per cent and 58 per cent of cases, the inverted sentences in 75 per cent, 50 per cent and 58 per cent of cases and the inverted imperatives in 58 per cent of cases, regardless of the subject. In contrast to the conclusion drawn by the authors, this does not seem to provide any evidence of early syntactic judgement. In fact, the syntactically incorrect sentences are accepted in more than half the cases. It simply appears that the well-formed sentences are accepted slightly more often than the others. This fact may correspond to a vague refusal to accept sound sequences which differ from those with which the children are customarily surrounded or, alternatively, to the rejection of sentences whose distortion has made it more difficult for the children to understand their meaning.

The results of Gleitman *et al.* are therefore unconvincing, and their conclusions have been challenged by a number of authors. Thus de Villiers and de Villiers (1974) think that the judgements reported by the authors provide only a low level of data. They prefer to argue that the majority of the few corrections made by the subjects of Gleitman *et al.* bear on the meaning of the sentences (see the subsection on metasyntactic control below) and they thus cast doubt on the belief that from the age of 2 children can make judgements of grammaticality similar to those made by adults.

These authors (de Villiers and de Villiers, 1972) have elsewhere attempted to prove the hypothesis which holds that semantic factors play a more important role than syntactic factors in children's judgements.

They showed eight children aged between 2 years 4 months and 3 years 9 months a puppet to which they attributed a number of different utterances. The subjects were warned that this fictitious speaker was liable to make utterances which were 'all the wrong way round' and that they had to help it speak properly. They were told to judge the acceptability of each utterance they heard and propose a correction for those which they claimed to be incorrect (these corrections will be examined in a later subsection). The authors asked the children to judge the utterances 'right' or 'wrong', terms which in their opinion hold fewer semantic connotations than 'good' and 'silly'. Three types of utterance were presented to the children:

1. Correct imperatives, for example, 'Pat the dog';
2. Semantically abnormal imperatives: 'Drink the chair';
3. Imperatives which were rendered ungrammatical by an inversion of verb and object: 'Cake the eat'.

The children were categorized according to their linguistic development, which was determined by the mean length of the utterances they produced. While the semantic anomalies were identified by all the children, only those who were most advanced in their linguistic development rejected the utterances which failed to respect the canonical order, although these subjects were generally incapable of correcting them (see the next subsection).

From these results the authors inferred that it is semantic factors which determine the judgements of syntactic acceptability given by young children. In other words, if children can make sense of an utterance they accept it, otherwise they reject it.

Smith and Tager-Flusberg (1982) repeated the experiment of de Villiers and de Villiers (1972) using a group of children aged between 3 and 5. In this experiment only correct imperative sentences (for example, 'Read the book') and inverted imperatives ('Book the read') were used. After a training period, five sentences of each type were presented to the children, who had to decide whether they were 'right' or 'wrong' and, if they chose the latter option, propose a correction (see the next subsection). The level of correct judgements ran at 63 per cent for the 3-to-4-year-olds and 91 per cent for the 4-to-5-year-olds (significantly different from the 50 per cent in the case of random responses). Moreover, 22 per cent of the subjects aged between 3 and 4 and 78 per cent of those aged between 4 and 5 replied correctly at least nine times out of ten.

Beyond indicating a clear difference in performance according to the age of the subjects, the results remain difficult to interpret. In fact, the levels of success reported by the authors are global values in which it is not possible to distinguish the responses associated with the grammatical sentences from those associated with the ungrammatical ones. If we hypothesize that the grammatical sentences are always recognized as such (which corresponds to the data found in the literature for sentences of this degree of simplicity), a random response for the ungrammatical sentences alone would yield a global value of correct responses of 75 per cent (5 sentences out of 5 for the grammatical sentences and, on average, 2.5 sentences out of 5 for the ungrammatical sentences). Yet the 3-to-4-year-olds do not attain this percentage. The tendency to reject sentences whose meaning has been distorted by their ungrammaticality which was suggested at the beginning of the previous study would be sufficient to account for the success of the older subjects. These data are therefore insufficient to establish the early existence of metasyntactic judgements.

Hakes (1980), who has interpreted early judgements of acceptability in terms of the possibility of identifying meaning, has proposed an explanation which is compatible with the data reported so far. According to this interpretation, children under 4 years of age differ from older children aged between 4 and 5 in their lack of sensitivity to word order when performing tasks of comprehension. The younger children would thus accept the inverted sentences which, for them, would be perfectly comprehensible, while the older children would find the same sentences unintelligible and would consequently reject them. This analysis is compatible with a result provided by de Villiers and de Villiers (1974), who found a highly significant correlation (0.77) between the performances measured in a task involving the correction of word order and the understanding of reversible passive sentences.

Hakes (1980) confronted a group of children aged between 5 and 9 with a set of six sentences containing three simple declarative sentences of the form subject-verb-object and three sentences of the same nature but inverted to the form object-verb-subject (for example, 'The string chased the kitten'). Like his colleagues in the preceding experiments, the fictional speaker, this time in the guise of a toy elephant, sometimes says things which are 'all mixed up'. Each subject must then tell the speaker if what he has said is correct and, if it is not, explain why. The level of correct responses among the 4-to-5-year-olds was 63 per cent, with nearly all the answers provided by the 5-to-6-year-olds being correct. At 4 to 5, fewer than 5 per cent of rejections were explicitly justified on semantic grounds. However, it should be noted that at the same age the majority of responses were not justified, or only a fanciful justification was given. The first justifications to designate the ungrammaticality of the sentence correctly did not appear until the age of 6 or 7 and were provided only by a minority, even among the 8-to-9-year-olds.

As Hakes himself points out, we must avoid confusing the ability to understand the rules of grammar with the ability to explain them. Dealing with the same question, Pratt *et al.* (1984) have suggested that one child can correctly reject a sentence because 'it sounds wrong' without having the slightest idea of the cause of this dissonance, while another may reject it because of an awareness of the problem of order without being sufficiently at ease with the language to be able to articulate this. As a result of the absence of justification, the performances of these two children will be viewed as equivalent, despite the fact that they are based on two very different levels of judgemental ability. In other words, the ability to judge grammaticality will precede the ability to explain such judgements.

Scholl and Ryan (1975, 1980) have criticized the method used in the experiments described above. This method presupposes that the children are aware of the significance of the adjectives 'good' and 'silly' (or 'right' and 'wrong'). They further argue that the responses obtained by this research are biased by the fact that the children are asked only to correct the sentences which they consider 'silly' or 'wrong', and that the acceptance of a sentence completes the subject's task. Subjects might thus be tempted to accept sentences simply in order to avoid having to correct them. This experimental bias is avoided by Bohannon (1976).

This author asked children aged between 5 and 8 to attribute utterances, either well-formed or with a distorted word order, to one of two adult speakers, Norman, who speaks well, or Ralph, who mixes his words up. The children had heard both speakers talking, but the difference between them had not been explained. After each attempt the subjects were told whether they were right or wrong. Success in the experiment was defined as a maximum of four errors out of the twenty-four attributions of utterances the children were asked to perform. The level of success of the subjects was 22 per cent at 5–6, 58 per cent at 6–7 and 78 per cent at 7–8. These results agree with those obtained by Corrigan (1975) in a study of the comprehension of causal sentences. Corrigan found that not until the age of 7 did more than half the subjects reject inverted sentences (without, however, being able to provide a clear justification for their rejection). We should note that not only are the sentences used by Bohannon much longer than those used by other authors (sometimes containing more than fifteen words, whereas the sentences generally used contain between three and seven) but that the distortion of word order is also far more pronounced (for example, 'Dog the house barking and ran into the started', the correct word order for the sentence being 'The dog ran into the house and started barking'. At least four displacements are required to transform one form into the other).

Warren-Leubecker (1987) used Bohannon's (1976) material and procedure to study the link between awareness of word order and reading performance (see the chapter on writing below). She presented her subjects with 45 sentences, the items being subdivided into three sequences of 15 sentences. At the outset of the test, the instructions given to the children were exactly the same as those used by Bohannon (attribution to one of two speakers after the presentation of a sample of language from each of them). If the criteria for success were not achieved by the end of the first 15 attempts (8 consecutive correct answers or no more than 4 errors out of 15 responses), the particular nature of each of the speakers was explained to the children. If the criteria for success were still not achieved by the end of the second 15 attempts, the children were simply asked if each of the final set of sentences was 'good' or 'silly'. This method gives a number of criteria for success, the narrowest of which corresponds to success after the first 15 attempts and the broadest to success after the end of 45 presentations. For reasons connected with her study, the author used the same procedure in two consecutive experiments. If we collate the results of these two experiments (which effectively gives us 263 subjects) and recalculate the success levels, the results are very interesting. Using the strictest criterion, the success level of the subjects is 7 per cent at 6 and 34 per cent at 7. Using the widest criterion, these levels rise to 76 per cent and 94 per cent respectively – which only goes to show that such experiments, which have no clear-cut results, can be made to suggest whatever one wants.

The facts remain insubstantial: there is clearly some discrimination between different utterances. The children do not judge all the sentences to be equally acceptable. When the material is simple and/or undemanding criteria for decision-making are applied, these discriminations and judgements of acceptability may be identified at an early age (thus Clark and Barron, 1988, show that whereas 4-year-old children accept badly ordered compound nouns, for example 'puller-wagon', the majority of children aged over $4\frac{1}{2}$ reject them without being able to provide an acceptable correction). However, an interpretation in terms of the semantic determination of these early judgements remains the most likely.

Other judgements of grammaticality

During the same series of experiments as those already presented, Smith and Tager-Flusberg (1982) attempted to get children between the ages of 3 and 5 to distinguish grammatical sentences from sentences rendered ungrammatical by the final morpheme of a word.

Three times out of five this ungrammaticality consisted of an incorrect verbal inflection (absence of the present continuous marker, incorrect verbal agreement of either person or tense), in one case out of five it consisted of the absence of the plural marker at the end of a noun, and in the final case an incorrect possessive marker. The experiment used two puppets – Cedric, who has not yet finished learning to speak, and Raggedy Ann, whose task is to teach Cedric to speak correctly. The puppets' voices are provided by two experimenters who give examples of correct and incorrect sentences. The children are asked to help Raggedy Ann judge ('right' or 'wrong') Cedric's productions. A picture is provided to aid the identification of each item. For example, the children are shown a picture representing a large dog and a small dog and Cedric is asked 'A small dog is called a . . .'. Here the correct response is 'doggie'. The subject is then asked to take the place of Raggedy Ann. This procedure is repeated for ten items, with the judgement referring each time to Cedric's production. If the subjects reject the suggested answer, they are asked to provide a correction (see below).

The level of successful judgements was 71 per cent for the 3-to-4-year-olds and 88 per cent for the 4-to-5-year-olds. The percentage of subjects passing at least nine correct judgements out of ten was 22 per cent and 83 per cent respectively. There is no need to repeat here the criticisms already levelled at the authors in connection with the task of judging word order. These criticisms also obviate the optimistic conclusions which Smith and Tager-Flusberg draw from this experiment. Moreover, the results obtained by Ryan and Ledger (1979) show a much lower level of performance. Children of 6, 7 and 8 years of age have to say if the sentences presented to them are 'right' or 'wrong'. At all ages the level of acceptance of the grammatical sentences is significantly higher than the random response level (68 per cent at 6, 85 per cent at 7 and 88 per cent at 8). In contrast, the level of correct responses to the ungrammatical sentences falls from 53 per cent at 6 to 43 per cent at 7 to 31 per cent at 8. Although the authors do not go into detail, it seems that the ungrammaticalities used have only a meagre effect on the meaning of the sentences (for example, the incorrect usage of the definite or indefinite article or the regularization of irregular verbs). The results suggest that while the 6-year-old subjects give a random response, an increasingly large proportion of the older children reject only the sentences which genuinely seem incorrect to them. The fall-off in performance thus seems to point to an increased metasyntactic ability.

In order to avoid the use of the terms 'good' and 'silly' (or 'right' and 'wrong'), which they consider semantically charged, Scholl and Ryan (1975) designed a nonverbal experiment in which the subjects were simply asked to indicate the photograph of the presumed author of a proposed utterance. One of the photographs was of a child who was said to be a bad speaker; the other showed an expert adult speaker. This study shows that even at 7 years of age the ability to distinguish well-formed sentences (for example, 'We cannot go home' or 'What can the cow say?') from deviant sentences ('Not we go home' or 'What the cow say?') is still restricted.

It is noteworthy that the sentences submitted by Scholl and Ryan are more complex than those used in the preceding studies and, most important, that the ungrammaticalities found there are common in the language of children. This remark provides a partial validation for the material in that it seems very likely that in such cases the meanings of the ungrammatical and grammatical sentences are equally easy to comprehend. On the other hand, this test may be seen as a task of attribution, either to an adult or to a child, of linguistic configurations which effectively correspond to the productions of one or the other without the need for any syntactic analysis. This interpretation is reinforced by the observation that more than half the well-formed interrogative utterances of the form 'Wh-' (i.e. 'Who?', 'What is?', 'When?') are attributed to the children by Scholl and Ryan's subjects. The justification given for these attributions is that it is only children who ask such questions.

A certain number of studies have focused on the child's ability to identify sentences which violate the rules of lexical selection. For the most part they use the ± animate selection restriction. Thus James and Miller (1973) presented children aged between 5 and 7 with grammatical sentences and sentences of the type 'The large rock walked down the hill' (here the violation concerns the relationship between subject and verb) or 'The happy pencil rolled off the desk' (here the violation concerns the relationship between adjective and noun). The subjects were asked to pass the judgement 'silly' or 'okay'. From 5 years old onwards, they gave properly adapted responses. In a related experiment, Glass *et al.* (1977) obtained the same results for children aged 6, 8 and 10.

Howe and Hillman (1973) reported results which, on first analysis, appear to contradict those of James and Miller. In their study, the violation of the rule of lexical selection concerns either the subject (for example, 'The story believed the teacher') or the object ('The dog frightened the car'). The children, who were aged between 4 and 9, were asked to decide which of the pairs of sentences was not acceptable. The results show that children of school age still have difficulty performing this kind of discrimination, and that ungrammaticalities concerning the subject are identified at an earlier age than those concerning the object. However, an examination of the sentences used shows that the ungrammaticality can also be defined as an inversion of subject and object. This makes it possible for the subjects who do not attribute much importance to the order of enunciation to accept such sentences, and suggests that these results might be better compared with the performances observed in connection with the judgement of word order than with those concerning the judgement of lexical selection.

However this may be, Howe and Hillman emphasize that correct discrimination may be determined in two different ways. It may be based on the identification of poor selection, or it may just as easily be due to the rejection of assertions which contradict the subject's experience. The results obtained by Carr (1979) point towards the second interpretation. In a longitudinal, three-year study of children who were 2 years old at the start of the research, she examined the development of judgements concerning the ± animate selection restriction. In the first test the majority of incorrect sentences were rejected, together with the majority of correct sentences. When they were older, the children generally accepted the correct sentences together with a not insignificant proportion of the other sentences. Finally, a third test (generally after the children had reached the age of 4) showed that more than 70 per cent of responses were correct whatever the nature of the sentence, but there was still a tendency to reject the correct sentences. According to the author, the acceptance of a sentence at an early age should be based on the recognition of something familiar to the subjects' experience. Awareness of the limited nature of their own knowledge of the world should later bias them towards an acceptance of the sentences. Finally, the children again base their responses on their experience, which has grown in the meantime. In fact, it seems that when young children have to judge the truth value of an utterance, they are influenced more by extralinguistic factors than by syntactic or lexical rules.

The same type of evolution is found in the results obtained by Hakes (1980) who, apart from judgements concerning word order (see above), asked subjects aged between 4 and 9 to distinguish between sentences containing other types of ungrammaticality:

• Violation of the rules of lexical selection concerning the relationship between verb and complement (for example, 'The teacher read a chicken'), the relationship between subject and verb ('The playground walked to the store'), the relationship between adjective and noun ('The sleepy rock was in the middle of the road'), inalienable possession ('The nurse blinked the doctor's eyes'), or incorrect usage of 'some' or 'any';

- Violation of the rules of subcategorization concerning transitive and intransitive verbs (for example, 'The teacher coughed the car').

Whatever their age, the children found it more difficult to reject the incorrect sentences than to accept the correct ones. However, the acceptance of the correct sentences increases consistently with age. As these sentences are grammatical, the improvement in performance cannot be interpreted in terms of increased awareness of the rules which determine the grammaticality of sentences. In fact, the determining factors here are of a semantico-pragmatic nature. This is demonstrated by the justification of the subject who rejected the sentence 'The big rock was in the middle of the road' because 'a car might run over it and get a flat tyre', or that of the subject who rejected the sentence 'Yesterday Daddy painted the fence' because 'daddies don't paint fences, they paint walls'.

These results confirm those reported by Gleitman *et al.* (1972) who, apart from their observations on the judgements of word order passed by very young children (see above), also compared the way eight children aged between 5 and 8 judged sentences, some of which violate the rules of selection, with the judgements made by adults. Only the oldest children resembled the adults in basing their rejections on poor lexical selection, whereas the youngest rejected the sentences which did not conform to their experience. Thus a 5-year-old child rejected the sentence 'I am eating dinner' because he did not like dinner. The same child accepted the sentence 'I am eating breakfast'.

Taking some of this work as their basis, Tunmer and Grieve (1984) summarized the evolution of judgements of acceptability in three successive stages:

1. At around the age of 2–3 judgements seem to be based solely on whether the child understands or does not understand the sentence;
2. At around the age of 4–5 the criteria of content become predominant;
3. It is not until 6–7 years of age that the child becomes capable of separating the form of a sentence from its content and basing judgements on linguistic criteria alone.

Nevertheless, it is important to remember that the available data are particularly difficult to compare and, above all, that the difficulty of the tasks required of the children varies greatly.

Judgements of grammaticality versus judgements of acceptability

Hakes's results (1980), like those of Ryan and Ledger (1979), show that ungrammatical sentences are more difficult to detect than grammatical sentences. In a study of the performance of a group of adults in tasks demanding the judgement of the grammaticality of sentences belonging to a second language, Bialystok (1979) demonstrated the existence of a scale of increasing difficulty in:

1. Judging the grammaticality of incorrect sentences;
2. Judging the grammaticality of correct sentences;
3. Identifying the incorrect section of a sentence;
4. Identifying the specific rule which has been violated.

In a more recent study, Bialystok (1986*b*) attempts to identify a developmental discontinuity which might reflect these different levels of difficulty.

The experiment she designed consisted of a judgement test followed by a test in which the sentences judged to be ungrammatical were corrected (see the next subsection). The judgement test involved the first two levels of difficulty. The subjects, aged 5 to 9, had to choose from a set of sentences those which they thought ungrammatical. They had been shown by means of examples that semantically abnormal sentences should be accepted if they were grammatical. The verbal material was composed of:

• sentences which were grammatically and semantically acceptable (GS);
• sentences which were ungrammatical but semantically acceptable (gS);
• sentences which were grammatical but semantically abnormal (Gs; for example, 'If I am sick again tomorrow, I will have to see my fireman');
• sentences which were grammatically and semantically abnormal (gs).

Only the sentences which were both grammatically and semantically acceptable were the object of a significantly larger number of correct judgements as age increased. The level of acceptance of these sentences grew from approximately two-thirds at 5 years of age to 90 per cent at 9 years of age. Moreover, only a third of the grammatical but semantically abnormal sentences (Gs) were accepted, irrespective of age, and an identical level of rejection was observed at 5 and 7 years of age for the ungrammatical but semantically acceptable sentences (gS), although in this case the success level approached 50 per cent at 9. The semantically and syntactically deviant sentences (gs) were rejected in more than two-thirds of cases from the age of 5 onwards.

A comparison of the performances relating to the sentences which are semantically acceptable provides a clear indication that grammatical sentences are recognized earlier and more readily than ungrammatical sentences. However, the global pattern of these data might cause us to doubt whether these judgements follow from any reflection on the syntax of the sentences. Bialystok (1986*b*; Bialystok and Ryan, 1985*b*) go on to suggest that implicit grammatical awareness is sufficient for the passing of such judgements. *In fact, the idea of grammaticality, however it is formulated, is probably meaningless for the young child, whose response is determined by the global acceptability of the sentences. Grammaticality is only one of a number of components in this acceptability, a component which is in no way a privileged (or even a particular) object of reflection for the young child.* When ungrammaticality lies at the root of the early rejection of sentences, it is mediated by the effects of distortion of meaning or by the dissonances it provokes. Although these factors are very difficult to control experimentally, this has nevertheless been attempted in the course of an extremely astute experiment.

Berthoud-Papandropoulou and Sinclair (1983) perfected an experimental procedure which was designed to make it difficult – indeed, impossible – to extract the meaning from sentences. This was intended to force children to take account of the form of the sentences alone when judging them. The subjects were children aged between 4½ and 10, French-speaking Genevans who were asked to judge sentences in Italian, a language which they did not understand but with which they were nevertheless familiar. The children were presented with two puppets. One of these fictitious speakers spoke a sentence in French and the other tried to translate it into Italian. The subjects' task was to judge the exactness of the translation and to explain this judgement. The source sentence was '*Le chien a mangé le bifteck*' ('The dog has eaten the steak'), which was incorrectly translated into Italian as '*Cane cane cane*' ('Dog dog dog') or '*Cane bistecca*' ('Dog steak'). It should be noted that even if the children could not judge these sentences on the basis of their proven existence within their linguistic experience, their meaning still remained partially accessible. The word '*cane*' is capable of evoking the French word '*caniche*' ('poodle') and the word '*bistecca*' the word '*bifteck*' ('beefsteak'). The repetitive translation was rejected by almost all the subjects, whatever their age, and the second translation by a third of the subjects aged 6 and under, half of those aged 7 and three-quarters of those aged 8 and over.

The distribution of the arguments used by the children who rejected the repetitive sequence is difficult to interpret. In fact, the majority of the subjects between 9 and 10 years of age were able to translate the pseudo-sentence, and arguments referring to its repetitive form were given by nearly half of the children aged 4–5 and approximately two-thirds of those aged 8. Here it is probably the configuration of the sounds of the utterance rather than its syntactic structure which determined the responses. The observation that the youngest subjects were readier to reject the repetition of a sound and the older subjects the repetition of a word no doubt reflects what they have learned at school about the use of the metalinguistic term 'word'. The arguments for the rejection of the incomplete translation are more interesting. If we ignore straightforward translations, not one of the justifications provided by the children aged between 4 and 6 referred to the form of the utterance, while almost all the justifications given by the children of 7 and over were based on the absence of elements. The relatively high number of subjects of this age who rejected the utterance thus seemed to do so after the conscious identification of a syntactic anomaly. Of all the data reported, this result is the only one which seems to us to be unambiguously concerned with the emergence of metasyntactic awareness.

Proof of the possibility of making metasyntactic judgements is thus furnished at the age of 7 – that is to say, at the age at which formal education commences. While episyntactic judgements appear at an early age, they are incidental to extrasyntactic, and often extralinguistic, considerations on the part of the children. This type of nonanalytical apprehension of language also seems to survive in adults when they are confronted with material whose meaning they can perceive. On this subject, Bredart and Rondal (1982, p. 89) indicate that 'it is likely that in practice, subjects do not distinguish clearly between purely grammatical factors and semantic and stylistic factors in their judgements of acceptability'. In fact, the term '*judgement of grammaticality*' is more often than not an illusion. In general this is a question of the *judgements of the acceptability of ungrammatical sentences*, a term which does not prejudge the true determining factors in these judgements. When confronted with an utterance, it is seldom useful to evaluate its syntax for its own sake. Most often the syntactic problems cannot be detected unless the subject has been alerted by a difficulty in semantic interpretation.

Tasks of judgement therefore appear to be only poorly adapted to the study of metasyntactic abilities, at least as long as these judgements are not analyzed in terms of the productions of the same subjects in the subsequent tasks of correction.

Metasyntactic control

The ability of individuals to control the grammaticality of their own productions intentionally is studied through the observations of spontaneous and externally provoked self-repairs and other-repairs. This latter type of behaviour corresponds to a productive activity which follows the perception of a linguistic production generated by someone else.

The study of syntactic self-repairs

It is partly due to the observation of the existence of activities of self-repair in the young child (from the age of 2 onwards) that E. V. Clark (1978) asserts the existence of early metalinguistic behaviour. This observation is not new. As early as 1914, Snyder had already seen a child aged $2\frac{1}{2}$

performing spontaneous self-repairs of word order (for example, the child said, 'Down sand beach I been' and then corrected this to 'I been down sand beach'). Since then similar observations have been reported by a large number of authors. For their part, Berko (1958) and Gallagher (1977) have noted that under certain circumstances young children can repair their linguistic productions if stimulated to do so by an adult interlocutor (for example, in response to the question 'What?').

For Clark and Anderson (1979, quoted by Tunmer and Grieve, 1984), who observed that the frequency of syntactic self-repairs increased with age in a group of three children aged between 2 and $3\frac{1}{2}$, the children must become aware of their language errors at the start of the acquisition period if they are to realize that their elementary versions of the language are inadequate. When such errors are produced, the children will reflect on their own production in order to repair them.

Slobin (1978) observed self-repairs and reformulations in his daughter Heida (an early polyglot and an extremely gifted linguist) between the ages of 2 and 6. For example, at the age of 3 years 2 months she said, 'It's watching we cutting ... our cutting ... we cutting ... our's cutting'. Or again, at 3 years 4 months, 'You didn't give me a fork .... You didn't gave me a fork'. However, Slobin asserts that these are the manifestations of low-level metalinguistic abilities which correspond to a 'preconscious' control of speech (which we shall call epilinguistic behaviour). Kolinsky (1986), Levelt *et al.* (1978) and Van Kleeck (1984) have developed the same point of view, and Pratt and Grieve (1984*b*), who base their arguments on the fact that outside prompting fails to cause young subjects to make any comments about their own activities of syntactic self-repair, think that this linguistic behaviour 'may reflect their tacit knowledge of the rules of language, rather than their conscious awareness of grammatical structure' (p. 5).

Most of the available data on the phenomenon of early self-repair are anecdotal in nature, all the more so since they derive to a large extent from the observation of the researchers' own children, and it is doubtful whether such a group is representative. Two analyses of larger groups do, however, give us a better idea of the phenomenon, albeit among children of 5 or older.

First of all, Rogers (1978) has examined the self-repairs produced by children of 5–6 and 6–7 in three individual conversations, during the course of which the children were asked to comment on a picture which was shown to them and speak on subjects associated with their everyday school life. Self-repairs bearing on syntax or morphology but leaving the meaning unaffected (for example, 'Me go ... I go') account for between 6 per cent and 8 per cent of utterances, depending on age. Moreover, at 5 years of age the self-repairs implying changes of meaning are only half as frequent as those concerning formal aspects. At 6 they are equally frequent, and at 7 twice as frequent. Evans (1985), who conducted a similar analysis in less formal circumstances (the interactions between children), found that less than 0.5 per cent of the produced sentences were syntactically self-repaired, irrespective of whether this was among the 5–6- or the 7-to-8-year-olds. Most of the self-repairs were of a semantic nature, concentrating on lexical changes or introducing a greater degree of precision.

Though noteworthy, this phenomenon still seems to be limited in scope and is, moreover, difficult to interpret in terms of deliberate monitoring of syntax. As Tunmer and Grieve (1984) observe, syntactic self-repairs do not necessarily presuppose an awareness of grammatical rules, and may follow from the child's observation that the sense of the verbal message it has produced does not coincide with the meaning it wanted to transmit.

The study of syntactic other-repairs

Weir (1966) has indicated that from 4 years of age onwards, children are able to comment on or repair the syntactic errors of their younger interlocutors. Such observations lead E. V. Clark (1978) to say that at this age children seem to become aware of the errors made by those younger than themselves. These spontaneous other-repairs have also been observed in connection with the productions of adults (Horgan, 1981). Bonnet and Tamine-Gardes (1984, p. 119) give some examples of these corrective comments:

> GABRIEL (4;1): His mother makes a mistake, saying '*celle-là*' ('that', feminine) about a quince ('*coing*', masculine). He corrects her: 'You say *celui-là*' ('that', masculine).
>
> VALÉRIE (5;2): X – '*Ils peignent ces oiseaux, tu vois?*' ('They're painting those birds, do you see?')
> V – '*Il faut dire: il(s) peint, pas il(s) peignent, il(s) peint*' ('You should say: 'He's painting, not they're painting, he's painting')

Again the question clearly revolves around whether this behaviour is truly metasyntactic in nature or not. It will not surprise anyone if we question whether these repairs reflect anything other than the identification and pointing out of a dissonance, and whether the subject has the slightest intention of defending a rule which goes beyond the limitations of the current situation.

Whatever the answer, we have to base our analysis on a broader collection of data than these few individual cases. In our presentation of these data, we shall distinguish between data yielded by corrections requested after a judgement of ungrammaticality (or, more exactly, of unacceptability; see above) and data imposed on the subjects by means of sentences which are presented to them as ungrammatical from the outset. The second type of data will allow us to conduct a more far-reaching investigation than the first, which is essentially intended to explain the factors which determine judgement.

The correction of sentences judged to be unacceptable
The results which will be presented here were all obtained from a task in which subjects had to correct sentences which they themselves had rejected during the course of an immediately preceding judgement task. This initial task is reported in the subsection dealing with metasyntactic judgements (see above).

Two of the three 2-year-old children tested by Gleitman *et al.* (1972) were not content to produce occasionally adapted judgements. They also produced corrections of the badly ordered sentences which they held to be 'silly'. Nevertheless, out of 19 corrections reported by the authors, only 3 referred exclusively to word order, the others being semantic in nature. For example, 'Box the open' was corrected to 'Get in the box'. It was this observation which led de Villiers and de Villiers (1974) to cast doubt on the idea that the judgements produced by young subjects are syntactically determined.

In an experiment reported in 1972, de Villiers and de Villiers preferred to ask their subjects (eight children aged between 2 years 4 months and 3 years 9 months) 'the right way to say' sentences which they judged to be 'wrong' rather than asking them to 'fix them up', as Gleitman *et al.* had done. In this way they hoped to maximize the possibility of obtaining corrections which were focused on the variability of order. The unacceptable sentences presented consisted of both badly ordered sentences and anomalous sentences (for example, 'Throw the sky' – see above). After considering the judgements produced and the proposed corrections, the authors were able to propose a four-stage evolutionary scheme linked to the linguistic development of children (increase in the mean length of produced utterances; see R. W. Brown, 1973):

1. Only semantically abnormal utterances are distinguished, although the child is not able to correct them;
2. Children can identify inverted utterances but are not able to correct them. They do, however, propose corrections for semantically abnormal utterances;
3. Children reject and correct inverted utterances. However, their corrections appear to be determined by semantic considerations (for example, 'House a build' is corrected to 'Live in a house');
4. Only children who are most advanced in their linguistic development (mean length of utterance greater than four words) reestablish the correct order.

Using the same method with twelve 4-year-old children, de Villiers and de Villiers (1974) showed that three-quarters of their subjects made more corrections relating to word order than to semantic content. Moreover, they noted a significant correlation (0.77) between these performances and their subjects' understanding of reversible passive sentences. This led them to suggest that the increase in this type of correction is linked to linguistic development.

However, these corrections do not prove that the subjects had identified a grammatical error and decided to reestablish the sentence's conformity with a rule which had been violated in the original formulation. Moreover, neither de Villiers and de Villiers nor Gleitman *et al.* support such a position. Their experiments were designed to test the model of linguistic competence elaborated by Chomsky (1965). Thus de Villiers and de Villiers (1974) use their results to affirm that, contrary to what is implied by the generative theory, we have to wait until the age of 4–5 for this competence (that is to say, *tacit* knowledge, not conscious awareness of syntactic rules) to become established.

Smith and Tager-Flusberg's (1982) presentation of the results they obtained in connection with the correction of sentences which their subjects rejected (the ungrammaticalities concerning either word order or the final morpheme of a word depending on the experiment; see above) is particularly opaque. On the one hand, the two age categories are conflated; on the other, the number of properly corrected sentences is never brought into any clear relation with the number of sentences which each subject declared unacceptable and thus had to correct. In fact, the group was divided into two parts: those subjects who succeeded in the task of judgement for at least nine sentences out of ten (half of the correct responses demanded acceptances, five of the sentences being grammatical; the other half consisted of rejections) and those who did not attain this score. Two-thirds of the first group corrected the ungrammaticalities at least four times out of five, irrespective of whether the error concerned word order or a morpheme (agreement of verb, plural or possessive marker). Thus, on a first analysis, their judgements seem to have been determined by syntactic anomalies.

The other subjects produced differing performances in the tasks of correcting word order and the task of correcting morphemic ungrammaticality. As far as word order is concerned, three-quarters of these subjects failed to make any corrections, the remainder producing between one and three corrections out of five. Here it would be useful to establish a relationship between these corrections and the judgements passed. In fact, it is possible that these subjects effectively corrected all the ungrammatical sentences which they rejected. However, this cannot be determined from the presentation of the data. This problem becomes clearer in connection with an examination of the levels of correction of morphemic ungrammaticalities. Here, nearly a quarter of the subjects performed four or five corrections. As the level of correct judgements passed by them never exceeds eight sentences out of ten, it becomes clear that at least one or two of the incorrect judgements made by this group must have consisted of the rejection of a grammatical sentence. However, this phenomenon is at no point considered by the authors in their analysis of the subjects' responses. Moreover, no information is given about the corrections proposed for the grammatical sentences which were rejected by the subjects. If we also consider that the authors do not specify the criteria for a good correction and that at no time do they speak of the semantic corrections which must necessarily exist in their data, it will be understood that these frequently cited results seem to us to have a very limited heuristic potential in the form in which they are currently presented.

Grammatical other-repairs
Pratt *et al.* (1984) are right to emphasize that the tendency, recognized up to the age of 6 or 7, to evaluate sentences on the basis of their semantic content may mask a real metasyntactic ability. In fact, it is difficult to know whether young children are truly unable to reflect on the grammatical structure of sentences or whether they are capable of doing so but prefer to evaluate the content. Furthermore, these authors recall two major problems which are intrinsic to the task of judgement: on the one hand the risk of confusing children's understanding of grammatical rules with their ability to express them; and on the other the possibility that a sentence may be rejected simply because 'it doesn't sound right', without the subject knowing the cause of this dissonance.

Pratt *et al.* (1984) attempted to avoid these potential sources of bias by using a procedure designed to focus the attention of the subjects, children aged 5–6 and 6–7, on considerations of form rather than content. Here again the subjects were asked to correct the ungrammatical utterances produced by puppets but, in order to avoid the sources of bias introduced by the passing of judgements, the subjects were warned that all the sentences presented to them were ungrammatical and that all therefore had to be corrected. Moreover, the type of ungrammaticality was specified: sometimes the sentences possessed an inappropriate word order (VOS, VSO or SOV sentences, article or adjective following the noun, auxiliary following the verb) and the children were told that the sentences were 'all jumbled up' and that they had to 'unjumble them'. Sometimes the ungrammaticality was the result of a single morpheme (agreement of verb, person or tense, marker of the continuous form, omission of the article or the plural or possessive marker) and the children were warned that the sentence was 'a bit wrong' and that they had to 'fix it up'. The second type of error was the object of corrections which bore on the syntax alone (without affecting the meaning of the sentence) in more than 90 per cent of cases for the 5–6-year-olds and older children. The badly ordered sentences were corrected in the same way at only the lower level of 50 per cent at the age of 5–6 and 75 per cent at 6–7. The authors concluded that from the age of 5 onwards, children possess the metasyntactic abilities which are implied in the corrections of detail but that, in contrast, the reestablishment of order is a more difficult task. In their interpretation of the latter result, they construct the hypothesis that this difficulty is associated with the fact that the change of order profoundly disturbs the meaning of the sentence. In such a case the children have to solve two tasks: (1) identify the meaning of the sentence; (2) correct the ungrammaticality. In the case of the other sentences, only the second task is necessary. Results similar to those of Pratt *et al.* have been obtained by Tunmer *et al.* (1987), who used an identical procedure to demonstrate a further link between observed performances and the reading level of the child (see the chapter on writing).

For our part, we have performed a series of experiments (Gombert and Boudinet, 1988) in which the experiment of Pratt *et al.* was adapted for use in French. The goal of this repetition was essentially to verify our hypothesis of a low level of success at 4–5 years old, an age band not studied by the Australian authors. Our results showed that at this age the success level does not exceed 17 per cent for the sentences with distorted word order or 41 per cent for sentences made ungrammatical by an incorrect morpheme. The clear difference in performance between children aged 4–5 and older children should not be allowed to hide the fact that these results demonstrate the undeniable existence of early syntactic corrections. This can be seen as support for the argument that from 4 years of age onwards, children are able to reflect on the syntactic dimension of language and monitor it intentionally in their own productions. However, this is not our hypothesis. In fact, we are of the opinion that these early corrections are largely determined by an unintentional process. More precisely, this hypothesis holds that each time the child can grasp the meaning of the ungrammatical sentence presented to it, it is content, in its own production (which follows the task of correction), to verbalize the representation of the sentence which it has constructed. As children of this age are often able to express themselves correctly, the ungrammaticality can thus become the object of an incidental correction without the child ever paying the slightest attention to syntax.

This hypothesis is supported by the results of Tyler and Marslen-Wilson (1978), who showed that when 5-year-old children are asked to repeat a sentence from a story 'verbatim', they make numerous syntactic and lexical modifications while retaining the overall meaning of the sentence. The same phenomenon has been observed, albeit to a lesser degree, among children of 7–11 years of age.

If our hypothesis is correct, the correction level should be the same whether the task is to correct the sentence or simply to repeat it. By confronting the same children with two tasks, we were able to reinforce the plausibility of this hypothesis, since the correction levels did not differ significantly from one task to the other.

Thus, for the change of word order, the levels of syntactic corrections following the correction task and the simple repetition task were 17 per cent and 16 per cent respectively. For morphemic ungrammaticalities these levels were 41 per cent and 34 per cent respectively. In contrast, the levels of simple repetition differ sharply and point to a differentiation between the two tasks on the part of subjects.

Far from being linked to a grammatical awareness, early corrections thus seem to be determined by the difficulties which young children experience when repeating linguistic constructions which are unfamiliar to them.

Similarly, Bowey (1986) also used the twin tasks of correction of ungrammatical sentences and repetition of errors with a group of children aged between 5 and 11. The verbal material consisted of ungrammatical sentences which, for the most part, had been observed in the speech of children (for example, 'John and Tom is a brother'). The level of success in the correction task was 44 per cent at 5, over 60 per cent at 5–6 and 6–7 and more than 80 per cent at 7–8 onwards. The level of corrections performed despite the instructions to repeat the error fell from 21 per cent at 5 to less than 10 per cent at 5–6. Using a similar method with children aged between 6 and 8, Ryan and Ledger (1979) encountered success rates lower than 20 per cent at all ages for the corrections, and additional correction rates of 5 per cent to 10 per cent for incidental corrections made during repetition.

In fact, it should be pointed out that Bowey's procedure maximizes the success rates for corrections. When subjects provided a correction which changed the meaning or the complete structure of the sentence, they were asked to start again and told that there was another way of eliminating the error. If this second attempt also failed, the item was moved back to the end of the series. The same procedure was used for the task of simple repetition and may be responsible for the introduction of a bias. The results of our research show that among children aged between 4 and 5, semantic changes occur nearly twice as frequently in connection with the correction task as with the repetition task. This leads us to hypothesize that for children of this age, this type of correction task is often interpreted as a simple sentence-changing task and not specifically as a syntax-changing task. Bowey gives no detailed account of the execution of the test, but there is reason to think that, with the youngest subjects at least, modifications to the meaning of the sentence occur more frequently with the correction task and that, in consequence, the responses obtained from the repetition task generally necessitated fewer attempts on the part of the subjects than those following the correction task. This may make it more difficult for us to compare the results. Such an observation might lead us to discount the difference of 23 per cent between externally provoked corrections and incidental corrections at 5 years of age. It is, however, insufficient to explain the difference of more than 50 per cent measured from the age of 5–6 onwards.

An interpretation of Bowey's results together with ours suggests a way of completing the hypothesis which we have formulated: up to the age of 5, grammatical corrections would appear to be incidental to the verbalization of the meaning of the ungrammatical sentences presented, with intentional syntactic corrections appearing later. In fact, as a number of authors have already noted (see, for example, Bialystok and Ryan, 1985*b*), the repetition of deviant sentences requires an effort of control on the part of the subject, who has to suppress the natural tendency to normalize such utterances. Of course, this tendency for normalization will manifest itself only if the subject is able to understand the sentence. Furthermore, this comprehension and the subsequent normalization developmentally precede the spontaneous production of the implied syntactic forms by the child.

Thus Kuczaj and Maratsos (1975) report the case of a child who normalized the repetitions of sentences in which the verb and the future auxiliary were swapped (for example, 'The boy push will the elephant') even though the child did not yet produce these auxiliaries spontaneously.

If, however, the fact that from 5 years of age children can produce corrections to ungrammatical sentences on request reveals an undeniable ability to monitor the form of the sentence, this still does not prove that the child is aware that it is applying rules of grammar with a scope which extends beyond the current situation.

It remains true that normalization can be performed only if the child is able to ascertain the meaning of the sentence. Bohannon (1975, 1976) found that among children aged 5 to 7 the level of non-normalized repetitions of badly ordered sentences did not vary with their ability to distinguish grammatical utterances from ungrammatical ones. However, it is clear that whatever the age of the children, the level of comprehension of the ungrammatical sentences used by the author (sentences of between 5 and 15 words) is very low. This absence of any elaborated representation of the meaning of the sentence prevents the subjects from manifesting any tendency for normalization without, however, casting any doubt on its existence.

Moreover, the tendency to normalize is not limited simply to formal aspects. Thus Bialystok (1986*b*) asked children aged 5, 7 and 9 to correct the ungrammaticality of sentences which were also semantically deviant. The children were asked to correct the syntax of these sentences but not their meaning. The success levels were approximately 20 per cent for the 5 and 7-year-olds and rose to no more than a third of the responses given by the 9-year-olds. Thus for a long period, the behaviour involved in such corrections seems to correspond to a process of normalization indistinctly applied to the semantic and syntactic aspects of the sentences. As such semantic aspects are necessarily closely linked to the presented items, it is possible that the same might be true of the syntactic aspects. In fact, in a study of an African population whose everyday language is a tribal dialect, Scribner and Cole (1981) showed that the ability to correct deviant ungrammatical sentences is

closely linked to education. Only those subjects who could read and write
were able to perform this type of correction.

Conclusion

Tunmer and Herriman (1984) invite us to distinguish between two types of
awareness: the awareness of errors and the awareness of linguistic structure.
These authors maintain that only the second type is metalinguistic in nature.
The results reported above – and in particular the near impossibility of
proving the metasyntactic nature of the processes which determine
judgements and corrections – incline us towards this viewpoint. However, as
almost all the available data concern only the judgement and/or correction of
grammatical errors, we are forced to try to infer the second type of
awareness from the behavioural evidence found for the first.

The limitations of the available data are aggravated by the way in which
the results of most of the experiments are processed. We have implicitly
based our account of the data on the statistical significance of the differences
reported by the authors. It is curious to note that in these days of sometimes
extreme statistical sophistication, the most suitable methods of analysis are
sometimes systematically ignored. An examination of the detail of our own
results will provide an illustration.

The verbal material used in the tasks of judgement and correction is
highly varied. Thus in the study which we adapted from Pratt *et al.* (1984)
the verb-subject-object sentence '*Chante la fillette une chanson*' ('Sings the
girl a song') is corrected by only 35 per cent of the 5-year-old subjects,
whereas a sentence with the same structure '*Jouent les enfants au ballon*' ('Play
the children ball') is corrected by 59 per cent of the same subjects. Generally
speaking, the level of success in reestablishing word order among subjects of
this age varies between 6 per cent and 88 per cent, with the level for the
correction of morphemic ungrammaticality varying between 18 per cent and
94 per cent. This fact, which has too great a scope to form part of our
current study, is never reported by authors. Moreover, whatever the study,
the analyses of variance used in connection with the results apply only to the
average values of the performances achieved by the subjects. Such an
approach smothers the variations between sentences under an overall score
which corresponds to none of the items actually tested. This fact has two
implications. First, the calculated significances are invalidated by the failure
to consider the variable 'sentence' as a source of uncertainty along with the
variable 'subject' (assuming that it really is so, otherwise it should be counted
as one of the factors manipulated within the experiment). The results should
thus be recalculated in such a way that only clear differences are considered
as such. Secondly, in the future we should concentrate on discovering the
factor or factors which lie at the origin of the differences between sentences.

Our initial investigations suggest that such factors are linked to the global acceptability of the sentence rather than to the specific ungrammaticalities which it contains.

Episyntactic behaviour

Berthoud and Sinclair (1978), basing their ideas on the results of experiments comprising both metalinguistic judgements and comprehension tests, remind us that reflection about sentences is possible only long after a generalized level of success in the comprehension of them has been attained. In the same way, de Villiers and de Villiers (1978) insist that there is an interval of several months, or even several years, between the use of the rules of production and metalinguistic awareness of these rules.

Nevertheless, in the field of spontaneous linguistic behaviour, it is possible to observe the effects of ungrammaticality at an early age, in particular in the case of the self-repairs which are observed from 2 years onwards and the other-repairs which are witnessed after the age of 4. Furthermore, 4 appears to be the age at which it is possible to get children to distinguish ungrammatical sentences and, to a certain extent, to correct these ungrammaticalities. However, the reported data suggest that these early manipulations of syntax long remain incidental to a consideration of the meaning of the presented sentences and the 'normality' of their sound configurations.

When the experimental context is such that referencing is impeded, it is nevertheless possible to provoke manipulations of syntax. For example, Berko (1958) has shown that children aged 5–6 and 7–8 are able to add an (s) to meaningless words to make them plural ('wug', 'two wugs'). However, as Pratt and Grieve (1984*b*) have suggested, these performances seem to be more closely linked to a tacit knowledge of the rules of language than to a conscious awareness of grammatical rules.

Whether we are talking about the first intuitions of acceptability or the first corrective abilities, this episyntactic behaviour is probably an *ad hoc* response to each specific provoking utterance and does not mean – to borrow an expression from Gleitman *et al.* (1972) – that there is a budding grammarian in the child of pre-school age. These early manipulations of language are nevertheless often effective and probably constitute the object of an emerging awareness which can later develop into a true metasyntactic ability (see Chapter 8).

Metasyntactic behaviour

It is necessary to wait for the age of 6–7 to encounter judgements which seem to reveal a conscious identification of the nonapplication of a syntactic rule (see Berthoud-Papandropoulou and Sinclair, 1983). Bialystok's results

(1986*b*) suggest that the conscious application of these rules appears even later.

In parallel with what we have seen in connection with metaphonological development – and despite the failure of an attempt by Ryan and Ledger (1979) to demonstrate this – it is possible that suitable training may cause such behaviour to emerge earlier, probably as soon as the corresponding epiprocedural behaviour has become well established (at about the age of 5?). Beyond the effects of such training, it is through school work on the formal aspects of language, in particular in the explicit learning of grammatical rules and in the corresponding practical exercises as well as in reading tasks focusing on comprehension, that the necessity for metasyntactic behaviour, of no use before this age, might be seen to emerge.

Chapter 4

Metalexical and metasemantic development

Introduction

Metasemantic awareness refers to both the ability to recognize the language system as a conventional and arbitrary code and the ability to manipulate words or more extensive signifying elements, without the signified correspondents being automatically affected by this. In theory, it is distinct from *metalexical awareness, which corresponds to the subject's ability on the one hand to isolate the word and identify it as being an element of the lexicon, and on the other to endeavour to access the internal lexicon intentionally.* Nevertheless, since the elements of the lexicon constitute minimal units of meaning, it is very difficult to dissociate the two aspects in the observation of real linguistic behaviour (except perhaps in neuropsychological studies of subjects manifesting specific problems in lexical or semantic processes). We have therefore chosen to present the development of these two components of metalinguistic awareness in parallel, although we repeat the distinction, albeit somewhat artificially, within the first subsection.

The logic underlying the experiments investigating this aspect of metalinguistic development has led us to divide its treatment into two separate parts: the word, on the one hand, and more extensive linguistic elements, on the other. One subsection will be devoted solely to metaphors, which are usually lexical but for the most part make sense only in a linguistic context. It is difficult to define a strict separation between the declarative and procedural aspects of the experiments cited. Therefore, in contrast to the practice of the preceding chapters, this structure will not be adopted here except in connection with the production and comprehension of metaphors for which such a classification is possible.

The data given below concern only the processing of spoken language. Similar studies bearing on written language are cited only when they illustrate the implementation of metalexical and/or metasemantic awareness in spoken language. The remaining studies will be presented in the chapter devoted to written language (see Chapter 7).

The awareness and deliberate manipulation of the word

Nelson (1974) has observed that many of the first discursive forms used by children are purely expressive in nature. She gives the example of games, greetings and ritual forms like 'boom', 'go away' and 'stop it' which serve to regulate interpersonal relations but possess no stable referents. These vocal games seem to be more closely linked to the field of action than of language. These utterances, often intended to produce the same response from the adult, have a repetitive character which strongly resembles circular behaviour. In other words, it is principally a question of the implementation and exercise of schemes which are indispensable to later language development.

All the same, the capacity which very young children have for adapting their attitudes and actions in response to the verbal messages addressed to them is not the manifestation of linguistic comprehension. Indeed, it has been established that in these reactions it is the prosodic factors which are the determining ones, while the semantic content of the discourse appears to play no role (Mehler, 1976).

If, therefore, many forms of behaviour observed in young children show that they can understand many things well before learning to speak, it is doubtful whether they understand many words. It is the intention of the speaker which seems to be perceived by children much more than the semantic content of the message being addressed to them. For young children it is the prosodic factor, soon to be assisted by the perception of certain key words (which are, in addition, accentuated by the adult speaker), which determines identification of the objective of the speech addressed to them. From then on, children attach meaning to this speech in the same way as they attach meanings to the multiple events taking place in their physical environment. Speech is thus significant, but that does not imply in any way that it is a signifier in itself; rather, it is the act of speech which has meaning, not the language itself. It is doubtlessly misleading to say that the very young child understands words. What is evident is that the child reacts in an identical manner to identical words, and this response springs more from the formation of concepts than from lexical awareness.

E. V. Clark (1978) recalls that when children begin to use a word, they do not necessarily know what it means. It could be added that they do not know that they are using a word, or even that they are emitting a sound or series of sounds which makes any sense. As Bonnet wrote (1986), even if they are aware of speaking, young children still have no awareness of signs or the relationship which signs have to their referents or to other signs.

Metalexical development

Lexical segmentation

In much the same way as children were asked to segment syllables into phonemes or words into syllables (see the chapter on metaphonological development above), a number of researchers have studied the child's ability to segment sentences or word sequences into words.

As in their tasks of segmentation into phonemes or syllables (see above), Fox and Routh (1975) asked children to repeat 'just a little bit' of a sentence said to them. The length of the sentences used ranged from two to seven words. Using this technique, the authors obtained success rates of over 60 per cent in 3-year-olds and almost 90 per cent in 4-year-olds. As was the case when this technique was used for phonemic or syllabic segmentation, we remain unconvinced by the results. Here too, we should note that the experimenters continued to ask for further segmentation of segments longer than a word until the child produced a sound sequence corresponding to one word. Thus this experiment seems unable to establish the existence of any real early metalexical competence.

To our knowledge only one other piece of research shows early success in a task involving the segmentation of word sequences into words. Tunmer and Bowey (1981) preceded the experimental segmentation task with explicit demonstrations. During this training phase they continually provided their subjects with corrective feedback. During the actual experiment the children had to identify each word by tapping on the table (word-tapping task). The authors obtained a 73 per cent success rate from 4-year-olds for sequences of two or three words. The subjects' performances were better for sequences comprising just nouns and adjectives than for those including verbs and quantifiers. The success rate rose to 90 per cent in 5-year-olds and 98 per cent in 6-year-olds. Criticizing their own experiment, Bowey and Tunmer point out (1984) that only words containing a single stressed syllable were used in the experiment, and that it was therefore possible that the children were simply tapping the table on each accentuation. This interpretation coincides with the results obtained by Holden and MacGinitie (1972), which show that children tend to segment phrases at the most accentuated points, and those obtained by Ehri (1975), which obtained incorrect responses when both syllables of a bisyllabic word were stressed.

In a repeat of their initial experiment, Tunmer *et al.* (1983*a*) used pronounceable sequences of nonmeaningful words (for example, '*loust namp denster*'). In all age groups the 'success rates' for these items were as high as for the sequences of meaningful words. This disqualifies an interpretation of the results in terms of the conscious identification of lexical elements. Also, in some of the sequences presented in this study, the authors used bisyllabic words comprising two independently meaningful morphemes (for example, 'outside'). In confirmation of Ehri's results (1975), it appeared that the 5-to-6-year-old children tended to tap on the table for each of the morphemes, and it was not until the age of 7 that the children identified the words correctly.

Several other studies seem to indicate that the ability for lexical segmentation is not at all prominent at pre-school age. In a study carried out in Russian, Karpova (1966) asked children aged 3–7 to count the number of words in a sentence which she spoke to them, and then to list each of the words. The subjects aged 4–5 split the sentence into semantic units, the 5-to-6-year-olds gave the principal components (nouns, verbs, theme), and it was not until the age of 6–7 that some children were able to say the first three words of the sentence separately. However, even at that age the success rate in the counting task was very poor. Even the subjects who produced the best performances still made frequent errors in connection with prepositions and conjunctions. Moreover, words were often deconstructed into syllables. Analogous results have been obtained in English (Hall, 1976) and in French (Berthoud-Papandropoulou, 1978, 1980; Papandropoulou and Sinclair, 1974).

Berthoud-Papandropoulou (1980) shows that the ability to perform lexical division is very rare in children under 7 and that such divisions are performed correctly in only a third of cases in 7-year-olds and a half of cases in 8-to-10-year-olds. It is not until the 11-to-12-year-old age group that total success is achieved in this kind of test. The majority of 4-year-olds and almost a quarter of 5-year-olds gave responses corresponding to a count (or, more exactly, most of the time a pseudo-count) and an enumeration not of the lexical elements but of the real elements referred to in the sentences. Thus for a child of 5 years 4 months there are nineteen words in the sentence *'Le cochon a mangé beaucoup'* ('The pig ate a lot') *'parce qu'il mange beaucoup, beaucoup, beaucoup'* ('because he eats lots and lots and lots'). For another child of 4 years 1 month (cited by Berthoud-Papandropoulou, 1978), there are six words in the phrase *'Six enfants jouent'* ('Six children are playing'), namely *'Moi, mon petit frère, et Christiane, Anne, Jean, etc.'* ('Me, my little brother, and Christiane . . . etc.'). This kind of response disappears at the age of 7.

In a study undertaken with children aged 5 to 7, Bialystok (1986*a*) used verbal material in which she tried to distinguish between a number of factors. Four types of item (sentences or clauses) were used:

1. Sentences comprising only monosyllabic words (for example, 'The birds in the old tree sang so well');
2. Sentences containing bisyllabic words ('The lovely princess tripped over a pumpkin');

3. Sentences containing multisyllabic words ('Do gorillas wear flannelette pyjamas?');
4. Sentences containing words composed of independently meaningful morphemes ('Jane knows that snowmen melt in the sunshine').

Moreover, each type of sentence was sometimes presented in its normal form, and sometimes jumbled up (for example, one of the sentences above becomes 'Old so birds the sang in tree well the').

The subjects had to count the words by picking up a cardboard square for each unit they considered to be a word. The results reveal that whichever type of jumbled-up sentence was presented, a third of 5-year-olds and more than three-quarters of 7-year-olds counted correctly. When the sentences were presented normally, the words were counted correctly in less than 10 per cent of cases by the 5-year-olds, while the 7-year-olds' results were affected by the type of sentence, with a 75 per cent success rate in sentences composed of monosyllabic words, a 58 per cent success rate in sentences containing bisyllabic or multisyllabic words, and a 28 per cent success rate in sentences containing words composed of independently meaningful morphemes.

These results are particularly interesting. The type of word to be counted has an effect already noted by other authors, but only in connection with 7-year-olds. What is especially interesting is that at all ages a meaningful word sequence appears more difficult to segment than a meaningless one. It is possible to hypothesize that the word divisions made by the subjects (or at least by the younger subjects) are divisions into units of meaning. Thus in sequences with a jumbled word order such a strategy extracts the content words and isolates the function words, which are never allocated a position in which they form phrases with content words. All words positioned in such an isolated way are therefore relatively easy to count. In sentences presented normally, the same strategy led to an underestimation of the number of words on the part of the younger children, who were, in fact, counting phrases. At age 7, the destruction of meaning imposed by the chopping up of sentences (an acceptable destruction for those who had started to learn the alphabet) sometimes led to too great a segmentation, with a syllable being given the status of a word. Unfortunately, Bialystok does not provide detailed reports of the incorrect responses made by her subjects, so the validity of our hypothesis cannot be confirmed here.

Christinat-Tièche (1982) has used a somewhat different technique. Subjects had to make up a story in pairs, each taking turns to invent '*un tout petit bout*' ('a tiny little bit'). Two examples were given, the first being composed of single word segments (*Le / chat / noir / joue / toujours / avec / la / grosse / pelote / de / laine* – The / black / cat / always / plays / with / the / big / ball / of / wool) and the second being composed of nominal and verbal groups (*Quand il fait sombre / la grand-mère / met ses lunettes / sur son nez / pour lire / le journal* – When it gets dark / Grandmother / puts her glasses / on her nose / to read / the paper). At age 4, neither of the models was followed; at age 5, 19 per cent of the stories were composed of divisions into nominal and verbal components, as were 36 per cent of those made up by 6-year-olds, but this model was not observed after that age. Lexical divisions appeared in 56 per cent of the stories produced by the 7-to-8-year-olds, and 78 per cent of 9-year-olds also followed this model. For the author, these performances show that from the age of 7, children recognize the word as a linguistic sign.

There is one criticism which has often been levelled at certain of the above-mentioned studies. In the instructions given to the children several of them actually use the metalinguistic term 'word', which is not understood until later (see below). It is possible that these results show more a lack of awareness of this term on the part of the children, and therefore a difficulty in interpreting the instructions, than a lack of ability to segment discourse into units corresponding to words. The same criticism can also be made of other experiments in which the child has to represent each word with an object (for example, a cube) or by tapping on the table. These studies, like the preceding ones, indicate that the 6-to-7-year-old child still has difficulty in segmenting a sentence into its constituent words (see Evans *et al.*, 1979). However, authors like Christinat-Tièche (1982), whose studies do not use the term 'word' in their instructions, have not found any evidence to suggest the existence of an early ability to operate lexical segmentation – despite observations confirming the existence of word substitution in young children's spontaneous verbal activity (see, for example, Weir, 1962). In fact, as Hakes (1980) points out, in order for these word-replacement exercises to be able to establish the subjects' awareness of the word, it would be necessary to demonstrate that these games have a deliberate, rather than fortuitous, character and, as Dale notes (1976), that their content is clearly subordinated to the linguistic form.

The results of a study by Huttenlocher (1964) throw some light on this subject. This author asked children of 4–5 to invert two-word utterances. The children did not seem able to separate and swap the words. The difficulty was even greater when the item presented was meaningful (for example, 'You are' or 'Man runs') rather than a simple juxtaposition of words (for example, 'Child lady'). The author concludes that the difficulty of the task was linked partly to children's inability to segment sentences into words and partly to their reluctance to produce semantically absurd utterances.

As we have already noted, numerous authors have indicated that in segmentation tasks concrete nouns and adjectives are more easily identifiable as words than are prepositions, conjunctions, possessive pronouns and other function words. Friederici (1983) asked children aged 5–12 to identify, in sentences presented to them orally, target words which had previously been presented to them in writing (lexical decision task). While virtually all nouns and adjectives were perceived by all age groups, numerous determiners, demonstratives and adverbs were not identified (the number of omissions diminishing progressively from age 5 to age 10–11). Moreover, the response time for function words was greater in all cases up to the age of 8–9, after which this tendency was reversed.

These results confirm those of Swinney and Cutler (1979) which show that, unlike adults, children aged 5–7 require longer to recognize function words than content words in sentences presented to them orally.

According to Van Kleeck (1984), function words are more difficult to identify because they do not have an autonomous semantic status, but are dependent on context. Furthermore, as Barton (1985) points out, when asked to repeat a sentence word by word or to tap on the table for each word, even children who have started learning to read count the article plus noun or verb phrase (for example, 'has gone') as a single word. Barton and Hamilton (1982, cited by Barton, 1985) find this tendency to count meaningful units in adults with little schooling. These observations lend weight to Kolinsky's viewpoint (1986), which suggests that the ability for lexical identification could be dependent on learning to read, since words are clearly isolated from each other in writing.

Deliberate control of access to the lexicon
Lexical access has provoked a large number of studies into adult behaviour. The models proposed by the different authors can be summarized as three principal conceptions.

The two oldest of these differ as to the obligatory character of phonological analysis in the recognition of written words. The first postulates that hearing (or reading) a word activates its phonological (or graphemic and then phonological) representation, which in turn activates its conceptual representation (see, for example, Chomsky and Halle, 1968); the second, the direct-access hypothesis, does away with the phonological stage in cases where words are presented visually, and passes straight from the graphemic representation to the conceptual representation (see, for example, Kleiman, 1975). However, many authors believe that both modes of access are possible. As Engelkamp (1983) points out, these two conceptions take it for granted that the recognition of a word precedes the activation of its meaning. This notion is challenged by the interactive models.

Johnston and McClelland (1980) propose a model for the recognition of the word which starts with the perception of the stimulus and works up to the activation of the relevant word in the subject's internal lexicon ('bottom–up' or 'data-driven' process). Broadly speaking, each new element (phoneme or grapheme) perceived would activate a collection of words in the lexicon (more exactly 'word detectors' in the vocabulary of McClelland and Rummelhart, 1981; 'logogens' in that of Morton, 1969) and would inhibit the activation of others until the selection of the single relevant word had been completed. This process would demand the complete (or at least extensive) analysis of the word presented, and this analysis is discussed by certain authors, mainly on the basis of the findings of two experiments.

First of all, when a subject is presented with an utterance in which one phoneme is masked (for example, by a cough) or omitted, the subject is unaware of this omission (phenomenon of 'phonemic restoration': Warren, 1970; Marslen-Wilson and Welsh, 1978). Secondly, a word is recognized very rapidly – between 175 and 200 milliseconds – when sometimes only half or less of the acoustic signal has been heard by the subject (Marslen-Wilson, 1973; Marslen-Wilson and Tyler, 1975). These facts led Marslen-Wilson to postulate an interaction between 'bottom–up' processes and processes which start from the internal lexicon and work down to the presented stimulus ('top–down' or 'concept-driven' process). More precisely, the first phoneme perceived would be treated in the 'bottom–up' fashion, thus limiting the number of lexical elements which could correspond to the word presented, and then the 'top–down' process would come into play to restrict the selection of any following phonemes and restore any missing phoneme (this model is known as 'the initial cohort'). Recognition thus takes place as soon as only one word remains possible, perhaps even before phonemic analysis of the presented word has been completed.

While supporting the model elaborated by Marslen-Wilson, Engelkamp (1983) postulates the existence of two types of stimulus analysis: an overall analysis which serves to determine the category to which it belongs (for example, to decide whether or not a stimulus is a word) and a task-specific analysis which is invoked whenever it is necessary to determine the element of the category to which the stimulus corresponds.

This summary of the models of access to the lexicon in word recognition in the adult reveals that in no case is the possibility of the subject's conscious control of the processes envisaged. On the contrary, the shortness of the response time demonstrates that this is a question of automatic processing.

As far as we know, the possibility of adults consciously controlling access to the lexicon is rarely considered, and this is even rarer in the case of children. Nevertheless, some studies have shown interest in the 'tip of the tongue' phenomenon (see, for example, Brown and McNeill, 1966), but this is generally with a view to constructing hypotheses about the way in which word representations are stored in the memory.

The fact that we sometimes recall the approximate sound and number of syllables of a word, but not the word itself, and at other times a synonym with a different sound, argues in favour of a double system of storage, comprising both the phonological and the semantic aspects.

The existence and developmental implementation of metaprocesses for lexical access thus remain to be established and studied, although it appears, a priori, very difficult to find adequate methods for experimentation.

The only data available for children concern their ability to recognize that they have not understood a word (i.e. that it is not in their lexicon) or that a sound sequence is not a word. Thus, Flavell *et al.* (1981) demonstrate that children of 4–5 are conscious of their incomprehension of a rarely used word ('hypotenuse'), and Baker (1984*a*) shows that the majority of 5-year-olds and a large majority of 7-year-olds can detect 'words which are not real words' (namely bisyllabic logatomes) in simple stories presented to them orally. Nevertheless, this early observation of one's own inability to access the lexicon reveals only general, but not specific, control of the processes of lexical access.

Given the current level of knowledge, it appears that lexical representations develop at a later age than the first linguistic productions. Bates (1979) asserts that the first words are not something children 'have' but something they 'do'. A similar idea is proposed by Grieve and Hoogenrad (1979), for whom the words produced by young children are uttered in order to communicate experience rather than meaning. Nelson (1983) proposes a detailed model of the developmental implementation of a first lexicon. She regards the first productions of words as being associated with 'scripts' which structure the knowledge young children have of each event they speak about (for a presentation and discussion of the idea of scripts, see Fayol and Monteil, 1988). These scripts would then later divide progressively into their internal elements which, in turn, would lead to the implementation of concepts and categories. At first, words would refer to these scripts or to elements contained in a particular script. Only after the process of script division could words begin to be used to refer to objects. Taking Nelson's model to its conclusion, Barret (1983) assigns scripts the role of accentuating certain of the objects which they imply. These objects could then be used as prototypical referents around which lexical categories are constructed. Of course, this process of developing a lexicon necessarily precedes any reflective behaviour concerning the lexicon itself.

The development of metasemantic awareness of the word

Piaget (1945) characterized the appearance of the symbolic function (at around 2 years of age) by the child's ability to distinguish between signifier and signified.

For him, the appearance of 'a set of behaviour which implies the representative evocation of an absent object or event "presupposes" the construction or employment of differentiated signifiers since these must be capable of referring both to elements which cannot currently be perceived as well as to those which are present' (Piaget and Inhelder, 1966).

For Piaget, the clearest manifestation of this differentiation was the verbal evocation of objects or events not present at the time of utterance.

It is possible to conclude from the temporal interval between perception and evocation that there is a differentiation between signifier and signified only if, like Piaget, we consider the mental image to be a signifier. This is not our view. We locate the signified in the activity of the subject and, from a psychological point of view, we consider that the represented image, just like the perceived image, is an internalization of the object. Of course, any internalization of an object implies a coding. The internalized object is not the physical object, but that is just as true for the represented image as it is for the perceived image. That which the speaker manipulates verbally is always an encoding of the object, and the signifier used corresponds to the signified, which is never the physical object itself but the image of that object. To limit the process of differentiation between signifier and signified to the differentiation between internalized object and physical object (a differentiation to which the temporal interval effectively attests) is psychologically inappropriate, since the physical object never intervenes unmodified in the cognitive activity of the subject. The point of departure for the psychological process can only be an image of the object.

Nature contains no such thing as the signified, only events and objects. These events and objects become signified only within the context of a sign, from the moment when the signifier confers this status on them. In other words, the signified does not exist outside the psychological activity of the subject. It is never a physical object but the psychological realization of this object.

To record the use of a word in the absence of its referent is thus insufficient to affirm that there is a differentiation between signifier and signified. In fact, at the time of verbal evocation, the signified is present in its conceptual form in the memory of the subject and is likely to influence the manipulation of the signifier.

The differentiation between the word and its referent

In the early part of this century, Piaget (1926) demonstrated that young children regard the name of an object as being one of its intrinsic properties, in the same way as its colour, shape or size. In his study of the child's representation of the world, he asked children aged 5–11 questions concerning the origin of names and the possibility of changing the names of objects. He reported four stages of development:

1. At 5–6, although children can distinguish the name and the object, they consider that the name is an (invisible) quality (for example, if the sun is called 'sun', that is because you can see it, or because it is hot), so the name cannot exist before the object.
2. At 7–8, many children claim that the object's name was invented by the object's creator (namely God or the first human). Even if the name has been given by humans, the object was baptized with it at its very creation. Names are thus inherent in the objects themselves; they can be

dissociated from the objects but are not considered to be purely conventional labels. They contain within themselves the idea of the objects they designate, and are not interchangeable.

3. At 9–10, the name is recognized as being conventional but, for the child, this is still not totally arbitrary. Even if the object existed before being baptized, its name was still its perfect match.

4. Not until the age of 9–10 is the name recognized as a simple sign.

Vygotsky's observations (1934) were much the same. He noted that children of pre-school age, when asked to explain the names of objects, rely on the attributes of these objects to explain their names. For example, a cow is called 'cow' because it has horns. In the same way, if children are asked if a cow could be called 'ink' and ink could be called 'cow', they reply that this is impossible, since ink is for writing and a cow is for giving milk.

This development – and in particular the fact that words do not seem to have an autonomous existence for 4-to-5-year-olds – has been confirmed by numerous authors. The research carried out by Berthoud-Papandropoulou with French-speaking children (Berthoud-Papandropoulou, 1978, 1980; Papandropoulou and Sinclair, 1974) is without doubt the most extensive and complete in this field. This researcher asked children aged 4 to 12 to explain what a word is and to give examples of words possessing particular characteristics.

Children under 5 are generally incapable of giving a definition of the term 'word', and the examples they provide are most often nouns referring to objects or animals.

The definitions offered by most of the 5-to-6-year-old children show that they do not differentiate between signifier and signified. Among their definitions were:

'*Un mot c'est quand je fais quelque chose.*' ('A word is when I do something.')

'*Un mot c'est quelque chose de vrai . . . c'est quelque chose . . . c'est n'importe quoi, ça peut être une chaise ou une tasse ou un livre ou une feuille ou un chien ou des gens ou une bouteille ou à boire ou un cube.*' ('A word is something real . . . it's something . . . it's anything, that could be a chair or a cup or a book or a leaf or a dog or some people or a bottle or something to drink or a cube.')

Thus words do not appear to have any existence independent of their referents, as is clearly illustrated by the child who, when asked how you can know something is a word, replied '*parce qu'on voit que c'est*' ('because you can see what it is').

When asked to give an example of a long word, these children generally offer a phrase designating a long object (for example, 'a train'); for a short word, a small object is named (for example, '*un œil [. . .] parce qu'il est petit*' – 'an eye [. . .] because it's small' – or '*une cigarette dans une petite boîte*' – 'a cigarette in a little box'). If they are asked to give a difficult word, they describe an action which is difficult to do (for example: '*quelqu'un qui enlève la clé [. . .] parce que c'est difficile*' – 'someone who takes the key away [. . .] because it's difficult' – or '*il range [. . .] parce qu'il doit ranger tous ses jouets*' – 'he tidies up [. . .] because he has to tidy up all the toys'). All these responses indicate that the children are unaware of any differentiation between the physical world and the world of language.

Other 5-to-6-year-olds and many of the 6-to-7-year-olds defined the word as being the act of speaking itself ('*c'est quelque chose qu'on parle*' – 'it's something you say'; '*c'est dire quelque chose*' – 'it's saying something'). A long word could thus be '*J'entre dans la maison pour quitter mes chaussures*' – 'I go into the house to take off my shoes' – this is a long word '*parce qu'on dit deux choses à la fois*' – 'because you're saying two things at once'; a short word could be '*il s'en va [. . .] parce qu'il s'en va seulement*' – 'he goes away [. . .] because he just goes away' – or again '*je vais là*' ('I go there') is a short word because '*y'a qu'une chose*' ('there's only one thing'). For these children the length of the word is no longer defined by the physical size of its referent but by the length of the speech chain.

At age 6–7, some children begin to apprehend words as 'labels' designating referents, and it is only at this age that words begin to acquire a reality distinct from that of the signified correspondents. These children identify constituent units in words ('*un mot c'est des lettres*' – 'a word is letters'). However, they refuse to regard articles or certain pronouns as words '*parce qu'il y a pas beaucoup de lettres*' – 'because there are not many letters'. Berthoud-Papandropoulou appears satisfied with this justification. Nevertheless, it seems that at this level again it is essentially semantic criteria which govern the rejection of articles and pronouns. Thus a child who rejects the pronoun '*elle*' ('she') as a word, on the grounds of insufficient letters, accepts the shorter string of letters '*âne*' ('donkey') as a word '*parce que les ânes ça existe*' ('because donkeys exist'). These same children reject the possibility of inventing words because '*j'ai toujours entendu les mots qui étaient vrais*' ('I've always heard words which are true').

From the age of 7, the word is considered as a part of the speech chain ('*c'est un bout de l'histoire*' – 'it's a piece of the story' – or '*on a une phrase, il y a des mots*' – 'there's a sentence, there are words in it'). Moreover, a growing number of children make use of what they have learned at school and tend to define words in terms of grammatical terminology ('*un mot, c'est un nom, un adjectif et un verbe*' – 'a word is a noun, an adjective and a verb'). Nevertheless, at this age most definitions correspond to that of a noun ('*un mot c'est quand on peut mettre "le", "la" ou "des" devant*' – 'a word is when you can put "the" or "some" in front'. It is not until about the age of 10 and over that semantic criteria begin to appear explicitly in the definitions ('*c'est quelque chose formé de lettres et qui veut dire quelque chose*' – 'it's something made from letters and which means something').

When this study was repeated in English, the same results were obtained

(Templeton and Spivey, 1980). These data have been further confirmed by results obtained by other researchers in similar tasks. Thus Francis (1973), who asked children to give an example of a word, obtained appropriate responses from only 44 per cent of 6-year-olds, 66 per cent of 6½-year-olds, 72 per cent of 7-year-olds and 92 per cent of 7½-year-olds. The other children answered with numbers, proper nouns, sentences or nothing at all. Nevertheless, the fact that phrases did not appear in the categorization of the examples provided suggests that the article-noun combination was considered as a good response and that the true level of performance was therefore much lower than that reported. In a quite different test, Feldman and Shen (1971) showed that while 5-year-old children can learn to designate an object by a nonmeaningful word (for example, 'wug', this being confirmed in children of 3–5 by the results obtained by Smith and Tager-Flusberg, 1982), less than a third of them will accept the idea of calling a cup 'plate'. Osherson and Markman (1975) further note that when children of this age accept the possibility of changing the name of an object – for example, when they accept that you can call a dog 'cat' – for them the dog thus renamed will no longer bark but will miaow. In this verbal game, therefore, the name carries with it the whole range of other qualities of the object to which it is linked. On the other hand, when a new name is used, the differentiation between signifier and signified does not operate and the children simply accept the addition of a supplementary signifier to an existing signifier/signified pair. Thus it makes no difference whether the object, dog, is called 'dog' or 'doggie'. A final – very significant – example is that reported by de Villiers and de Villiers (1978) of a child who rejected 'ghost' as a word 'because it isn't real'.

Results obtained by Costermans and Giurgea (1988) agree with the above data.

After a training period, children aged 3 to 7 were asked to segment multisyllabic words into syllables, each word containing a meaningful constituent element. When this element corresponded to the syllable asked for (e.g. *pin-gouin* – /pɛ̃-gwɛ̃/ – penguin, of which /pɛ̃/ ['*pain*'] in French means 'bread'), virtually all the 4-to-5-year-olds and all the older children were successful. However, when this correspondence did not exist (e.g. *fleu-riste* – florist), 40 per cent of the 4-to-5-year-olds, 19 per cent of the 5-to-6-year-olds and 8 per cent of the 6-to-7-year-olds isolated the meaningful segment (*fleur-iste* – '*fleur*' means 'flower' in French) instead of the first syllable. The younger children, 3-to-4-year-olds, seemed unable to segment any item into syllables.

This study thus reveals the tendency of children up to the age of 6 to segment words in such a way that at least one item constitutes a meaningful unit, and this tendency can be interpreted in terms of the difficulty they experience in regarding a word as a phonological chain independent of its meaning.

Bialystok (1986*a*) used a forced-choice method to obtain figures which go some way towards relativizing the observational data presented above. The children had to decide which word was the longer out of the pairs of words presented to them. In some pairs the longer word corresponded to the referent with the larger size (for example, 'hippopotamus' / 'skunk'), in others the opposite was the case ('train' / 'caterpillar'). When there was congruity of size between word and referent, the success rate was 79 per cent in 5-year-olds and 97 per cent in 6-year-olds. When there was no such congruity, the success rate was 28 per cent and 67 per cent respectively. Thus two-thirds of 6-year-olds can give a correct answer when the task of dissociation is extremely simplified.

There is, nevertheless, a remarkable congruity between all the data illustrating the lack of autonomy of the signifier in the manipulation of words by young children. A similar phenomenon is observed as children's comprehension of the written word develops (see below, Chapter 7). The case recorded by Cazden (1976) of a nursery-school child who declared: ' "little" is a big word and "big" is a little word' should therefore be considered as an exception. Also conforming to Piaget's observations (1926), Ianco-Worrall (1972) demonstrates that awareness of the fact that names are arbitrarily assigned to objects develops even later than the ability to separate the qualities of an object from its name.

As is the case with metaphonological awareness, the behaviour which reveals difficulties in focusing reflection on language itself does not appear to be any more specific to young subjects than to individuals of any age who have not yet encountered the *necessity* of manipulating language as an object *per se*.

Thus Kolinsky *et al.* (1987) found responses characteristic of young children in illiterate Portuguese adults. These subjects were asked to provide examples of short words and long words. If all responses indicating an intention to produce long or short segments of the speech chain are considered to be correct (whether or not they correspond to a 'word', as the unschooled subject would not necessarily be aware of this concept), then 52 per cent of the answers would have to be regarded as wrong: 24 per cent being based on the size of the referent (for example, *'nogueira'* – 'walnut [tree]' – is a long word because it is a big tree, and *'galinka'* – 'chicken' – is a short word because it is smaller); 14 per cent taking into account the emotional weight of the objects or events referred to; and the remaining 14 per cent being based on the characteristics of the actual act of saying the relevant segment (thus an expression which is uttered slowly and/or in a loud voice is regarded as longer). In a second experiment, ten other illiterate adults were asked to designate which of two pictures represented the object with the longer name. For each item, one of the two names was actually longer than the other, but sometimes the difference in the size of the objects referred to corresponded to the difference in the length of their names ('*camelo*', 'camel' v. '*olho*', 'eye'), sometimes there was no correspondence between the linguistic and extralinguistic dimensions ('*casa*', 'house' v. '*televisao*', 'television'), and sometimes the objects referred to were much the same size ('*pato*', 'duck' v. '*galinka*', 'chicken'). Two of the ten subjects gave correct answers whatever the item; four gave correct answers for the 'concordant' items, based their answers on the size of the referents for the 'nonconcordant' items, and seemed to guess the answer for the 'neutral' items (about 50 per cent correct answers). The remaining four subjects gave correct responses for the 'concordant' and 'neutral' items but failed on half of the 'nonconcordant' items. These results, like those obtained from pre-school children, reveal the importance of learning to read and write for the ability to distinguish between signifier and signified. This learning leads to higher success rates in most subjects (as is shown by the performance of the control groups used by Kolinsky *et al.*), although a reasonable proportion of illiterate subjects also succeed in this kind of test. The consequences of these findings will be discussed in the chapter devoted to the relationship between metalinguistic development and writing (see Chapter 7).

The final data regarding the signifier/signified dissociation concern the child's manipulation of lexical ambiguity and synonymity. Horgan (1981) gives the following report of his daughter, not yet 4, saying: 'There are two jeans, Jessica's mommy named Jean and jeans to wear'. This is a good example of early awareness of lexical ambiguity – provided, it is true, by the eldest daughter of a philosopher and psycholinguist. On the other hand, at age 3 years 2 months, Slobin's daughter (1978) seemed troubled by an apparent synonymity: 'Why cause you have two names, "orange" and "tangerine"? '

Tasks of lexical ambiguity make it possible to study children's ability to accept that several referents can be designated by the same word (for example, 'letter'). Studies of the child's awareness of this kind of ambiguity are often interpreted as revealing an ability to dissociate the word from its referent, since the detection of lexical ambiguity presupposes a recognition that at least two referents can have the same phonological realization. Most of the research uses tasks of paraphrasing or designating the referents in pictures. Depending on the degree of difficulty, success appears between the ages of 6 and 9 (for a review of this, see Bowey and Tunmer, 1984).

As far as we know, only Bialystok (1986*a*) has set children tasks of judging lexical synonymity (or rather, quasi-synonymity). For example, the word 'dog' was given to the subjects, who then had to decide which of the two words 'frog' and 'puppy' have the same meaning. At age 5, a correct response was given in 65 per cent of cases; at age 7, 76 per cent. Since random choice could give a 50 per cent success rate, these performances (in particular those of the 5-year-olds, but also those of the 7-year-olds) could be regarded as relatively low, and even more so since success at such a task does not really demand a truly reflective processing of synonymity but can be obtained by the simple activity of classification of the referents. These poor early performances in recognition of synonymity support the hypothesis defended by Markman and Wachtel (1988), who postulate that for the young child lexical elements are mutually exclusive, one object being unable to have two designations. This functioning, which the authors show to be evident in 3-to-4-year-olds in the case of hierarchically ordered terms (for example, 'car' v. 'vehicle') and in cases where new names are attributed to an object whose name is already known to the child, could very well be applied to the early processing of synonymity.

The correct recognition of lexical ambiguities does not seem to require the conscious ability to dissociate the name from its referent. If the name is a feature of the object for the young child, then nothing *a priori* prevents this feature from being shared by other objects in the same way that other properties are shared. This is not the case for synonymity, awareness of which requires the recognition of the fact that the same object can be randomly named in one way or another, and this recognition assumes a prior awareness of the arbitrariness of the linguistic sign. Several studies have investigated the understanding children have of the synonymity of sentences (see below), and this phenomenon deserves to be studied much further at the lexical level, where experimental control is perhaps easier to implement.

The awareness of the metalinguistic term 'word'

As we have already pointed out, the principal criticism to have been levelled at some of the work which has just been presented is that the metalinguistic term 'word' is generally used in the instructions given to the subjects. There is a suspicion that this term is difficult to comprehend, and that this comprehension is dependent on formal training. Correct usage of the term has been observed in the speech of children as young as 1 year 9 months (Bohn, 1914) and 3 years 4 months (Slobin, 1978), but this correct use of the term in certain contexts does not prove that it is correctly used or comprehended in others. The results recorded are thus very likely to underestimate the metasemantic competence of children who are studied solely with reference to their ability to understand (and sometimes define) a metalinguistic term.

It has often been observed that many children just starting to learn to read (at approximately 6 years of age) do not understand the terms used by their teachers ('word', 'sentence', etc.). These observations have been validated experimentally.

Downing (1969, 1970, 1972) presented children of 5 with a variety of sound stimuli (various nonhuman noises, phonemes, sentences, words, etc.). The children then had to say 'yes' if the sound was a word, and 'no' if it was not. None of them was successful. In another study, Downing and Oliver (1974) noted that all children up to age 8 overextended the meaning of the term 'word'. However, the scope of this overextension diminished between the ages of 5 and 8. At age 5, the children had a tendency to reply 'yes' in all cases, while at age 8, although phonemes and syllables were still being designated as words, sentences were generally not. Here, no doubt, schooling has an effect, as is suggested by the results of Hirsh-Pasek *et al.*, (1978) which show that, from the age of 5, it is relatively easy to teach a child the distinction between the concepts 'word' and 'sentence', but not between the concepts 'word', 'syllable' and 'sound'. Furthermore, Hamilton and Barton (1983, cited by Barton, 1985), who asked adults at different levels of learning to define the term 'word' and to judge whether certain items were words or not, obtained the same range of success levels as those found in children by Berthoud-Papandropoulou (1980, see above), except that none of the adults posited the requirement for a minimum number of letters, or gave sentences as examples of words.

Bowey *et al.* (1984) believe that Downing's results underestimate children's understanding of the term 'word'. The presentation of nonhuman noises together with different kinds of linguistic stimuli which do not constitute words (phonemes, syllables, sentences) at the same time as words would require the ability, not yet acquired by 5-year-olds, to perform multidimensional classifications. By asking for discriminations between pairs involving only two categories (word v. sound or word v. noun phrase) and assisting comprehension of the instructions by giving prior training with explanations of differences and corrective feedback, these authors obtained much better performances than those reported by Downing, with success rates of over 75 per cent in 5-to-6-year-olds and more than 90 per cent from 6–7 onwards. In a similar experiment using nouns and nonmeaningful syllables (*pim, pleck, fod, drin, ab* and *gesh*), Smith and Tager-Flusberg (1982) obtained 64 per cent success in 3-to-4-year-olds, and 84 per cent in 4-to-5-year-olds. However, the fact that all the words used in both the above-mentioned experiments were substantives rather limits the import of the results.

In another experiment, formally similar to the preceding one, Bowey *et al.* (1984) used content words (nouns, adjectives, verbs) and function words (quantifiers, prepositions and conjunctions). The success levels of 70 per cent in 5-to-6-year-olds, 97 per cent in 6-to-7-year-olds and 98 per cent in 7-to-8-year-olds with the content words dropped to 45 per cent, 85 per cent and 92 per cent respectively in the case of the function words. Thus in the younger subjects, the response for function words was no more than that of random choice.

While it may be greater than Downing's results suggest, comprehension of the term 'word' nevertheless remains limited at pre-school age. Lastly, the particularly good performances recorded by Smith and Tager-Flusberg (1982) may correspond to the simple strategy used by young children of designating as words those items which are meaningful to them.

This collection of data thus justifies the criticism levelled at studies which use the metalinguistic term 'word' in their instructions. However, the evident risk of underestimating the child's awareness of the lexical unit does not necessarily imply that researchers are guilty of this underestimation. Furthermore, the few studies to which this criticism cannot be applied – for example, those concentrating on lexical synonymity and ambiguity – provide no more evidence for an early metasemantic awareness of the word.

Conclusion

Bowey and Tunmer (1984) point out that there are three requirements for full awareness of the word:

1. awareness of the word as a unit of language;
2. awareness of the word as an arbitrary phonological label;
3. comprehension of the metalinguistic term 'word'.

The data reported above seem to indicate that there is no clear evidence for the existence of these abilities before the age of 7. This might appear to contradict the phenomenon, described in the preceding chapters, of the factors determining the young child's processing of language being essentially semantic in nature. This is not the case. Indeed, it is one thing to be restricted by the evocation of one's own pragmatic experience in the fulfilment of metalinguistic tasks, and another thing to be able to explain what is implicit in the use of language – for example, in a task of definition.

Sentential metasemantic development

The pre-school infant's inability to manipulate language without being constrained by the external reality to which it refers is evident in linguistic units which are greater than the word. A notable illustration of this is given by Gérard (1981).

This author asked children of 5 to shorten a sentence composed of several juxtaposed clauses without removing any of its meaning. In response to this instruction, some children contented themselves with repeating the sentence with a negative element introduced into one of the clauses. On the surface the sentence had not been shortened but, on the contrary, made longer by the addition of this negation. However, the effect of this negation was such that one of the facts related by the sentence was removed (by virtue of its negation) and the sequence of action referred to was thereby stripped of one of its elements and made shorter. This example provides us with a striking illustration of the lack of differentiation between signifier and signified in the processing of sentences.

Boutet *et al.* (1983) systematically studied 6-to-12-year-old children's conception of the sentence. The subjects had to *read* handwritten sequences and were then asked which of the sequences constituted sentences, and why. The verbal material used was as follows:

1. *les enfants mangent la soupe* (the children eat the soup)
2. *marie cueille* (marie picks)
3. *la table mangera à la cantine* (the table will eat in the dining-hall)
4. *quand ta grand'-mère arrivera-t-elle* (when will your grandmother arrive)
5. *sortie de camions* (lorry exit)
6. *oui* (yes)
7. *je vais aller à l'aéroport et après j'arriverai à la maison et j'irai à un spectacle de marionettes* (I am going to go to the airport and afterwards I shall arrive home and I shall go to a puppet show)
8. *arrivons demain gare de lyon* ([implied we] arrive tomorrow gare de lyon [name of station])
9. *ce matin maman a fait un gâteau et on l'a mangé dimanche* (this morning mummy made a cake and we ate it [on] sunday)
10. *pierre il est très gentil* (pierre [he] is very nice)
11. *ne pas marcher sur les pelouses* (do not walk on the lawns)
12. *quelle drôle de poupée* (what a funny doll)
13. *je suis à l'hôpital j'ai des ennuis* (I am in hospital I'm ill)

The arguments most frequently given by children of 6 to 8 concerned either the referents (for example, a child of 6 years 8 months rejected item 7, explaining: 'but that's not true, all that – because I never go to the airport – it's my sister' [*Translator's note*: The original French of the speech quoted in this study has been omitted henceforth] and, in response to the experimenter insisting 'so it isn't a sentence', replied 'not for me – but my sister, if she was me – she'd say yes') or the quantitative aspects (a child of 6 years 10 months accepted item 7 'because it's big'). This latter type of argument was also the most frequently used by 8-to-9-year-olds.

One argument appeared at around the age of 8 and was the most frequently used from the age of 9–10. This concerned the syntactic relationships between the elements (a child of 8 years 8 months rejected item 8, arguing that there should be a '*nous*' ['we'] with a word ending in o-n-s [French verbs are conjugated such that the first person plural of, for example, '*arriver*', to arrive, is '*arrivons*']). Two other types of argument were also given. The first, which constituted about 10 per cent to 15 per cent of the arguments in all age groups, pointed to the semantic properties of the items (item 13, age 9 years 3 months: 'You can't say that I'm in hospital okay – "I'm ill", you could have said that first – because "I'm ill then I'm in hospital", that explains better, but "I'm ill", that bothers me because I don't know where I should put it – "I'm ill then I'm in hospital", for me it's like that – because for me it says that someone is ill and then he wants to get better and then he's in hospital – I can see that, but there he's in hospital then after he's ill, well, that I don't understand' [for the development of the child's processing of the order of utterance, see below]). The second type of argument also occurred in about 10 per cent to 15 per cent of cases, but appeared only at the age of 7–8 onwards. This argument took account of the situation in which the sentence might have been spoken (item 11, age 9 years 9 months: 'that's okay because it could be a park keeper saying it'). The authors, who are linguists, legitimately consider that apart from those which unambiguously centre on referents, all the above arguments are metalinguistic in nature, since they refer to language or to its enunciation. Viewed from this perspective, more than 60 per cent of the metalinguistic arguments were given by children aged 6 and older. A psycholinguistic point of view would be much more restrictive. In fact, only those acceptances or rejections which are based on the syntactic relationship between elements provide irrefutable evidence of a dissociation between signifier and signified. This type of argument was the latest to appear (in terms of age) and was never used by children younger than 7 to 8.

Similarly, it has often been noted that for children of pre-school age the ordering of a sentence with several clauses should correspond to the order of occurrence of the actions referred to (see, in particular, Ferreiro, 1971).

E. V. Clark (1970, 1971) observed this order-of-mention-strategy being used by 3-year-olds, both in their temporal description of events and in their comprehension of sentences containing 'before' or 'after', in which they ignore these prepositions. Barrie-Blackley (1973) obtained similar results, noting that whatever preposition ('after', 'before' or 'until') was used to link the clauses in sentences given to 6-year-old children, almost two-thirds of subjects, when asked to repeat the sentences, would change them around if the spoken order did not correspond to the order of events. For our part (Gombert, 1983a, b, 1984), we used tasks of repetition and commentary with sentences composed of two clauses and presented in each of the two possible orders of utterance to demonstrate that the child's first way of accounting verbally for a temporal sequence is to apply a rule of strict correspondence between the order of utterance and the chronology of events. Our results further suggest that this functioning is not reflected on before the age of 5, and that it is the simple consequence of nondifferentiation between language and the events referred to by the sentence. Until the age of 7, the arguments for rejecting a noncorrespondence always concern the factual, never the linguistic, ordering of events.

Here we have further proof that young children do not consider language to have an autonomous existence at the representative level. This nondissociation of the order of utterance and the order of temporal succession of the referents has also been observed in studies devoted to the interpretation of causal sentences and passive sentences.

There are signs of a similar phenomenon in some studies of the child's judgement of synonymity. Some authors (see Harvey, 1985) suggest a distinction between referential synonymity (for example, 'the Queen of England' v. 'Elizabeth II') and linguistic synonymity ('he is angry' v. 'he is furious'). The former designates two referents which our knowledge of the world deems to be one and the same. The fact that the latter refers to the same referent can be perceived only on the basis of linguistic knowledge. It is (conscious) awareness of this latter kind of synonymity which requires the ability to reflect on language.

Beilin (1975) asked children aged 4 to 8 to compare the meanings of sentences presented to them first in the active and then in the passive form (for example, 'The boy pushes the girl' v. 'The girl gets pushed by the boy') or in cleft and uncleft forms ('It's the boy that pushes the girl' v. 'The boy pushes the girl'). It was not until the age of 7–8 that the subjects affirmed synonymity more often than could be obtained by random choice. Hakes (1980) obtained similar results but also proposed other synonymous pairs. Synonymity based on spatial or temporal relationships (for example, 'The old lady is in front of the boy' v. 'The boy is behind the old lady') is not recognized until the age of 8–9 (the results regarding temporal relationships confirm the one we observed in an unpublished study of 173 children aged between 3 and 12). Synonymity corresponding to logical implication (for example, 'There is more cake than ice cream' v. 'There is less ice cream than cake') is not identified more often than it could be by random choice even at the age of 8–9. Finally, synonymity of the type 'There is an apple on the table' v. 'The table has an apple on it' is recognized from the age of 5–6. Sack (1973, cited by Beilin, 1975) has demonstrated that children of this same age identify sentence synonymity which can be reduced to lexical synonymity ('The puppy sleeps' v. 'The baby doggie sleeps'). Finally, both Beilin (1975) and Hakes (1980) have shown that success in these tasks of recognition comes later than success in the comprehension of the individual sentences involved.

The authors agree in recognizing that to be certain of success in tasks of judging synonymity, it is necessary to find a balance between a comparison of the surface forms of the two sentences and a comparison of the semantic representations they engender. However, there is disagreement as to the explanation of the failure of children of pre-school age. For Hakes (1980), it is because they base their responses on a surface comparison alone. This would explain why, when the sentences to be compared are not synonymous, the success level of 4-year-olds is greater than that of random choice, whereas when the sentences are synonymous, the success level long remains significantly lower than that of random choice. This interpretation does not seem able to account for the fact that performances vary from one type of synonym to another. For this reason, Beilin's hypothesis (1975) seems more probable. Young children compare only the semantic representations provoked by each of the sentences, not the sentences themselves. This means that it is an error in the interpretation of one of the members of a synonymous pair which causes nonrecognition of synonymity. The frequency of such errors broadly correlates with the complexity of the sentences and the possibility of correct interpretation despite poor differentiation between signifier and signified. In other words, the first judgements of synonymity, whether appropriate or not, are based not on metalinguistic reflection but rather on classification of the referents. One final way of expressing this hypothesis would be to suggest that for children of pre-school age, there is only referential synonymity.

It is true that this is only a hypothesis which should be compared and contrasted with that of Hakes in further experimentation. It is by no means impossible that both of these hypotheses could be partially valid and that the two suggested processes might alternate depending on the task, the items within that task, or the age of the subject attempting it. Another factor which would need to be experimentally controlled is that of the mnemonic ability of the subjects, which, as Hakes (1980) points out, is of fundamental importance in tasks requiring the subjects to retain the representation of the meanings evoked by each of the two sentences after they have been compared.

However this might be, the data regarding the sentence, like the data concerning the word, do attest to the child's tendency to confuse the linguistic and the extralinguistic.

The development of the processing of figurative language

Philosophers have always been fascinated by the *tropes* which correspond to the use of language in a figurative sense. For their part, the cognitive psychologists have focused on the processing of *metaphor*, the stylistic device which consists of deliberately violating the rules of lexical selection by replacing or qualifying one referent (*topic*) by invoking another (*vehicle*) which has, in common with the first, a characteristic (*base idea*) which the speaker wishes to emphasize (for example, 'this man is a beanpole' for 'this man is tall and thin').

The processing of metaphor by the adult is not discussed here. In fact metaphor is of interest to this study only in so far as it causes a conflict between two modes of interpretation: the literal interpretation and the figurative interpretation of a metaphor. In the comprehension of metaphor the former type of interpretation should be replaced by the latter, and this seems to demand *a priori* the ability to recognize that a single structure can correspond to several different meanings. It is the implementation of this ability, as well as the ability to use this faculty of language deliberately to signify something different to what is actually said, which is of interest in the study of metasemantic development. For this same reason, no mention is made of research into the development of the ability to pair objects 'metaphorically' in nonverbal tasks (for a review of these studies, see Dent, 1987).

Children's production of metaphor

There are a number of reports of young children who, from the time they first begin to speak, produce utterances of a metaphorical type, mainly when playing games of make-believe in which they rename certain of the objects they are playing with or playfully assimilate the real situation into another situation. Thus Winner *et al.* (1979) note how an 18-month-old child made a toy climb up its mother's arm, calling this toy 'a snake'; and Carlson and Anisfeld (1969) describe how a 2½-year-old child declared: 'I'm drinking juice' while sitting in the bath and sucking its soapy fingers. Similar utterances have also been observed outside the play situation in connection with objects which the child finds particularly interesting. Bowerman (1978) gives the example of a child calling a grapefruit 'moon', while Hakes (1982) gives that of another child calling the moon 'ball'.

The available literature reveals that there are two divergent interpretations of this type of utterance. There are those who believe that it reflects a lack of awareness of language and, in particular, errors of categorization (Chukowsky, 1927/1968), while others regard it as deliberate violation of the rules of lexical selection, and thereby truly metaphorical in nature (for example, Winner *et al.*, 1979, 1980).

In a longitudinal corpus-based analysis of a child from the age of 2 to 5, Gardner and Winner (1979; Winner, 1979; Winner *et al.*, 1979, 1980) found that around 80 per cent of the overextensions produced were metaphorical in nature – that is to say, they were produced even when the child knew the real name of the objects which were metaphorically designated. However, many of these metaphors appeared when the child was playfully using the metaphorically designated object in the same way as the referent of the metaphorical name would be used. Around the age of 4, metaphors appeared to be based on physical resemblance (Billow, 1981, who observed 73 3-to-6-year-old children for an entire school year, found that 94 per cent of the metaphorical utterances produced were of this type). None of the metaphors produced was conceptual in nature. Similar findings have been collated from the results of games during which the authors asked children to give new names to familiar objects. The observation of two further children revealed a variability between individuals. While the metaphors produced by one of them were mainly metaphors 'of action', the metaphors produced by the other were almost all based on similarities of perception.

As Kamhi (1987) emphasizes, although the metaphorical nature of such overextensions is often pointed out in the literature, there is nothing to establish clearly that the children themselves appreciate this.

Hudson and Nelson (1984) further develop the point of view which holds that many of the overextensions reported in the literature correspond to children's general strategy for indicating similarities between objects but do not reveal any early awareness of metaphorical relationships. They postulate that in order to be able to speak metaphorically the child must know not only the real name of the renamed object but also the real referent of the name used. However, by controlling these factors in situations of games of make-believe, the authors still found that metaphorical overextensions were produced from the age of 2 onwards.

For these overextensions to be attributed to reflection of a metalinguistic type, however, it would be necessary to establish that the young child plays with names without confusing the objects themselves. When a child puts a pot on its head and calls it a 'hat', it is the whole object, along with its nominal quality, which is wrested from its normal usage, not just the name. In the activity of playing, the pot has effectively become a hat. While this is clear in the case of the effective manipulation of an object, the internalization of an action leaves only the nominal substitution apparent. None the less, the underlying process could be the same, in which case the utterance which is taken to be metaphor is only denotation. The passage from these metaphors 'of action' to metaphors of physical comparison could be a reflection of the passage from the predominance of action to the predominance of the first transductive categorizations in the child's activity. Moreover, as noted by Hudson and Nelson (1984), young children often appear to connect the meaning of a word to a number of attributes such as shape, colour or function, which could lead to them calling all four-legged animals 'dog', or all objects that can be worn on one's head 'hat'.

Fourment *et al.* (1987) observed groups of children aged 3–4, 5 and 7 in free-play situations. Whatever the age of the subjects, around 4 per cent of their linguistic utterances were interpreted by the authors as metaphorical. Two types of metaphor were distinguished: metaphors based on action (following a symbolic action) and metaphors based on perception (of physical resemblance between topic and vehicle, and preceding the symbolic action). The first kind was used by the majority of 3-to-4-year-olds (54 per cent); the second by 5-year-olds (67 per cent) and 7-year-olds (69 per cent). Here again, a very broad definition of the term metaphor seems to have been adopted. Even when the children knew the real names of the objects they renamed, they never juxtaposed the real name and the metaphorical name (for example, in a formulation of the type 'N1 is N2'). Moreover, the relevance of the differentiation between 'metaphor based on action' and 'metaphor based on perception' poses a problem here. It is, in fact, debatable whether this latter category can include, as the authors assert, utterances of the type 'this is my hat' which precedes the action of putting a yoghurt pot on one's head. More generally, it is doubtful whether utterances of the type 'I am Musclor' (a muscular cartoon character), also considered to be a metaphor based on perception, can truly be said to be metaphorical in character. On the whole, there is no doubt that we must consider that many of the utterances observed by the authors are either playful denotations or used to mark the adoption of social roles. This also seems implicit in the position of the authors, who hypothesize that a decrease in the number of 'metaphors' between ages 3 and 7 indicates that the utterances they were studying were not the product of a developed metalinguistic activity.

Several authors have noted that the number of spontaneous metaphorical utterances decreases with age. Gardner and Winner (1979) put forward two hypotheses to explain this phenomenon. One is that the formalism imposed by conventional schooling leads to a diminution of the language of fantasy; the other is that as children's vocabulary grows richer, so the necessity to use these 'approximate' metaphors is reduced. Kolinsky (1986) offers an additional explanation: that the development of the notion of the arbitrary nature of the referent reduces the child's predilection for metaphorical description (she cites an example borrowed from Bonnet and Tamine-Gardes, 1984, of the substitution of the metaphorical nickname *giant's ears* for the term 'burdock', the scientific name for a type of broad-leaved plant). It is notable that the latter two explanations both assume that early metaphors are by nature nonmetalinguistic (in the psycholinguistic sense of the term). As Bredart and Rondal (1982) point out, we should guard against mixing up metaphor and lexical confusion. Most authors who note a decrease in metaphorical utterances around the age of 6 use criteria for determining early metaphors which lead to this designation being applied to any apparently nonliteral utterance which is meaningful to an adult listener. This being the case, the decrease could have been greatly overestimated.

Vosniadou (1987) believes that early metaphorical competence is based on children's ability to perceive similarities between objects and events. This ability would play a fundamental role, not only for activities of classification but also in enabling the children to use their knowledge to understand new phenomena. In other words, metaphor is the linguistic path and preferred tool for transferring knowledge of a known area to an area which is being discovered. While this hypothesis seems well founded, we are nevertheless dealing with a process of conflation of vehicle and topic which does not constitute sufficient evidence of true metalinguistic awareness of metaphors at an early age. Such an awareness would presuppose that the communicative intention is concerned not with the effective designation of a new referent but with the basic idea itself. This use of language to express a concept corresponding to the metaphorical link between topic and vehicle has never been confirmed in observations of children.

Finally, certain researchers (Gardner et al., 1975; Vosniadou and Ortony, 1983) asked children to complete sentences by choosing from a selection of sentence endings, some of which were metaphorical and some of which were not. In this type of task, the youngest children (aged 4), unlike their seniors, made as many 'metaphorical' choices as adults. This U-shaped development curve suggests that the factors determining the choices of different subjects vary. In such play situations the children might choose, quasi-systematically, utterances which appear incongruous to them. Indeed, it should be noted that it is also in 4-year-olds that the most choices of totally inappropriate sentence endings for the presented sentence are found.

The child's comprehension of metaphor

Asch and Nerlove (1960) studied the understanding which children of 3 to 12 have of adjectives which refer sometimes to physical properties and sometimes to psychological properties (soft, hard, sweet, bitter). They found that before the age of 6 children are broadly unaware of the psychological meanings. They report the case of a child who, when asked 'Can a person be sweet?', replied 'Not unless he was made out of chocolate'.

In a more general sense, Winner *et al.* (1976) describe three phases of development in the understanding of metaphors. This is based on the results of a study in which children had to choose between several interpretations of a number of metaphorical utterances:

1. In 6-to-7-year-olds, a magic approach to metaphor invokes action by a superior force (for example, the psychological meaning of the adjective 'hard' is explained by the fact that God has turned the heart of the 'hard' person into stone). Other children of the same age replace the relationship of identity (person = hard) with a relationship of contiguity (the 'hard' person is envisaged as being surrounded by walls of stone).
2. In 8-to-9-year-olds, the interpretation is dominated by physical characteristics (a 'hard' person has hard muscles).
3. It is not until the age of 10–12 that children become aware of the psychological meaning of such adjectives.

That full comprehension of metaphors appears very late is confirmed by several other authors and has often been related to the ability to perform concrete operations or to the onset of the stage at which the child is able to perform formal operations (see, for example, Cometa and Eson, 1978).

Studies showing the early understanding of metaphor are much less numerous than those which report the metaphorical overextensions which appear in the speech of young children. It is true that Gardner (1974) demonstrates that from the age of $3\frac{1}{2}$ children obtain success rates of between 57 per cent and 76 per cent in tasks of designating colours, faces and objects respectively with the adjectives 'cold' / 'warm', 'light' / 'dark', and 'happy' / 'sad'. Further, Gentner (1977) shows how 4-to-5-year-olds can indicate the 'knee' of a mountain or tree on a picture. However, as Gardner (1974) points out, this behaviour simply bears witness to an analogical ability which is probably based on intuition.

Vosniadou (1987; Vosniadou *et al.*, 1984; Vosniadou and Ortony, 1983) defends the idea of early awareness (at about the age of 4) of metaphorical meaning in tasks of comprehension. She believes that the results of studies showing late development of comprehension of metaphors are due to the poor control of variables (in particular, the absence of linguistic or extralinguistic contexts for the metaphors presented, and the fact that the tasks of paraphrase and explanation used have often been poorly adapted for young subjects). Understanding of metaphor would appear to be acquired at an early age but is masked in these studies by task-related difficulties.

In order to avoid this kind of bias, Vosniadou *et al.* (1984) asked children to use toys to act out stories whose final sentence was metaphorical. This metaphor corresponded either to the predictable end of the story or to a less probable ending. The results showed that when the metaphorical sentence corresponded to the probable outcome, 85 per cent of the 4-to-5-year-old subjects acted out the story correctly. The authors use these results to support their theory of an early-acquired understanding of metaphorical language. This conclusion does not seem to be justified by a detailed examination of the results.

In the first place, when the metaphor corresponds to the probable outcome of the story, it is sufficient for children to act out the end of the story in the way that seems most normal to them, even if they have not understood the last sentence. The success rate for 4-to-5-year-olds acting out stories ending in a metaphorical sentence corresponding to a less foreseeable outcome was 25 per cent in one experiment and 12 per cent when it was repeated. These results seem to us to provide a better reflection of the children's understanding.

In the second place, even the success achieved with these less likely endings does not necessarily require the ability to decode metaphor. For example, one of the stories to be enacted was that of a little boy who was being silly, when all of a sudden his mother arrived. The metaphorical sentence corresponding to the literal sentence 'He ran to hide' was 'Paul was a rabbit running to his hole'. If the subjects accept that Paul is being qualified as a rabbit, a literal interpretation of the sentence will lead them to run to a hiding place, and this action corresponds exactly to the metaphorical sense of the sentence. Further, the results show that when the literal acting out differs from the metaphorical sense (for example, with the sentence 'Paul was a rabbit hopping to his hole') the success rates were no greater than 5 per cent in 5-year-olds and 25 per cent in 7-year-olds. The authors argue that these results confirm their view that increasing the difficulty of the task hides the child's true ability to understand metaphor. For us, however, these results show that when success is clearly conditional on understanding the metaphor, the children's rate of failure is extremely high. This suggests that success obtained under other conditions is not achieved through the decoding of the metaphor.

While the preceding results appear to fail to establish the existence of an early understanding of metaphor, it nevertheless remains true that the methodological criticisms addressed by Vosniadou are justified. In a later experiment, Vosniadou and Ortony (1986) show that although children of 6–7 succeed in acting out metaphorical utterances (see, however, the above reservations), many of them fail when asked to perform tasks of paraphrasing. Moreover, Waggoner *et al.* (1985) show that linguistic context has an effect. In 8-year-olds, the levels of correct explanation of metaphorical sentences of the type used by Vosniadou rise from 39 per cent to 50 per cent after the sentences have been inserted into a story.

Examination of the data given in the literature clearly shows that not all metaphors are equally accessible. In particular, metaphors which are based on perceptual comparisons (which, for example, liken hair to spaghetti, or a river to a snake) are much more easily comprehended than those which are conceptual in nature (for example, 'necessity is the mother of invention'). While the former are understood at a relatively early age – about 5–6 – the latter are not understood before adolescence (see Billow, 1975). Siltanen (1986) tested the comprehension of different kinds of metaphor in 246 people aged between 3 and 31, and was thus able to show a gradual increase in the comprehension of more and more difficult metaphors between age 5 and adulthood.

Gentner (1988) distinguishes between two types of metaphor, those based on the sharing of attributes between objects (for example, 'the sun is like an orange') and those based on a common relational structure (for example, 'a roof is like a hat'). The former are correctly interpreted by 5-to-6-year-olds, while the latter are not. The most interesting result among those obtained by the author reveals that double metaphors, which combine both the above-mentioned types (for example, 'a lake is like a mirror'), are interpreted in the same way as the first type by children of 5–6 and in the same way as the second type by 9-to-10-year-olds, while adults perceive both the physical similarity and the shared relational structure, though they show a marked preference for the latter interpretation. This result suggests that the increasing comprehension of metaphor is accompanied by a growing preference for the more sophisticated interpretations.

In fact, as Keil believes (1986), the development in the child's processing of metaphor essentially seems to reflect conceptual development and is thus scarcely affected by metalinguistic development. It nevertheless remains the case that children's limitations in signifier–signified differentiation make it impossible for them to perceive metaphor in tasks whose formalism requires them to focus on the linguistic message itself. The literary genius which some may wish to see in the early production of metaphor bears no comparison to the poetic productions of the expert. Even if the linguistic productions of the two are sometimes alike, young children produce accidental poetry by ignoring lexical convention as a result of a lack of control over language, whereas poets deliberately go beyond strictly denotative language in order to draw attention to the characteristics of the referents they want to emphasize. The transition from one to the other presupposes a disappearance of the early pseudo-metaphors, which is effectively affirmed at school age. As Gardner (1980) points out, early metaphors are a result of a lexical poverty in children, while those which appear in adolescence are deliberate violations of category boundaries.

Young children appear to possess basic metaphorical competence, which is probably indispensable to the later appearance of good understanding and control of the production of metaphor. However, this competence does not appear to require a reflective manipulation of language, and is therefore epilinguistic by nature rather than metalinguistic.

Conclusion

It is worthy of note that in view of the behaviour reported in this and the two preceding chapters, the age of 6–7 seems to be an age of transition. To plagiarize the formulation of Boutet *et al.* (1983), it is at this age that we observe the passage from a use of language based exclusively on experienced reality to a possibility of apprehending linguistic objects in a metalinguistic way, which implies that they are distinguished from their extralinguistic referents.

Epilexical and episemantic behaviour

Children of pre-school age seem to play with words and meanings. From the first appearance of language, they are capable of rejecting incorrect designations. Very soon they make comments on the meanings of words, can detect lexical synonymity, create metaphors and even use the metalinguistic term 'word'. This behaviour has often been confirmed in observations of spontaneous language, but does not appear capable of stimulation when the formalism of the situation forces the subjects to focus exclusively on language. It has long been emphasized that it is context which creates meaning for young children (Laguna, 1927). In fact, at this age the manipulation of the semantic dimension of language is incidental to the cognitive manipulation of very large entities, encompassing the signifier, the signified, and sometimes even the context of the utterance. The manipulation of language in the narrow sense is only the tip of the iceberg, and prefigures the later metasemantic and metalexical manipulations, although it has a completely different cognitive status. Metalexical competence does not exist at an early age, since words do not have an autonomous existence for young children. Metasemantic competence presupposes the manipulation of the signifier as distinct from the signified, while at this age the only effective differentiation is between signs and referents.

Metalexical and metasemantic behaviour

The available literature reveals that there is a significant discontinuity associated with the difficulty of the verbal material or the tasks. While the first segmentations of sentences into words, the first clear signs of a differentiation between signifier and signified and the first metalinguistic explanations of synonymity and simple metaphor all appear in 6-to-7-year-olds, it is not until the age of 10 or 12 that elaborate lexical division, the conceptual understanding of metaphor and the correct definition of metalinguistic terms like *word* or *sentence* become evident.

Just as in the case of the other metalinguistic behaviour which we have already discussed, we believe that as soon as the corresponding epilinguistic behaviour is well established, metalexical and metasemantic abilities can also be implemented, however little use they may be to the child. In general, these abilities become useful when children start to attend school and come into contact with written language. However, it is probable that their earlier actualization could be stimulated. The discontinuity emphasized above could stem both from the progressive character of school learning, which leads to a gradual emergence of the metaprocedural abilities required, and from the fact that certain of the proposed tasks, over and above their metalinguistic characteristics, require cognitive abilities which are not yet operative in children of school age.

Chapter 5

Metapragmatic development

Introduction

The breadth of conception concerning the meaning of the term *metaprag-matic* and the relevance of the broadening of the metalinguistic field to include the reflexive behaviour which concerns the use of language have both been mentioned in the introductory chapter and have led us to support Hickmann's (1983) position, which defines metapragmatic abilities as 'a specific metalinguistic ability, notably the ability to represent, organize and regulate the use of speech itself' (p. 21).

A simple and convenient method of delimiting the field of metapragmatic behaviour *a priori* is to exclude from it all behaviour which does not imply reflection on or deliberate control over the pragmatic aspects of language (for a presentation and discussion of the pragmatics of language, see Caron, 1983). This is the approach chosen by Bruner and Hickmann (1983), who defined metapragmatics as those uses of language which 'imply an act of reference or representation which has as its object the use of the signs themselves' (p. 287). They implicitly situate metapragmatic behaviour with reference to the definition of pragmatics in terms of 'indexical rules that link a linguistic form to a given context' as proposed by Bates (1976, p. 3).

Things become more complicated when we start to consider not only the variable geometry of the domain of pragmatics, which can be extended to embrace all the communicative aspects of language (theoretically distin-guished from its representative function), but also the theoretical presup-positions which determine the use of the concept. In effect, pragmatics can be thought of as a theory of linguistic actions, a theory conceived in reaction – indeed, even in opposition – to truth-value theories in which the sole interface between language and the extralinguistic is of a semantic nature (for a discussion of the implications of these different conceptions, see Grewendorf, 1984). It would not be appropriate for us to take a position in this debate, which does not concern us here.

If we might be allowed to exploit the polysemy of the term, our own pragmatism inclines us, in the first instance, to allow the term *metapragmatics* a wider meaning by adopting the definition given by Pratt and Nesdale (1984, p. 105) which speaks of the '*awareness* or *knowledge* one has about the relationships that obtain *within* the linguistic system itself (e.g. across different sentences) and the relationships that obtain *between* the linguistic system and the context in which the language is embedded'. In contrast to the metaphonological, metasyntactic and metalexical fields which centre on the language system alone, the metapragmatic field includes aspects which go beyond the components of language in the strict sense. In effect, beyond the awareness and the intentional control of the linguistic parameters which determine the efficiency of the message, reflection on the management of the extralinguistic parameters of the situation in which the utterance is made plays a central role here. The pragmatic abilities permit the effective use of language in its (social) context, and the metapragmatic abilities allow the comprehension and control of this use.

Bruner and Hickmann (1983) make a distinction in the *pragmatic basis of language* between *deictic relationships*, which refer to the relationships between the linguistic signs and the extralinguistic context, and *intralinguistic relationships*, which exist between the signs and their linguistic context. This allows them to define the *metapragmatic level* as having both types of relationship as its object. Seen from this viewpoint, it is the relationship between the signs and the context of the utterance (which encompasses both the intra- and extralinguistic contexts) which constitutes the focus of metapragmatic behaviour. However, we shall limit the scope of this chapter to an account of the extralinguistic parameters in the treatment of language (both in comprehension and production) and reserve the problem of intralinguistic relations (as arise, for example, in connection with intersentence compatibility, anaphora or reported speech) for the following chapter, which deals with textual metalinguistic development. The result of this is a *de facto* reduction of metapragmatics, in the sense in which we shall study it, to the *awareness of the relations which exist between the linguistic system and the context in which it is used.*

We should not fail to mention that there is a strict but arbitrary delimitation between metasemantics and metapragmatics. This is especially true in view of the fact that we number ourselves among those who, as far as the analysis of language behaviour is concerned, would be happy to see the emergence of a pragmatico-semantic field covering everything which does not concern the specifically structural characteristics of language. It seems just as difficult to distinguish between semantics and pragmatics as to separate signification from experience, and we are therefore unconvinced of the wisdom of dealing with anything in this chapter which was not dealt with in the preceding one. However this may be, it may be of some pedagogical use to respect established classifications here and attempt to focus our attention on the communicative dimension of language, just as in the last chapter it was focused on language's representative dimension.

An important condition for the effectiveness of the verbal message is the absence of any ambiguity. The emergence and development of the identification and management of the referential adequacy of language will be the subject of the first subsection before we go on to discuss, in the next subsection, the adequacy of language with reference to the parameters of the situation of utterance and, most importantly, the objective characteristics of the interlocutor. Awareness of the social rules of language will be discussed in a third subsection, followed by the presentation of the development of a particular aspect of linguistic behaviour: linguistic humour. A final subsection contains an overall developmental scheme.

The referential adequacy of the verbal message

In the previous chapter we discussed the lexical ambiguities which correspond to polysemies. There are other types of linguistic ambiguity which may affect the comprehensibility of verbal messages:

- The ambiguities of surface structure which are determined by the form of the sentence (this is what happens in relations of co-reference: 'Mary argued with Jane. She wasn't happy'. Who? Mary? Jane?).
- The ambiguities of deep structure which do not depend on the surface realization (de Villiers and de Villiers, 1978, give as an example 'The shooting of the hunters was terrible').
- A final type of ambiguity has given rise to a large amount of research. These are referential ambiguities which indicate a lack of precision in the message with reference to what is demanded by the context in which it is emitted.

Evaluating the explicitness of a verbal message

A series of studies exists into the ability of children to estimate whether a message contains the necessary information, in its context of production, for its comprehension by the addressee. Markman (1977) explained the rules of a card game to children aged between 6 and 9. While explaining these rules, she specified that the winner was the one who had the most cards at the end of the game, and spoke of a 'special card' which played a decisive role in the game. However, she deliberately omitted to say which card this was and how it was possible to take cards from opponents. The children had to evaluate the adequacy of her explanation of the rules. At 6–7 years of age, just one child out of twelve seemed to notice the omission before starting to play. This was the case with five children out of twelve at 7–8 and ten out of ten at 8–9. The judgement of the adequacy of the explanation of a magic trick yielded slightly better results, although again it was not until the age of 8–9 that the majority of the children asked for further explanation. Markman hypothesized that these results derive from the fact that the young subjects do not execute the instructions in their minds and are thus unable to detect their incomplete character. Moreover, when she accompanied her incomplete explanations with a demonstration she obtained a significant improvement in performance at all ages.

Riesbeck (1980) increased the complexity of the task and obtained the same type of result from adults who were asked to judge the clarity of instructions describing the journey necessary to get to a set destination. Most of the subjects accepted the ambiguous instructions and did not become aware of the problem until they had to describe the journey themselves.

Numerous experiments have used the procedure followed by Glucksberg *et al.* (1966). Two interlocutors, separated by an opaque screen, both have a collection of objects or pictures. The speaker describes one of the objects and the addressee has to discover which it is (on the basis of the verbal information alone). The original research revealed a very low level of success at pre-school age; performance improved progressively with age.

A certain amount of research work based on this experimental paradigm (see Patterson and Kister, 1981) has shown that it is not until 10 years of age that a listener will ask for supplementary information when confronted with a manifestly incomplete instruction. Furthermore, it has been shown that some children will explicitly state that they have understood an ambiguous message (Karabenick and Miller, 1977). In this type of experiment, the adult speaker presents a description which corresponds either to one of four cards laid out in front of the addressee, or to two of them, or to all of them. The addressed child must select *the* card which corresponds to the description. The authors themselves emphasize that the fact that better results are obtained at a later age may be connected with a poor interpretation of the task. It is, in fact, possible that the children believe they have to guess the card the speaker is thinking of. Moreover, when the children are urged to listen better and the researchers are insistent about the need to ask questions if they are uncertain of their choice, the children aged between 6 and 8 ask for clarification, whereas those aged 4 do not.

Unlike their elders, children younger than 6 do not benefit from being trained to ask questions when this is necessary (Patterson *et al.*, 1980) whilst, as Sonnenschein has shown (1986*a*), training based on corrective feedback has a clear effect on the 6-to-7-year-olds: one week after the training, 95 per cent of the ambiguous instructions led to demands for clarification and these instructions were judged to be inadequate in 91 per cent of cases (compared with 23 per cent in a control group). The ineffectiveness of incitements to ask questions was identified by Donahue (1984) among 9- to 12-year-old learning-disabled children. In contrast, Dollaghan and Kaston

(1986) have shown that from 6 years of age onwards this type of child benefits from a long training period (three weekly sessions of twenty minutes for approximately a month). One month after the end of the training, three-quarters of the insufficiently explicit messages led to a request for explanation (training has been seen to produce a similar effect for other types of message inadequacy: hearing impaired by noise; impossibility of performing the action prescribed by the message; excessive lexical or syntactic complexity).

The young child's apparent inability to ask for clarification does not imply that referential ambiguities have no effect on its behaviour. Patterson *et al.* (1980) note that from 4 years of age onwards, children hesitate before choosing a card. These hesitations seem to show that the ambiguity has a functional effect. The early effect of ambiguities, even when the child is not conscious of them, is also demonstrated in the data collected by Flavell *et al.* (1981) and Beal and Flavell (1982), who asked young subjects to follow prerecorded instructions for building-block constructions. The results showed that the imprecision of the instructions made the 8-year-old children doubt whether they had understood them correctly. In contrast, even though the 6-year-olds hesitated during the building stage (though less than their elders), they claimed to be certain that they had understood and constructed the expected building correctly.

Similar results were obtained by Robinson and Robinson (1983). The subjects studied by these authors were given three identical rows of horses and were asked to choose one, and only one, horse from each row in response to instructions given by an adult. The children were asked to take 'the horse with the collar', although each row contained one horse with a brown collar and one horse with a black collar. Most of the children chose different horses from each of the rows. The authors interpreted this as a sign of the children's awareness of the ambiguity, even though they were demonstrably unable to explain the factors determining their choice. The subjects declared themselves to be sure of having taken the correct horses and in general did not ask for more precise instructions.

However, Robinson and Whittaker (1985) have demonstrated a link between the degree of certitude and the identification of ambiguity among children aged between $4\frac{1}{2}$ and 7. Faced with ambiguous instructions, some of the subjects were certain that they had understood correctly and did not point out the ambiguity. Others identified the ambiguity and also questioned whether they had understood the message correctly, whilst yet others showed their uncertainty but failed to identify the ambiguity. *None of the subjects who had identified the ambiguity declared him- or herself certain of having understood the instruction.* Although this result might appear trivial, it shows that before even being able to identify referential ambiguities young subjects can respond differently to ambiguous and unambiguous messages, depending on their certainty or uncertainty concerning the interpretation of these messages. In other words, verbal messages are functionally differentiated by the subject before this differentiation is performed consciously.

One point should not be neglected: the memory burden imposed by this task. If, in all the examples given, children under 5 or 6 do not seem to identify the potentially ambiguous character of the messages which are addressed to them, the performance of the older children seems to depend on the complexity of the message.

In a test for the identification of ambiguous instructions, Patterson *et al.* (1981) used messages which referred to collections of four, eight or sixteen pictures. Whatever the age of the subjects (6, 8 or 10), their performances improved as the number of referents was reduced. Moreover, whilst the performances differed only slightly with age for the small collections, the ambiguity of instructions referring to the largest collection was significantly better detected by the oldest subjects. Since the only difference between the items is the volume of information which has to be managed in working memory at any one time, the explanation in terms of processing capacity is the one which best accounts for the improvement of performance as a function of age.

This may be seen even more clearly when the proposed tasks do not consist simply of the detection of ambiguities, but also require the formulation of requests for clarification. The results obtained by Brown *et al.* (1987) show that adolescents aged 13–14 whose performance in such tests is poor are quite capable of perceiving the ambiguity but have great difficulty formulating adequate requests for additional information. The authors link these difficulties to problems of working-memory capacity.

Robinson and Robinson (see Robinson, 1981) placed the children in the position of spectators at a situation of referential communication. For example, the subject watches a sequence in which a speaker takes a picture representing a man holding a red flower and tells the listener that in order to choose the same picture he must take one that depicts 'a man holding a flower'. As we might expect, the addressee selects a picture depicting a man holding a blue flower. The children are then asked to identify the person responsible for the failure in communication. In some of the experiments it is the child and the experimenter who take the roles of speaker and addressee, and these roles are periodically reversed. The overall results obtained are as follows:

- below the age of 5 the children designate the addressee 'who should have listened better' (the same type of response has been obtained by Meline and Brackin, 1987, working with 8-year-old language-impaired children);
- at 5–6 years of age the children frequently blame the experimenter. The experimenter has played the role of speaker half of the time and addressee the other half (none of the subjects systematically designates him- or herself as being the cause of the failure: Robinson and Robinson, 1976);

- it is only from the age of 7–8 onwards that the fault is attributed to the speaker alone.

When asked to judge the adequacy of the message, some of the children were more easily able to evaluate it as inadequate if it resulted in an incorrect choice or a refusal to make a choice than if (by chance) it was followed by the correct choice (Robinson and Robinson, 1977). Thus, between the ages of 6 and 8, 51 per cent of the judgements of ambiguous instructions preceding correct choices are positive, whereas 34 per cent of the judgements of unambiguous instructions which preceded an incorrect choice are negative. Thus at an early age the subjects seem to be aware that one yardstick for the adequacy of a message is the intention of the speaker.

Thus Robinson and Whittaker (1986) have shown that when the speaker produces an ambiguous verbal message whilst visibly indicating his choice and the addressee makes a different choice, children (aged between 5 and 7) correctly guess that the speaker's choice is the correct one.

It is possible that it might be the characteristics of the participants rather than the message itself that determines the subjects' judgements.

This is what seems to be indicated by the results obtained by Pratt (1982, cited in Tunmer and Grieve, 1984), who asked children to judge whether the designations of one card from a set of four given by a puppet, *who was reputed to speak badly*, were good descriptions or not. From 4 years of age onwards, 70 per cent of the judgements were correct. Nevertheless, as the authors did not report the detail of the results, it is difficult to interpret them. In particular, if half the designations are effectively unambiguous and designated as such (as might be surmised in view of the tendency shown by young children to give an affirmative response to a task of judgement), then the level of adequate judgements of the ambiguous utterances would be close to the level for random response. The same reservations should be made in connection with the 76 per cent success rate at 5, but would not disqualify the 90 per cent success rate at 6.

The results produced by Sonnenschein (1986*b*) are much clearer. At 6–7 years of age all the children rejected the ambiguous messages if they were produced by another child. In contrast, the same messages were accepted in 70 per cent of cases if the speaker was an adult, unless the adult was explicitly designated as stupid. At 9–10, differences in evaluation which depend on the nature of the speaker had disappeared. However, the effects of a poor awareness of ambiguity do seem to be present. At 6–7, those deficiencies in the message (for example, its potentially incomplete nature) of which the children are well aware are pointed out to an equal degree, regardless of the speaker. In contrast, at 4–5 all the messages are considered equally adequate despite the fact that they are ambiguous, incomplete or contradictory (Patterson and Kister, 1981).

Bredart (1980) has further shown that the detection of the cause of a failure in communication may appear earlier or later, depending on the nature of this cause:

- from 8 years of age onwards, the child can accurately determine the adequacy of the verbal message with regard to the reality to which it is supposed to refer;
- between the ages of 8 and 10, children find it more difficult to suppose that a foreign listener cannot understand their own language than to suppose that a speaker of their own language is unable to understand a foreign language;
- the lexical and syntactic difficulties and the length of the message are the last problems to be invoked.

In the same way, differentiation as a function of the semantico-pragmatic characteristics of the verbal messages appears at a relatively late age. Finn (1976, cited by Pratt and Nesdale, 1984) asked 5-year-old children questions containing meaningless words (for example: 'Are there more yukkays or more oakkeys?'). He observed not only that the subjects responded to the questions as if they were meaningful, but also that they explicitly affirmed that they were correct. Hughes and Grieve (1980) obtained the same results with children aged between 5 and 7, noting, however, that the 7-year-olds were more inclined to hesitate than the younger children. However, Wales (1974) has shown that in a task of judging questions, some of which could be answered and some not (the latter type being meaningless), 76 per cent of judgements were correct at 5 years of age and 86 per cent at 6. Even when we take account of the reservations already stated concerning tasks of judgement, it seems very much as if the first appearance of the subjects' conscious monitoring of their own comprehension occurs at around the age of 5–6.

Within this framework, the poor performances of young subjects can be interpreted as a result of the consideration of elements external to the verbal messages themselves. Thus Surian and Job (1987) have shown that when selecting pictures in accordance with ambiguous instructions, 7-year-old children apply either Grice's (1975) 'Maxim of Quantity' – the speaker must be as explicit as the situation demands, but not more so – or Clark and Haviland's (1977) 'Maxim of Antecedent' – the speaker must construct his production in such a way that the listener can find in what has already been said a direct antecedent for the current utterance. The maxim selected depends on the actual situation. In the first case, when the children are shown a set of pictures depicting a clown who is happy or sad and is or is not holding a flower, and asked to point to 'the happy clown', they indicate the one who is not holding a flower (as, moreover, the majority of adults do in the same situation). In contrast, if the children have already been asked to describe the picture depicting the happy clown who is holding the flower, it is this picture which they indicate (Maxim of Antecedent). However, nothing in the reported data indicates that the choices made are conditioned by the identification of the ambiguity. The application of these maxims may well accompany a lack of awareness of the ambiguity amongst the youngest subjects or be intentionally used for the purposes of disambiguation by the oldest.

One particular instance is when the speaker deliberately introduces a contradiction between information and context. This occurs, for example, in the case of sarcastic utterances. Ackerman (1986) told short stories to subjects aged 7, 10 and 18. Each story contained a description of an event, the comment made by someone about this event, and the response of another person to whom the comment was addressed. The comment is either literal or sarcastic (for example, after Billy has just played lamentably badly in a baseball match, Billy's trainer tells Cheryl that Billy has had a great match) and the response of the addressee (Cheryl) shows whether the sarcastic intention has been understood or not. The subjects are then asked questions designed to reveal whether they have understood the speaker's intention (Is the trainer happy with Billy's match?), whether they think they have understood what was said and whether they think the addressee has understood or not. The subjects are asked to respond to each question with a simple yes or no. From 7 years of age onwards, 75 per cent of the responses to the first question seem to indicate an understanding of the sarcastic intention (81 per cent at 10 and 90 per cent among the young adults). However, while the subjects aged between 10 and 18 think they have understood the speaker in 95 per cent of cases and judge the understanding of the addressee correctly in more than 90 per cent of cases, at 7 the subjects think they have understood the sarcastic utterances in 73 per cent of cases, and their level of success in judging the comprehension of the addressee does not differ from that expected for random response. At 7 years of age, the subjects thus appear to possess a good understanding of the sarcastic intention but find it difficult to judge the understanding of others independently of their own comprehension. Nevertheless, it is possible that the subjects base their responses solely on the description provided of the event referred to and on the intonation used, which is very different for the sarcastic and literal utterances. When the 7-year-old subjects are deprived of any intonational clues, their level of understanding of the sarcastic intention falls to 60 per cent; and when they are given only these clues (not being told the details of the event which is being commented on), their level of comprehension does not exceed 31 per cent. Children of this age thus often seem to reestablish the compatibility between verbal messages and the context in which they are emitted. However, it would be useful to establish that in this type of experiment the understanding of the sarcastic intention is accompanied by a consideration of the utterance itself and not by a correction (conscious or not) of this utterance by the children, as is often the case when they are confronted by utterances which they consider unacceptable (see Chapter 3).

Whilst an awareness of the referents of the messages can cause young subjects to misconstrue those messages which do not refer to these literally, it also seems that knowledge of the speaker's intentions prevents them from perceiving the referential ambiguities. Thus Beal and Flavell (1984) have shown that at 6–7 years of age, children are unable to detect the ambiguity of imprecise verbal designations of objects when the speaker points to the intended object ('give me the big block' when the available collection contains several large blocks of different colours and the speaker points to one of them), whereas they are able to detect such ambiguities when the speaker makes no such indications of intention (39 per cent judgements of ambiguity in the first case and 86 per cent in the second). This difference disappears at the ages of 7–8 (96 per cent and 94 per cent of correct judgements respectively). Similar results had already been obtained by Robinson *et al.* (1983) among children aged 4–5.

Torrance and Olson (1987) have shown that this is not a memory problem. Even children who remember the exact terms of the message do not seem to be able to differentiate between what has been *said* and what the speaker *meant*. Furthermore, Bonitatibus (1988) has shown that at 6–7 years of age those children who are able to designate the author of an ambiguous message as being to blame for a failure of communication are, unlike the others, also able to extract the manifest intention of the speaker and concentrate solely on the literal meaning of the message. In a recognition task, it is only these children who can distinguish between what was actually said and what the speaker meant.

Up to the age of 7, the analysis of the meaning of verbal messages thus seems to be greatly restricted by the contextual indices of the speaker's communicative intention. The same phenomenon is observed when an adult addressee incorrectly claims to have understood the referent designated by an ambiguous message. Amongst children aged 5–6 this affirmation overrides the analysis of the message itself (Beal and Flavell, 1983). Moreover, at this age children seem to be able to perceive what the recipient of an ambiguous message knows after listening to it (they are able to respond negatively to questions of the type 'Does he know where the chocolate is?') without being able to evaluate the level of explicitness of the message itself (Sodian, 1988).

The monitoring of explicitness in self-produced verbal messages

All the results produced so far concern the identification of ambiguities, the conscious character of which appears at a relatively advanced age. There is also a smaller body of work which focuses on the monitoring of the explicitness of the produced message. These studies have shown that when children under 6 are cast in the role of speaker, they produce ambiguous referential descriptions (see, for example, Sakata, 1987) and find it difficult to respond to the addressee's requests for clarification (Peterson *et al.*, 1972) unless the feedback provided specifies the required information (see, for example, Spilton and Lee, 1977). The recodings of messages observed by Wilcox and Webster (1980) among children under 2 in response to feedback indicating the incomprehension of the addressee were in fact mostly gestural recodings which reveal the instability of the initial verbalizations. At no point at that age was there any realization of the inadequacy of the produced message.

It seems that young children are unable to detect the inadequacy of the messages they produce (Asher, 1978). However, from the age of 6 onwards suitable training seems to lead to a considerable and long-lasting improvement in performance (Sonnenschein, 1986*a*).

Furthermore, Robinson and Robinson (1978) have shown the existence of a link between the ability to designate the person responsible for the failure of communication and the child's ability to point out the ambiguity of a verbal message voluntarily. Moreover, being taught to criticize the communicative performances of others improves the performances of pre-school-age children in both the comprehension and the production of referential messages (Sonnenschein and Whitehurst, 1984*b*). In contrast, training focused specifically on comprehension or production improves performance in that mode without being transferred to the other (Sonnenschein and Whitehurst, 1983) unless, at the same time as being trained in one particular mode, the children had the opportunity to act the role corresponding to the other mode, although in this case no specific training is given (Sonnenschein and Whitehurst, 1984*a*). However, there was no case in which specific training improved the children's judgement of the communicative exchanges of others. These results seem to show that tasks of criticizing the productions of others, such as the tasks used by the Robinsons (see above), involve other competences than those which are at work when the child participates as either addressee or speaker in a communicative exchange. We should like to suggest that the first type of task, unlike the second, requires a reflective (metapragmatic) attitude towards verbal exchange.

Kossan and Markman (1981) think that if children produce ambiguous verbal messages, this is because they do not rely on the verbal channel alone to transfer information. The physical presence of the interlocutor (even if separated from the child by a screen) could thus impair the explicitness of the message and, in consequence, result in an underestimation of the real abilities of the child. In a task in which one picture in a group was to be designated verbally, these authors showed that at 6–7 years of age the level of effective designations (i.e. those which led an adult partner to make the expected choice) rose from 60 per cent using the traditional method of the screen to 78 per cent if the addressee was not in the room and the child communicated with him on an intercom. Moreover, the adult addressee was asked to indicate, on a scale of 1 to 5, how certain he was of having made the correct choice on the basis of the instructions given by the child. The average score obtained when the screen was used was 2.72, and 3.91 when communication was performed via an intercom. Finally, the average number of deictics (terms of designation) used fell from 18 in the first situation to 2.38 in the second. The use of these deictics suggests that when the interlocutor is present, even if separated from the subject by a screen, the children behave as if a certain amount of information which they possess were also available to the partner ('it's *this* triangle', which presupposes that the addressee can see the designated triangle).

These results should be viewed in conjunction with those obtained by Maratsos (1973), who showed that between the ages of 3 and 6 the level of sufficiently explicit designations varied between 8 per cent and 42 per cent with age when the addressee could see the designated objects and between 71 per cent and 77 per cent when the addressee was blindfold. Moreover, simple pointing without comment, which was absent in the second case, was very common in the first.

Finally, the successes achieved in the simplest cases are not repeated when more complicated descriptions are used – for example, when a route has to be described by telephone. The success rate in such cases barely exceeds 50 per cent at 7 years of age, despite feedback from the addressee and the subject's awareness of the results of a number of previous attempts (Lloyd, 1985). Similarly, a telephonic exchange of instructions intended to lead to the construction of a shape was completed successfully by only a quarter of 11-year-old subjects (Vivier, 1988).

We have already seen that the analysis of the explicitness of verbal messages seems to be late to emerge. The same appears to be true of its intentional monitoring. However, the volume of study directed at this question is still low and the data are often too generalized to be interpreted easily. The evolution of the monitoring of one's own productions can be seen more clearly in the body of research devoted to the way in which speech is adapted to the interlocutor. Furthermore, the ability to produce unambiguous messages is simply one particular aspect of the adaptation of speech to the addressee, an adaptation which takes account of the partner's perspective and state of knowledge. Thus, in a referential communication task conducted in Japanese, Sakata (1987) has shown that before the age of 7–8, children experience equal degrees of difficulty in producing explicit messages and in adapting their productions to the age of the addressee (adult, same age or younger).

Adaptation of speech to the addressee

Flavell *et al.* (1968) asked subjects aged 8, 12 and 17 to recount the same story first to an adult and then to a 4-year-old child (the interlocutors were represented by photographs). The story had previously been read by the subjects. The researchers noted that, unlike the 12- and 17-year-old subjects, two-thirds of the 8-year-olds modified the story only slightly to adapt it to the addressee. Beaudichon *et al.* (1978) repeated this experiment but substituted flesh-and-blood interlocutors for the photographs. In contrast to the results obtained by Flavell *et al.*, these researchers observed that even the 8-year-olds introduced a number of simplifications when the story was addressed to a 4-year-old child. The majority of these simplifications consisted of condensations and changes of presentation which did not affect the story's meaning.

It would thus seem that at 8 years of age, children are able to adapt their speech to suit the age of the addressee. However, Brami-Mouling (1977), who obtained results very similar to those of Beaudichon *et al.* by asking children to tell a story either to someone of their own age or to a younger child, noted that of all the modifications made by the 8-year-olds, the only ones which the subjects named when asked to describe the changes they had decided to make were those of prosody (intonation, emphasis, pauses, speed of delivery) or lexical simplification. These thus appear to be the only changes to be performed knowingly.

However, adaptation of speech to the age of the addressee has been observed amongst much younger children in everyday situations. Everyone will have heard a small child using 'baby talk' to speak to its younger brother or sister. During the course of more systematic observations, Weeks (1971) has noted that a child aged 3 years 4 months spoke more loudly than usual, exaggerated his intonation and slowed his speed of delivery when talking to a child aged 1 year 9 months. Similarly, Gleason (1973) has observed that from the age of 4 onwards, subjects simplify their language when addressing younger children.

In the same way, in 1935 Smith had already observed that children (average age = 44 months) produce longer and syntactically more complex sentences when speaking to an adult than to a child of pre-school age. However, only the difference in length is statistically significant (and it is possible that the second difference is simply a consequence of the first).

In a controlled experiment, Shatz and Gelman (1973) asked 4-year-old children to explain the workings of a toy first to an adult and then to another 4-year-old child. When speaking to the latter, the subjects produced fewer sentences (Garvey and BenDebba, 1974, have reported that children of pre-school age adapt the number of verbal productions they make to the number produced by their interlocutor), shorter sentences and syntactically less complicated sentences, voluntarily substituting simple parataxis for subordinate and coordinate constructions. The authors found these same adaptations amongst the spontaneous productions of slightly more than a third of the subjects.

Similar results were obtained by Sachs and Devin (1976) in their analysis of mainly spontaneous speech. However, when these authors asked children of 4–5 to talk like babies, they observed prosodic, phonological and lexical modifications, but no syntactic modifications. Finally, Fey and Leonard (1984) have found that, in general, a group of language-impaired children used the same speech modifications as 'normal' children, but that this similarity was not manifested in the indices of syntactic complexity (mean length of productions and number of words before the verb).

As Bredart and Rondal (1982) have emphasized, the age of the interlocutor is not in itself an objective parameter which can be used to determine a change of linguistic behaviour in the speaker. What is important is to identify, amongst the entire set of changes observed during development, those of which the young speaker is aware.

Observing a group of 4-year-old children, Masur (1978) notes that in a situation similar to the one used by Shatz and Gelman there is an adaptation of speech as a function of the linguistic level of a 2-year-old interlocutor (determined by the mean length of the produced utterances and noted by the speaker in the feedback). This adaptation becomes all the more pronounced the worse the speech of the addressee. However, these adaptations are performed only at the start of productions and fall off as they progress. The linguistic level of the partner thus appears to have a role to play, as does his or her cognitive level. The significance of the latter is suggested by the results of Guralnick and Paul-Brown (1977) who, analyzing the spontaneous speech of children aged 5–6, found adaptations when the addressee was a mentally handicapped child of the same age. In such cases the productions were adapted to the linguistic level of the mentally retarded child, being shorter and syntactically simpler than when the children were addressing a nonhandicapped child of their own age.

Adjustments have also been identified in the speech of 2-year-old children of deaf parents when speaking either to a deaf person or to one with normal hearing (Schiff and Ventry, 1976). When speaking to a deaf person, the children make more gestures, produce shorter utterances and manifest distortions of language similar to those observed in the spoken productions of deaf people.

Menig-Peterson (1975) has conducted an experimental study of the ability of children of pre-school age to adapt their speech to the listener's perspective. After an interval of one week, the subjects were asked to report an event to one adult who was present at it and to one who was not. The author studied the introduction of new elements (for example, definite article v. indefinite article). The results show the existence of modifications adapted to the two situations. These data agree with those reported by Maratsos

(1973), who noted that the speech of 4-year-old children became more explicit when they were talking to an adult who was blindfold, but are partially contradicted by the data collected by Warden (1976). According to these data, the adaptation of articles as a function of whether the addressee can or cannot see the referents does not appear until 5 years of age and increases progressively until the age of 9–10.

Perner and Leekam (1986) have suggested that in Menig-Peterson's experiment the addressees might have appeared more interested when the children were telling them something new than when they were recounting something already known. In such a case, the subjects would have adjusted their productions not to the addressees' level of knowledge but to the attention they showed. To control these factors, the authors repeated the Menig-Peterson experiment with subjects aged 3–4, but with addressees (aged 4–5) who were either partially or totally ignorant of the reported facts. Faced with partially ignorant partners, the subjects adapted their productions to the limited knowledge of the interlocutor and generally mentioned only those events which were unknown to their partners. Nevertheless, faced by partners who knew nothing of the event, the youngest subjects (aged 3 to $3\frac{1}{2}$) also tended to report only some of the facts which they might potentially have related. To the authors, it still seems that it is the level of knowledge rather than the attitude of the addressee that lies at the origin of these adaptations. However, the fact that in the Perner and Leekam experiment the addressees ask explicit questions about what they want to know suggests that it is primarily the ability to provide accurate answers to factual questions which is brought to light by such an experiment.

On a first analysis, the results of the initial body of research, which suggest that the ability to adapt speech is late to appear, and those of the second body, which reveal the existence of early adjustments, seem to be contradictory. In fact this contradiction is apparent only. The situations which reveal the late emergence of adjustments which depend on the addressee are highly formal in nature, whilst the remainder of the research has examined situations of social interaction in which the addressees are not only actually present but also provide feedback during the course of the exchange. The speakers are then able to consider this feedback when deciding on their own verbal productions.

Spilton and Lee (1977) have shown that amongst 4-year-olds who were observed in free-play situations, two-thirds of the responses to the addressee's feedback were adapted. This suffices to differentiate these productions from those emitted without feedback.

In fact, the two types of situation do not seem to mobilize the same type of ability. As Menig-Peterson (1975) thinks, the first probably calls on the cognitive ability to resolve problems (applied here to the pragmatic dimension of language) and the second on the more general skills associated with the assumption of social roles. It is these skills which the sociocognitive perspective sees as lying at the base of the earliest communicative behaviour (Hale and Delia, 1976).

Even if these studies show the existence of adaptations from 4 years of age onwards, they do not establish the children's awareness of these adaptations. Their metalinguistic nature is thus uncertain. Indeed, as Van Kleeck (1984) reminds us, the field of social psychology has produced a large number of studies of the communicative behaviour of adults, and these indicate that the attitudes and way of speaking of the participants in a conversation tend to converge (quantity, intensity, volume, accent, linguistic structures, etc.). Moreover, these adjustments are often performed automatically in a more or less unconscious way (see, for example, Berger, 1980). We agree with what is suggested by these studies, and think that the adaptations to the speech of others observed in young children are nothing more than the verbal aspect of wider, unreflected behaviour modifications made by the child in reaction to the situation. The adaptation manifested at the level of language would then not constitute the phenomenon in its entirety but would simply be the most directly observable element of it. It would not be metalinguistic in nature (see Gombert, 1987).

Ghezzi *et al.* (1987) have studied the speech of pre-adolescents aged 11 discussing a film sequence, seen immediately before, with either a child of 6, someone of the same age, or an adult. The younger the partner is, the more often the subjects speak but the shorter the utterances they produce. Moreover, modifications are also made to the contents of the speech. The young speakers take themselves as the reference point when speaking to an adult (speaking about themselves, their families and their friends) but take the interlocutor as the reference point when speaking to a child younger than themselves (speaking then of the child's life, family and friends). These data seem to us to demonstrate that situations of social interaction are unsuited to the study of the ability to modify speech intentionally as a function of one of the parameters of the situation of utterance. The difference between the conditions obtaining is too great. The subject, confronted by very different circumstances, does not occupy the same position in the interaction and does not say the same things. We are here in a field associated with psychosociological (or sociocognitive) studies, and certainly not in the presence of formal metalinguistic tasks. An analysis of the structural modifications of language alone leads to erroneous conclusions.

For example, when a subject speaks for a long time without being interrupted (which is dependent on the attitude of the partner, a factor which itself varies in accordance with certain circumstances, the age of the two participants being one of them), we naturally observe the presence of longer productions, but also very probably of syntactically more complicated constructions in which a large amount of information is concatenated within the same production.

Moreover, in their commentary on the results of their study showing early syntactic adaptations (see above), Shatz and Gelman (1973) themselves suggested that the children did not choose to use a simpler syntactic form when addressing partners younger than themselves. Instead, they chose not to speak of certain things. As Schmidt and Paris (1984) have emphasized, the selection of different styles of speech depending on the characteristics of the addressee is more likely to be determined semantically than syntactically.

Some authors explain the difference in performance between experiments which reveal late adaptations and those which show early adaptations in terms of the factors of memory capacity. The former experiments, unlike the latter, would require a large volume of information to be held in memory (see, for example, Lafontaine, 1983). Even if the growth in the capacity of working memory is an important causal factor in the evolution of performance in tasks requiring the resolution of problems, whatever these might be, it is doubtful whether it constitutes, as current tendencies would often seem to suggest, the sole (or even the principal) explanation for the development made between pre-school age and the start of adolescence. For memory capacity to be the key factor here, we would have to see subjects attempting to memorize the initial message with a view to performing intentional modifications to its structure as a function of the circumstances under which it is subsequently produced. Such a strategy does not appear to be very relevant to children whose objective is not the completion of a stylistic exercise but the communication of information.

For our part (Gombert, 1985) we asked a number of 4-year-olds to tell a child aged 2 (the same child was used for all the subjects) either a straightforward story (simple model) or the same story in a version previously adapted for the child listener by its mother and presented by her to the subject in this form. At some other point (a balanced experimental order was used) the subjects were asked to tell one of the two versions of the story to a child of the same age (again the child was the same in all cases). Furthermore, pictures corresponding to each of the episodes in the story were available to the child speakers as memory aids. Finally, before each production, each subject was asked to tell us the story. This provided us with a reference version for any later adaptations. The results revealed no difference between the repetitions and the subsequent productions, either in the number and length of clauses or in the indications of syntactic complexity (number of words before the main verb, coordinated and subordinated expressions, tenses other than the present indicative). Moreover, no simplifications were found in the narration of the unadapted story addressed to a child of 2, whatever indications of syntactic complexity were retained. They are thus no more significant than those (also nonexistent) which might have arisen in the narration following the presentation of the adapted version. The existence of such a difference would have pointed to the presence of a real ability in young children to adapt the narrative to the characteristics of the addressee.

In fact, setting aside the problems of memory, early adaptations are never found when the formalism of the task requires the child to perform a manipulation which bears on language alone. This observation tends to support the point of view developed above concerning the unconscious – and therefore nonmetalinguistic – nature of the early adaptations observed in situations of social interaction.

Awareness of the social rules of language

Martlew *et al.* (1978) hold that young children adapt themselves to the expectations of their surroundings, which may vary according to different social circumstances. This adaptation would affect the children's use of language. According to the authors, the child should develop from a global perception of the interlocutor's role to a division into broad categories (adult/child – stranger/acquaintance) and then to increasingly fine categorizations. They analyzed the spontaneous speech of a boy aged 5½ playing alone, with a friend of the same age, and with his mother. The productions occurring with his mother were on average longer than with someone of the same age but were also often not completed, with the child trying to reformulate his sentence or abandoning the idea altogether. In fact, verbal exchanges with a friend consisted almost exclusively of discussion, whereas with his mother his utterances were primarily concerned with the play task that he was currently attempting to accomplish. Martlew *et al.* concluded that the child recognized the role required of him in each situation and identified this skill as a prerequisite for the ability to realize that the addressee might understand the world in a different way from the speaker, and that it is necessary to take account of this in one's own verbal messages in order to facilitate their decoding.

The adoption of a social role thus seems to emerge at a relatively early age, as is also shown by the observations of Hall *et al.* (1977), who pointed out differences in the speech of 3-to-4-year-olds depending on whether they were in class or in a supermarket. However, these early skills appear to be limited in scope.

Andersen (1977) asked children aged between 4 and 7 to provide the voices for three puppets (mother, father and baby). Even the youngest subjects adjusted their speech in accordance with the family role given to them. However, this adoption of roles was less successful when the children were asked to provide the voices for a doctor, a nurse and a sick child, or for a teacher and a pupil. These results seem to demonstrate that such behaviour is highly dependent on the imitative component of the roles which the children are asked to play.

A particular case of adaptation to the situation and/or the characteristics of the interlocutor is provided by the use of verbal forms of politeness. In a study conducted in Hungarian, Hollos (1977) showed that for children of 7–9 the adopted social role (in an experiment similar to that of Andersen, 1977) had an effect on the use of pronouns (which in Hungarian differ depending on the familiarity of the addressee). In 1978, James discovered that children of 4 and 5 also adapt the degree of politeness in the formulation of requests as a function of the age of the addressee.

As Ervin-Tripp (1977) emphasizes, the literature reveals a degree of consensus concerning the identification of two conditions for the ability to adapt the use of linguistic politeness: (1) the knowledge of the 'polite' linguistic form; (2) the knowledge of the pragmatic rules at work in a given social or situational context. These conditions make awareness of linguistic politeness a relatively late and complex ability.

In 1976, Bates identified three stages in the development of the use of linguistic politeness in the formulation of requests:

1. Up to the age of 4, children appear to produce direct requests only in the form of imperative sentences (for example, 'Give me the ball'). However, from 4 years of age onwards they are able to identify the least direct request as 'the nicest' in a forced-choice test;
2. At 5–6 years of age they appear to be able to produce all the syntactic subtleties of their mother tongue but are still unable to 'mask' the contents of their request in order to attain their objective (for example, they are not yet able to say 'It isn't very warm in this room' in order to persuade someone to close the window);
3. It is not until the age of 7–8 that children can manipulate both the form and the content of their requests in order to produce indirect requests (for example, 'Could you pass me the salt?').

This analysis is confirmed by Gleason's (1973) observations which show that even if the age of 4 does see the appearance of a modulation (for example, certain 'whinings' are reserved for the mother) it is not until about 8 years of age that certain routine verbal politenesses are reserved for adults who are unfamiliar to the child.

The majority of studies of linguistic politeness have focused on the ability to formulate indirect requests. This appears to be the most prevalent type of request amongst children of school age (see Wilkinson *et al.*, 1984). Nevertheless, Wilkinson *et al.* show that the use of indirect requests develops before the child's conscious awareness of it. Although it has been shown that the adapted comprehension of such requests exists at the age of 3 (see Elrod, 1983), it plays no major role (in French) until the age of 5–6 (Bernicot and Legros, 1987*a*). Before this, the child appears to base its interpretation primarily on the social situation of the production (see also Beaudichon, 1982).

Axia and Baroni (1985) have worked on the hypothesis that the ability to formulate requests politely (in other words, the ability to formulate indirect requests in a suitable way) is a complex ability which consists of a combination of linguistic and social skills. In order to be as polite as the situation requires, children must simultaneously be aware of the form and content of their requests, understand the signals given by the addressee, recognize the status of the participants, etc. In a study conducted in Italian (like Bates's studies of the same subject), these authors provoked requests from children aged 5, 7 and 9. The experimenter possesses a set of coloured pegs with which he constructs a shape on a slotted board. The children also have to construct a shape, but must continually ask the experimenter for the pegs they need. In order to obtain reformulations the experimenter resists the children's requests, sometimes pretending not to hear them and sometimes countering them with arguments which are obviously untrue (for example, he tells the child 'I can't give you any red pegs because I need them myself' while possessing a large stock of pegs of each colour). The percentage of 'polite' (nonimperative) requests, which at 5, 7 and 9 years of age amounts to 11 per cent, 20 per cent and 25 per cent respectively for the spontaneous requests, rises to 20 per cent, 56 per cent and 84 per cent in the reformulations which follow an explicit refusal on the part of the experimenter to satisfy the original request. From the age of 7 years onwards, the child thus seems able to formulate requests politely if the reaction of the addressee makes this necessary. However, it is not until the age of 9 that we encounter a fine awareness of this attitude and a difference in the reformulation depending on the type of resistance shown (repetition or reformulation when the addressee does not appear to have heard, change of request when the refusal is explicit). In the view of Piché *et al.* (1978) this evolution continues throughout adolescence, with the degree of adaptation to the attributes of the addressee becoming ever finer.

In a second experiment, Axia and Baroni (1985) asked subjects aged 5–6, 7 and 9–10 to attribute polite requests (for example, '*Vorresti spostarti, per favore*' – 'Could you move, please?') or impolite requests ('*Spostati*' – 'Move') either to a speaker talking to an adult or to one addressing a child. It was not until the age of 7 that the majority of responses attributed the polite requests to the speaker addressing the adult and the impolite requests to the one talking to the child. Furthermore, it was not until the subjects reached the age of 9–10 that the first justifications appeared (in 10 per cent of subjects) citing the deference due to adults.

If social conditioning can provoke the early use of polite language (Wilkinson and Genishi, 1987, further show that differences can relate to the culture of origin, in this case North America or Mexico), it still seems that it is only at a later age that the child recognizes the factors which determine this usage. In the same way, the comprehension of indirect requests seems to predate their production by a considerable period.

Bernicot and Legros (1987*a*, *b*) have shown that even though such requests are practically never understood at 3–4 years of age (at least where these concern unconventional formulations such as 'I can't manage to build a sand castle with my hands' as a request for a spade), they are correctly interpreted from 5–6 years of age onwards, especially if contextual signs which aid their comprehension exist. In contrast, at the age of 4 – but not at 2 – children seem to be capable of modulating their assertions when they are addressing an adult (Shatz and Gelman, 1977).

In the evolution of judgements of the degree of acceptability of requests, the development which takes place after 5 years of age essentially seems to concern the indices of which the child is aware. Thus Bernicot (1988) has shown that when judging whether a request is likely to procure the desired result, 5-year-old children base their evaluation exclusively on the characteristics of the situation of utterance (for example, the circumstance of talking to an unaccommodating person), whereas 10-year-olds also consider the linguistic characteristics (the more or less direct character) of the formulation of the request. In other words, what seems to take place between the two ages is a development from the simple judgement of the chances of success of a language act as a function of the situation in which it occurs to the possibility of modifying this judgement by a linguistic analysis of the production which constitutes this language act. As the results obtained by Bernicot suggest, this development may take the form of a complete reorganization of the modes of functioning which (at around the age of 7) are accompanied by a decline in performance. It is at this age that the situational indices are abandoned, although the linguistic indices have not yet been taken into account.

The developments described above are essentially concerned with 'stylistic' verbal politeness, awareness of which seems to appear at a relatively late age. The same is not true of the use of polite formulae and conventional formulations, which many authors believe to appear in the language of children at around 2–3 years of age, when the social status (which includes the family status) of the addressee demands it (see Ervin-Tripp and Gordon, 1985), especially when the child is strongly encouraged to act in this way by its parents (Greif and Gleason, 1980).

However, significant differences appear to exist, depending on the sociocultural environment to which the children belong. According to the only study which we know to have been conducted into this question – amongst the urban populations of Florida – the spontaneous use of routine formulae of politeness seems to occur more frequently in children of 4 who come from deprived backgrounds than amongst those belonging to the middle classes. The test group was composed of schoolchildren (Becker and Smenner, 1986).

Gleason *et al.* (1984) have noted the use of numerous polite formulae among American children aged between 3 and 5 ('please', 'thank you', 'I pleased be excused', 'you're welcome'). The use of such formulae is often encouraged by the adult ('What do you say?', 'What's the magic word?'). These authors think that at the same time that as children are learning to use specific polite formulae they are also learning, peripherally, to express their intentions in different linguistic forms. Early learning of polite formulae would thus have the advantageous effect of acquainting children with stylistic variations.

Viewed in their entirety, these data do not contradict our interpretation of the adaptation of speech with reference to the interlocutor. The social adaptations of language appear at an early age but correspond more to a sociolinguistic competence based on an implicit knowledge of the rules of use than to an ability to modify formulations voluntarily as a function of circumstantial objectives which are clearly perceived by the young speaker. If, at an early age, the messages are adapted to the social context of their emission, then metapragmatic control over them is still late to develop. Furthermore, the necessity for such a control probably does not arise before the child proceeds beyond a simple respect for social norms, and needs or wants to use language rhetorically – a step which leads him or her to experiment with formulations which, despite respecting the socially permitted rules, do not form part of the restricted body of conventional formulations.

Finally, the correlation, made implicitly in the literature, between politeness in verbal requests and the indirect character of these requests raises problems. In fact, in a study conducted in English and Hebrew, Blum-Kulka (1987) has shown that adults do not judge the most indirect requests to be the most polite. An essential element of politeness would appear to reside in the clarity of the message, and the indirect character of the message would appear to be no more than a secondary aspect which possesses the virtue of softening the coercive nature of the request. Thus the requests judged to be the most polite are the conventional indirect requests (their conventional character reestablishes the character of the message). Direct requests *and* requests containing hints are both judged to be less polite. The same hierarchy of politeness has been found in French by Bernicot (1988) amongst 10-year-old children.

Linguistic humour

It is only for reasons of simplicity that we shall attempt to deal in a single section with the mosaic of linguistic behaviour which constitutes linguistic humour. It is, moreover, a questionable decision to include this subject in a chapter devoted to metapragmatic development. In fact, any incongruous linguistic production may create a humorous effect, irrespective of whether the incongruity is borne by phonological, lexical, syntactic or pragmatico-semantic characteristics. It would therefore have been possible to approach one aspect of such behaviour in each of the preceding chapters. However, from the metalinguistic point of view, our interest must be focused on the intentional control of the humorous production and on the ability to identify the factors determining the humorous effects created by the linguistic productions of others. In this regard, it is the humorous intention which is the most important factor. In Austin's terms, we are interested here in the intentional management of perlocutionary effects (effects intended by a production without being explicitly declared by the speaker, as is the case, for example, with speech which is intended to console or whose goal is to provoke laughter or to relax the atmosphere). From this point of view, it is legitimate to consider all aspects of humorous language behaviour under the heading of metapragmatic behaviour.

Basing his ideas on the Piagetian description of cognitive development during the first seven or eight years of life, McGhee (1979) has proposed a four-stage model for the development of humorous behaviour (linguistic or otherwise):

Stage 1: At about 1½ to 2 years of age, children's newly developed ability to represent objects to themselves makes 'pretend' behaviour possible. The objects present are thus manipulated as if they were other objects, absent but none the less manipulable because of the force of the mental image. It may be that the same type of diversion is at work in the verbalizations which accompany the action. This type of behaviour is generally accompanied by laughter, which suggests its humorous nature.

Stage 2: At the start of the third year similar behaviour appears, and this is limited to the sphere of language. Children deliberately give inappropriate names to objects or events. It is the absence of any action directed towards the objects present which differentiates the behaviour seen in stage 2 from that in stage 1.

Stage 3: The age of 3–4 years sees the emergence of conceptual incongruities. The behaviour of simple substitution of objects seen in stages 1 and 2 becomes more sophisticated. From now on the child deconstructs concepts into their attributes and reacts humorously to the violation of one or more of these attributes, laughing at the idea of a bicycle with square wheels or a cat with two heads. In the same way, at language level, the child takes pleasure in the distortion of phonological characteristics or the creation of meaningless words.

Stage 4: Finally, at approximately 7 years of age, a form of humour appears which is related to that of the adult and which, at the linguistic level, is essentially based on the deliberate manipulation of ambiguities. McGhee explicitly relates this new ability to the acquisition of operational thought.

Working on the hypothesis that linguistic humour in children is based on the development of metalinguistic knowledge, Shultz and Robillard (1980) have reviewed the work concerned with the emergence of linguistic humour and distinguished between types of behaviour on the basis of the implied linguistic dimension. They were thus able to identify linguistic incongruities based on the distortion of articulation (phonological humour), the deliberate violation of morphological rules (as in Javanese play language or in *verlan*, a French backward talk, such playing with language is never observed at pre-school age), deliberate violations of the rules of lexical restriction and violations of the rules of usage (as, for example, the literal response to an indirect question: 'Can you pass me the salt?' – 'Yes, I can'). On the other hand, they find little evidence of the existence in children of humorous effects created by violations of the rules of syntax.

Phonological humour

A large number of authors have reported their observations of young children who 'play' with language by making up rhymes or distorting sounds or intonations (see Chapter 2 above). This behaviour, although characteristic of stage 3 of McGhee's (1979) model of the development of humour, has been observed at the age of 1 year 8 months by Horgan (1980): 'Cow go moo. Mommy go mamoo. Daddy go dadoo. Ha ha.' In a production such as this, the humorous effect is created by the systematic use of an incongruous rule for the production of phonemes. As we have indicated in the chapter dealing with metaphonological development, even if such productions undeniably constitute phonological manipulations there is nothing to suggest that for the subject this is anything more than a simple playful manipulation of sounds, the symbolic nature of these sounds never being taken into account by the young child. The same reservation must apply to the rhymes which appear at 2–3 years of age in certain playful verbalizations. Moreover, a number of authors have defended the idea that although young children enjoy playing with sound sequences, there is nothing to prove that such games reflect an explicit awareness of phonological segments (see Kamhi, 1987).

Humour based on linguistic ambiguities

As Van Kleeck (1982, 1984) reminds us, there are a number of studies which seem to show that before the age of 6–7 children do not understand humour based on lexical ambiguities, and that before the age of 8–9 they also fail to understand humour created by the ambiguities of surface or deep structure. This full degree of awareness does not seem to emerge before the age of 10 or 12. However, these ambiguities can be detected in the form of jokes at an earlier age than when they are presented in a nonhumorous form.

Humour based on ambiguity plays a large role in riddles, and we again have to wait until the age of 8–9 before children can, when requested, produce (and understand) guessing games which are effectively based on such ambiguities rather than on simple questions in which the aspect of guessing is limited to the riddle surface structure without a punch line (Sutton-Smith, 1976). Moreover, a number of authors have shown that 6-year-olds find 'nonhumorous' riddles (for example: 'What do giraffes have that no other animal has?' – 'Long necks') just as funny as humorous riddles (the same question as above, but with the answer 'Little giraffes'; example provided by Prentice and Fatham, 1975, p. 212). In a recent study conducted amongst French children, Lang (1986) has identified the entire evolution of the production of riddles by children (for a more complete review of humour based on linguistic ambiguities, see Bernstein, 1986).

Pragmatico-semantic humour

The first linguistic productions which can be classed in this category are those corresponding to stages 1 and 2 of McGhee's (1979) model for the development of humorous behaviour. These consist of violations in the naming of objects or events. For example, the child will call a bucket 'hat' (at stage 1, but to a greater degree at stage 2, these violations are accompanied by distortions of use which correspond to the use of the objects). Horgan (1980) has observed similar productions in her 1½-year-old daughter, the author assuming that the child's laughter is proof of her awareness of the humour. For example, at 1 year 4 months this child put a tennis ball on her foot, said 'shoe' and laughed. We have already (in the section of the previous chapter dealing with metaphor) expressed our doubt about the metalinguistic nature of the skills which underlie this type of behaviour.

De Villiers and de Villiers (1978) have given the example of a 6-year-old child who, in response to the indirect request 'Can you tell me the time?', replied 'Yes, I can'. For the authors, this response proves the child's awareness of the two possible interpretations of the utterance. Although children take evident pleasure in repeating the same play on words or the same riddle to saturation point (for the listener), we should be wary of inferring from this that they are aware of its humorous nature. To convince ourselves of this we need only think of the way in which these productions are distorted, and that even when these distortions suppress the humorous aspect of the production they in no way reduce the pleasure of the child.

In an experiment conducted in German, Sinclair (1981) asked children aged between 5 and 7 if there was anything strange or funny in the short scenarios which were presented to them. In fact, each of the scenarios contained one or two inappropriate speech acts (for example, someone responds literally to the indirect question 'Can you tell me the time?', or a shopper uses the formulation 'I have a kilo of bananas' in order to ask a shopkeeper for a kilo of bananas). Amongst the 5-year-olds, the incongruity seemed to pass unnoticed in 40 per cent of cases and, on average, no more than 13 per cent of responses indicated that the violation of these speech acts had been identified. Amongst the 7-year-olds, although the strange nature of the exchanges was almost always detected, only 40 per cent of the responses revealed that the violations had been identified. Furthermore, there were also significant variations between the scenarios, with the possibility of making use of extralinguistic clues in the staging of these short scenes greatly facilitating the subjects' task.

The intentional management of linguistic humour thus appears to be a complex ability which is late to emerge. The same seems to be true of other aspects of the subtle manipulation of language – lying, for example. De Villiers and de Villiers (1978) have reported the very rudimentary (and easily detectable) character of this in young children ('I didn't break the lamp' in a situation where no one knows of the event and the child has no reason to believe that it will be accused).

A final question remains to be discussed: *Is humour really a legitimate object of study for cognitive psychology?* In fact, it seems that the criteria used to qualify an act of behaviour or a task as humorous are inadequate. Generally speaking, two different types of case arise. A particular reaction by a child is qualified as humorous if it is accompanied by laughter. It is this criterion which a number of authors (see, for example, Shultz, 1976) apply when claiming that pretend play lays the foundations for humour in the child. However, that this motor response is certainly not exclusively reserved for manifestations of joy has been proved by early studies which show that laughter in young children may be provoked by physical activity, the same stimulations being able to cause either laughter or tears (Ding and Jersild, 1932), or by aggression (Sinnott and Ross, 1976). The second procedure, which is often used to determine *a priori* the humorous character of a situation, is highly adultomorphic. A situation or linguistic utterance is considered funny because the experimenter finds it so (or because it has been taken from a comic work).

The problem of preserving the humorous element in situations as formal as those of an experiment is rarely raised. Very often the supposedly humorous task is transformed for the subjects into the resolution of problems of incongruity. These are, of course, cognitive tasks, and it is simply the desire of cognitivists to show that they, too, can deal with sympathetic objects of study that permits them to preserve the illusion that they are studying humour. Cognitive researchers may investigate certain components of humorous situations. However, the limitations of their means of investigation should force them to leave the study of the overall phenomenon to specialists whose tools do not claim to possess the same rigour and who can thus analyze the phenomena in a more ecological way (this appears to be the approach adopted by Sinclair, 1981, who at no point in her article speaks of humour, preferring to focus on children's detection of inappropriate speech acts). After all, no one is going to forbid the cognitivists to enjoy, or even to practise, humour outside of their professional (and/or sacerdotal) research activities.

The detection of linguistic incongruities is an activity which demands metapragmatic abilities. It is late to appear because it is particularly complex and of little use to the child. This experimental fact does not prevent us encountering humorous behaviour at an early age, or even defining humour in such a way that it applies to behaviour which has nothing to do with the behaviour presented here.

Conclusion

For Lafontaine (1983), 'to know how to communicate is not just to know all the linguistic rules which make it possible to produce a message which is acceptable to the speakers of a given language, but also to know the social and cultural rules which lead to the production of an adequate message in a given situation while taking account of the different parameters of the situation' (p. 200). If we add to this the ability to monitor the referential adequacy of the produced messages and the ability to comprehend the different aspects of the relationship between language and the contexts in which it is used, we have a description of metapragmatic awareness.

The data presented above have brought to light a considerable age-related difference in children's ability to monitor the parameters of the situation of communication.

Epipragmatic behaviour

At a very early age, often at the time when language first appears, children adapt their own productions to the situations in which they are made and take account of contextual parameters in their interpretation of the messages produced by others.

In fact, far from testifying to an early awareness of the pragmatic aspects of language, these skills actually point to the young child's inability to separate language from the context of its emission. *What is processed is an unanalyzed whole. There is never a conscious identification of the links existing between the linguistic and the extralinguistic because there is never any distinction between the two.*

Epipragmatic behaviour is characterized by the incidental nature of the adaptation of language to its context. It is the aggregate of the young child's attitudes in its entirety which is affected by the undissociated body of information it receives. It is the linguistic organizations which are held piecemeal in long-term memory that are actualized and adapted whenever the situation requires the child to adopt any particular attitude.

When we turn to the question of comprehension, we see that for the young child language is simply one of the elements of its own context, with no special status, and that the child's early performances are interpretations of this context rather than instances of contextualized language.

Donaldson (1978) writes: 'Before the child has developed a full awareness of language, language is embedded for him in the flow of events which accompany it' (p. 88). This point of view, widely accepted in scientific writings, renders 'implausible an account which requires the child to reflect consciously on features of his language' (Elliot, 1981, p. 38).

The illusion of an awareness and intentional monitoring of the pragmatic aspects of language results, once again, from research which has concentrated on linguistic modifications alone without considering the other changes in behaviour. It is not the intention of young children to monitor language. Instead, situation-dependent variations provoke in them a modification of the communicative attitude – a modification which is marked by, amongst other things, their linguistic behaviour.

Metapragmatic behaviour

It is again at the age of approximately 6–7 that we see the emergence of behaviour which unambiguously reveals reflection on or monitoring of language in terms of the relationship between it and its context of emission. This applies equally to both the awareness of referential ambiguities and the young speaker's consideration of the addressee's characteristics.

However, it seems that this ability to process contextual indices continues to grow until adolescence as such indices become more complex and, probably, more familiar to the child. As far as this last point is concerned, we may find here an explanation of the differences between individuals in terms of the experiences to which the child is exposed by its environment. As for the possibility of taking account of increasingly complex organizations of contextual indices and responding to these with increasingly sophisticated linguistic organizations, this is undoubtedly dependent to some extent on the growth in the processing capacity of working memory.

Chapter 6

Metatextual development

Introduction

In the introduction to the preceding chapter we indicated that, for a number of authors, the field of metapragmatics includes the awareness or knowledge both of the relationships between linguistic signs and the extralinguistic context *and* of the intralinguistic relationships between signs and their linguistic context. With reference to the pragmatics of language, this grouping is justified in that it concerns all the rules governing the entire set of relationships between signs and their users, which includes the relationship of utterances to the discourse in which they occur. While we are not contesting either the importance of the suprasentential level or the necessity of distinguishing it from the classical syntactic and semantic levels of linguistic analysis, nor challenging its dependence on the extralinguistic parameters of the situation of utterance, we do believe that it should be thought of as a specific aspect of language which is liable to be the object of specific metalinguistic activities. In other words, we are postulating the existence of *metatextual operations involved in the deliberate control, in both comprehension and production, of the ordering of utterances in larger linguistic units.*

To our knowledge, no theoretical approach has yet dealt specifically with this particular instance of metalinguistic functioning. Besides the fact that it is frequently assimilated into the field of metapragmatics, two other factors have contributed to this state of affairs: (1) textual awareness is most often considered from the perspective of a study of writing (writing activity and reading); (2) the production of text in spoken language is largely neglected, most studies being concerned with the comprehension of oral texts and reported under the general heading of *metacomprehension.*

Here again, we shall be confronted with the difficulty of separating that which is linked to the textual dimension of the tasks we shall be dealing with from that which is associated with the characteristics of writing. In this chapter we have chosen to report those results relating to writing which agree (often with discontinuities between ages) with the small amount of data available for spoken language, or with the predictions made on the basis of processes not specific to writing. The remaining data will be presented in the next chapter.

Another difficulty is that most of the available studies are concerned with comprehension which will, therefore, be overrepresented in this chapter. For about ten years, a number of authors have been interested in *metacomprehension, which corresponds to the ability to know whether or not one has understood and to proceed to make appropriate adjustments in cases where one has not understood* (for a summary of current theories, see Baker, 1985; Markman, 1981, 1985). This perspective groups together the monitoring activities which bear on very different characteristics of verbal messages. Baker (1985) identifies three of these: lexical, syntactic and semantic characteristics. The monitoring of lexical characteristics concerns, for example, the identification of the fact that a sound sequence (or graphic sequence in the case of writing) does not constitute a word, or that the meaning of a word is not known. We have dealt with this in the section devoted to metalexical development (Chapter 4). Syntactic monitoring refers to the awareness of the grammatical contrasts of a language, and this problem has been discussed in the chapter on metasyntactic development (Chapter 3). What remains is the monitoring of the semantic characteristics which requires that the meaning both of individual sentences and of the text taken as a whole should be considered simultaneously. Indeed, a detailed examination of these characteristics, such as that conducted by Baker, reveals that they are as much textual as semantic: textual if we focus on the surface markers and rhetorical organization; semantic if we concentrate on the representations which these markers induce in the subject.

Baker lists five types of semantic characteristics:

- propositional cohesiveness, which concerns the links between the ideas expressed by adjacent propositions;
- structural cohesiveness, which refers to the thematic compatibility of different ideas expressed within a single text;
- external consistency, which corresponds to the correspondence (or lack of it) existing between the text and its listener's (or reader's) prior knowledge of the subject of the text;
- internal consistency, which depends on the possible presence of (explicit or implicit) contradictions in what is expressed by the text;
- finally, the informational clarity and exhaustiveness of the text.

In two of these headings, the term used by Baker is 'cohesiveness'. Authors like Karmiloff-Smith (1985) or Fayol (1985*b*, 1986), however, distinguish between *cohesion* and *coherence*. Coherence concerns the linking of ideas at the level of the representation yielded by the text (or, in contrast, the 'pre-linguistic' representation in production). Cohesion, on the other hand, 'refers to the linguistic markers which reveal the interrelations between concatenated utterences on the surface of the text' (Fayol, 1985*b*, p. 111). Baker, by using the more generic term 'cohesiveness', does not state her intention specifically. Nevertheless, in her discussion of semantic characteristics she appears to be dealing more with coherence than with cohesion.

While it is easy, in theory, to distinguish between coherence and cohesion, it is more difficult to decide the extent to which each is involved in the processes performed by the subject. In order for coherence to be manipulated in experiments, it is often necessary to manipulate the textual surface of the verbal material which is presented to the subject, and therefore to manipulate the cohesion of the text. *We will, however, attempt to respect this distinction by using the term coherence when the manipulated variables are semantic in nature, and cohesion when they are morphosyntactic in nature.*

The first subsection will deal mainly with coherence, and will report research into the development of the ability to detect possible contradictions within what is said in a text or between the statements which it contains and the subject's prior knowledge. This will necessitate an approach to the problem of inference, which has as much to do with detecting nonexplicit contradictions as with resolving them. The next subsection will focus on the processing of the surface markers which are intended to assure the unity of the text by linking the clauses of which it is composed. At this point our perspective will be that of the monitoring of cohesion. A final subsection will be concerned with the impact which the overall organization of the text has on the monitoring exercised by the subject and, in particular, whether this monitoring varies according to the type of text.

The monitoring of coherence

The question here is essentially one of the ability to detect contradictions at a conceptual level. These may be internal to the information provided explicitly or implicitly by the text itself. However, contradictions may also arise between new information and information which is already known to the subject.

Here we can observe functions similar to those – studied in the preceding chapter – which are at work in the detection of ambiguities in a referential message. In both cases it is necessary to compare what is being carried by the message with the extralinguistic data. However, while referential communication involves an evaluation of the prevalent situation, the monitoring of coherence requires the use of known information in order to evaluate new information. Nevertheless, what is brought to light is the arbitrary necessity of identifying differentiated classes of functioning in cases where continuity between these classes is more frequently encountered. In wishing to distinguish 'the metatextual' within what is traditionally thought of as 'the metapragmatic', we find ourselves confronted by the didactic necessity of defining a boundary. We have chosen to draw this boundary between the awareness of the extralinguistic situation and the overall processing of the text in both its linguistic and its conceptual aspects. It would also have been possible to place this boundary between the presence or absence of the necessity of taking account of information not present in the text. This last solution has been avoided, as it would have required us to deal with the influence of textual schemata (see below pp. 139–50), whose textual character is difficult to dispute, in the section devoted to metapragmatic development.

The monitoring of the compatibility of new information with the knowledge base

Tikhomirov and Klochko (1981) produced a narrative text containing three clauses which described phenomena violating simple laws of physics (for example, the water in a river flowing up a mountain slope). The subjects, who were educated adults, underwent six experimental stages. They were asked (1) to examine the text and assess its grammaticality; (2) to retell it (the text having been taken away from them; (3) to read it aloud; (4) to retell it again; (5) to say whether they had noticed anything abnormal about the text; (6) to look for the violations, whose existence had by this time been pointed out to them, while reading the text aloud for a second time. Only one subject out of forty-five identified the violations at the first stage, and two spotted them in response to the question posed at stage 5. In contrast, the level of detection at the final stage was 84 per cent. An electrodermogram which was used throughout the test revealed that certain subjects were affected by the incongruities even though they did not seem to detect them consciously. At the final stage there was a perfect correspondence between the electrodermal response and the explicit detections. *This experiment suggests that, even in the educated adult, the conscious comparison of the information contained in the text with that in the knowledge base does not occur spontaneously.* Nevertheless, the presence of incongruities does affect processing during the actual reading of the text (on-line processing). Finally, explicit instruction is all that is needed for the signal emitted during on-line processing to be decoded and the incongruities detected.

Going beyond the explicit ability to detect contradictions between information carried by a text and prior knowledge, the effect of such contradictions on the recall of text has been studied in children. Ceci *et al.* (1981) asked children of 7 and 10 to listen to descriptions of television stars which contradicted what the children already knew about these personalities. Three weeks later, when the children retold the descriptions, they had removed most of the contradictions. This, however, was not true of all the

10-year-olds, which suggests that some of them, unlike their juniors, had noticed the contradictions at the time of memorizing the descriptions.

However, as Owings *et al.* (1980) have demonstrated, it remains the case that incongruous information is the most difficult to recall. These researchers asked children of 10–11 to study written texts containing some information which was either incongruous or contradicted the children's past experience. While certain children – the good readers – identified the problematic passages, the others did not unless they were asked to evaluate the texts in relation to their own experience. In this type of task, the apparent difficulty in detecting contradictions could very easily be explained by the problem of excessive demands being placed on memory capacity. So for the poor reader, the burden represented by the activity of reading at a low level of ability makes the possibility of performing spontaneous comparisons at a conceptual level highly problematic. The results in tasks of detection would thus have been different if the tasks had been presented orally.

In a task requiring the judgement of the acceptability of texts, some of which contained clearly incorrect statements, Markman and Gorin (1981) found that the incorrect statements were detected by 27 per cent of 7-to-8-year-old listeners and 31 per cent of 9-to-10-year-old listeners. This result reveals a reasonable level of success in 7-to-8-year-olds and, at the same time, a surprising lack of improvement between this age and age 9–10. The operations necessary for detection were mobilized spontaneously in only a third of cases, whatever the age of the subjects. In a slightly different task, Pace (1979, cited by Baker, 1985) found similar levels of detection in younger subjects. These subjects, aged 5–6 and 7–8, were asked to detect incongruities in stories such as that of a woman making sandwiches with peanut butter and ice cream (violations of script – according to Schank and Abelson, 1977, a script is a 'standard event sequence'; for a presentation and discussion of this idea, see Fayol and Monteil, 1988). In both age groups, a quarter of the subjects were successful in this task.

While age does not cause a significant change in the overall levels of detection following a simple instruction to evaluate the presented texts, specifying what type of problem might arise (i.e. incorrect information) is all that is required for such an age-related effect to be observed. When they provided their subjects with such precise instructions, Markman and Gorin (1981) obtained success levels of 39 per cent in 7-to-8-year-olds and 61 per cent in 9-to-10-year-olds. This reveals that only the older subjects were able to benefit from this degree of precision. While improving the explicitness of the instructions did not help the younger children, some simple training helped them to maximize their performances. In fact, using a task of identifying violations of prior knowledge in simple stories, Baker (1984*a*) demonstrated that simple corrective feedback, followed by a second attempt to identify the incongruities overlooked in the first attempt, resulted in success rates of 60 per cent in 5-year-olds, 83 per cent in 7-year-olds and

97 per cent in 9-year-olds. These results suggest that simply making the instructions more explicit does not aid the comprehension of the younger subjects, while explicit correction of their mistakes is more effective. In all cases, at least from age 5 onwards, children are able to detect contradictions between new information and the knowledge base, even if they do not always perform this operation spontaneously. Lack of understanding of the task and the cognitive burden imposed by any indication of what should constitute the focus of attention may explain the modest performance levels attained in most of the experiments.

This is what seems to be indicated by the results obtained when the texts are read by the subjects themselves. In contrast to what has been reported above for poor readers, good readers seem to benefit from the mnemonic aid provided by the presence of a written text. Thus in one of the experiments reported above – that carried out by Pace (1979, cited by Baker, 1985) – only 25 per cent of 7-to-8-year-olds detected incongruities in texts presented to them orally, whereas this success level rose to 66 per cent for the detection of incongruities in texts the subjects had to read themselves. From age 9–10 onwards, the results were good whichever mode of text presentation was selected.

However, success levels vary between experiments. In particular, the results seem to be worse for expository texts than they do for narratives. Thus, instead of the near-perfect success rate obtained by Pace for short stories, Baker (1984*b*) obtained only 48 per cent success rates for the detection of violations of prior knowledge in good readers of 9–10 and 11–12 whom she presented with short expository texts. It would thus appear that the type of text does have an effect (see pp. 139–50 below).

As indicated above, one of the factors determining the ability to detect incongruities seems to be mnemonic in nature. Results obtained by Vosniadou *et al.* (1988) point in this direction. Thirteen out of forty 6-to-7-year-old subjects failed in a task involving the detection of information which contradicted common knowledge in short texts. Of these thirteen subjects, more than two-thirds (nine subjects) did not restore the incongruity in a later task of retelling the text. Thus, out of all the subjects examined, only 10 per cent did not appear to detect incorrect information, although they had perceived it correctly. This low proportion of subjects could very well correspond to those who had not understood the task or did not verbalize a detection they had actually made. However, this experiment does not establish that all the information had not been memorized. The subjects could, in effect, have omitted incongruous information from their retelling even though this information was present in their memories and could have been activated by a task of recognition, for example.

It therefore seems possible for the type of detection discussed here to occur at a very early age (approximately 5) when the verbal material provided is very simple. However, it is not put into practice without explicit instructions, even by adults. In fact, subjects do not seem to search their long-term memories spontaneously for the prior information which is required for a comparison with the new information stored in working memory. If this assumption is true, the results should be different when the two conflicting pieces of information are both presented in the text, which thus contains an internal contradiction.

The monitoring of intratextual coherence

This is a question of the ability to check whether the different ideas expressed in a text are compatible with each other. Markman (1979) asked children of 8 to 12 to make the short stories she presented to them more comprehensible. These stories violate the *modus ponens* rule of logic (thus being of the form $P \Rightarrow Q, P \wedge \bar{Q}$. For example, one of the stories contained the following passage:

> Fish must have light in order to see. There is absolutely no light at the bottom of the ocean. It is pitch black down there. When it is that dark, the fish cannot see anything. They cannot even see colours. Some fish that live at the bottom of the ocean can see the colour of their food; that is how they know what to eat. (p. 646)

Whatever their age, about half the subjects did not appear to notice the contradiction. Markman thus concludes that children do not monitor their comprehension and do not compare the information carried by different sentences.

The poor level of performance observed by Markman in an apparently simple task could be linked to the fact that the stories involved animals which were unknown to the children (for example, deep-sea fish or noseless ants). The children might credit such creatures with mysterious powers which defy logic. Moreover, using the same procedure as Markman, Tunmer *et al.* (1983*b*) have demonstrated that when the stories contain more familiar information, almost all children of 7 (success rates 97 per cent) and most 5-year-olds (thirteen subjects out of sixteen) are able to detect the anomalies. Furthermore, whatever the subjects' age, most of the justifications they give point to the presence of the contradiction. Harris *et al.* (1981) obtained the same results with subjects aged 8 and 11 in a reading task in which the children had to point out the statement which did not fit in with the others (78 per cent correct answers at age 8).

Markman explains the poor performances she obtained in tasks of detecting contradictions in terms of the children's tendency to apply a strategy of verifying the empirical validity of each of the statements made in the text, rather than a strategy of verifying the compatibility of the different assertions made in the text. This tendency is all the more pronounced the younger the child is, but also exists in adults who are faced with written texts (Baker and Anderson, 1982). Moreover, when the texts may contain a variety of problem types, lexical problems and violations of the knowledge base are more easily detected than internal contradictions. This is equally true whether presentation is oral or written (Baker, 1984*a*). The simple fact of telling children, whatever their age (from 5 onwards), precisely what problem is likely to exist in a text (a contradiction) improves their performance considerably (Nesdale *et al.*, 1985) and prior training is even more beneficial (Baker, 1984*a*).

Here again, the observations made above lead researchers to suspect the existence of problems associated with storage or retention in memory. Markman, who observed excellent levels of recall for each piece of contradictory information in her 1979 experiment, rejects this explanation in favour of one based on the difficulty of comparing these items of information. Other results, however, invite us to modify this author's interpretation. First of all, in 5-year-olds but not in 6-year-olds, the shorter the story – and thus the easier it is to encode and retain in memory – the better the performance (Nesdale *et al.*, 1982, cited in Pratt and Nesdale, 1984). Secondly, Markman's results (1979) reveal a related effect in 11-to-12-year-olds but not in 8-to-9-year-olds. She finds that performance improves the closer together the pieces of contradictory information are in the text (and hence the increased probability of their co-presence in working memory). Garner and Kraus (1982) have also made this same observation in connection with reading in good readers (but not poor readers) at secondary school. Finally, in contrast to Markman, Vosniadou *et al.* (1988) found that among the twenty-two subjects out of forty 6-to-7-year-olds who did not detect the contradictions in a text presented to them orally, only three restored the contradictory information in a task of retelling (in a similar task, involving reading, only three of the fifteen 8-to-9-year-olds who failed out of a total of forty acted in this way).

In fact, if there is a problem of a mnemonic order, it is not so much at the level of encoding or retention in the long-term memory as in the possibility of activating both pieces of information simultaneously in working memory in order to compare them. This hypothesis, which is compatible with the data presented above, also explains why a contradiction with the knowledge base should be detected more readily than an internal contradiction in the text. In fact, the prior knowledge violated in the experiments is most often very familiar to the subjects and is thus easily accessible in long-term memory, perhaps even being automatically activated when contradicted by the memorizing of new knowledge. In contrast, new information stored in long-term memory at the time of the previous hearing (or reading) of the text cannot be retrieved in working memory when another piece of new, contradictory information has just been entered there, except by means of conscious effort on the part of the subject. Moreover, when one of the two contradictory pieces of information within the text corresponds to a fact already known by the subject, the detection of the contradiction is as frequent, in 7-year-olds, as it is in the case of violation of prior knowledge (Vosniadou *et al.*, 1988).

The explanation proposed above also conforms to observations made in reading tasks. Several studies suggest that the comparison of pieces of information is carried out automatically when they are simultaneously activated in working memory. Only the older (and/or more expert) readers appear capable of searching the long-term memory for the information necessary for comparison, and probably do this only after reading the text and following an explicit instruction (see Baker, 1985).

It has thus been shown that at a very early age children are capable of detecting contradictions, however little the characteristics of the task permit contradictory pieces of information to be present simultaneously in working memory. Nevertheless, it remains true that certain studies have obtained astonishingly low performances at relatively late ages. As several authors assert (see Baker, 1985), this could be partly a consequence of strategies of inference developed by the subjects in order to suppress perceived contradictions. Moreover, McDevitt and Carroll (1988) have shown that, in a task resembling that used by Markman (1979), 8-to-9-year-old children were better able to discern contradictions in stories when the narrator of the stories was presented as trying to dupe them than when the narrator was presented as trying to inform them. In the first case, 75 per cent of the subjects spotted the contradiction in at least one of the five stories containing a contradiction, while this figure fell to only 55 per cent in the second case.

The monitoring of inference

Several studies suggest that the apparent nondetection of contradictions might be a consequence of the operation of inferential processes, intended either to complete explicit information by adding other information which is considered to have been omitted, voluntarily or not, or to interpret the text in an alternative way to that intended by its author (see Baker, 1985). When an ambiguity is noticed by the listener or reader, he can decide to wait for complementary information. When a contradiction is spotted, he can wait for its resolution or assume that what follows in the text will justify it. As Markman (1981, 1985) points out, this type of decision requires both inferential processing and, at the same time, an evaluation of the inferences for a later decision on their acceptability.

This evaluation of inferences is related to judgements of explanations intended to abolish apparent incongruities. Children seem to have difficulty judging the quality of such explanations.

Geoffrey (1979, cited by Markman, 1985) asked children of 10–11 and 11–12 to listen to essays which violated the script of the scene being described (for example, a girl goes into a shop to buy a pair of shoes. She enters, sits down and waits for the saleswoman. After choosing a pair of shoes she goes into the dressing-room, closes the curtain and tries them on). If subjects did not notice the violation spontaneously, it was pointed out to them and four explanations were offered whose acceptability was then to be assessed:

1. an adequate explanation (in the example given, the girl wants to see if the shoes match her dress, and the only foot-level mirror is in the dressing-room);
2. an irrelevant explanation which adds information but has nothing to do with the violation (for example: 'Some people have trouble picking out something to buy when they are shopping. Either they don't like anything they see, or they can't decide which thing to buy');
3. a pseudo-explanation which adds information but does not justify the violation (for example: 'You have to be able to tell if things are too big or too small. It is important to try things on to see if they fit');
4. a simple repetition which paraphrases the incongruous sentence, but without giving any new information.

Unlike the children of 11–12, the 10-to-11-year-olds judged that all the first three explanations were acceptable. Only the simple paraphrase was rejected.

Quite apart from the question of whether inferences can be made and retained in memory, we can thus suppose that children have difficulty in judging their relevance to the various pieces of information contained in the text. Furthermore, we cannot be sure that the inferences necessary for overall comprehension of the text are always made.

Flavell *et al.* (1981) asked children of 7–8 and 11–13 and adults to follow verbal instructions for moving an object. The subjects then had to say whether they were sure they had arrived at the intended destination. Some of the instructions were constructed in such a way that the first part of the message was ambiguous and the second, though not ambiguous if taken on its own, did not resolve the initial ambiguity and thus allowed the possibility of arriving at the wrong destination. Although the children understood and could recall that the initial part of the message was ambiguous, they tended to disregard this information when judging the explicitness of the instructions and thus concluded that they were certain that they had understood them. In contrast, the adults tended to retain the initial ambiguity in their minds and conclude, correctly, that they could not be certain of having arrived at the intended destination (82 per cent as against 44 per cent of 11-to-13-year-olds and 19 per cent of 7-to-8-year-olds). This result suggests that, unlike adults, when children notice the initial ambiguity they do not spontaneously make the inference which would lead them to expect a disambiguation in the following text, and that they therefore do not notice its absence.

The general problem is of knowing how children use the indices which are present in the text in order to make the inferences which might be necessary for its comprehension. It is this which Schmidt and Paris (1983) have studied in connection with narrative texts. Children of 5–6, 7–8 and 9–10 listened to a short story and then had to reply to questions concerning information which was either present in the story or could be inferred from it. The level of correct responses to inferential questions increased both with age and with the number of items of information confirming the inference (with a single piece of information the percentages of correct answers were 20 per cent in 5-to-6-year-olds, 17 per cent in 7-to-8-year-olds and 33 per cent in 9-to-10-year-olds; with three congruent pieces of information these percentages rose to 70 per cent, 84 per cent and 89 per cent respectively). In a second experiment the subjects had to answer inferential questions after only the beginning of a story had been presented to them. They were then invited to revise their inferences in the light of information contained in the remainder of the text. Again, this task was carried out more successfully with increasing age. Finally, the oldest children, unlike their juniors, showed themselves capable of using the separately presented items of information in the forming of inferences.

The difficulty which children experience in making the inferences necessary for comprehension is apparent in the poor performances they achieve when asked to identify inexplicit internal contradictions in a text. Such contradictions were present in several of the stories presented by Markman (1979) which contained passages of the type: '... There is absolutely no light at the bottom of the sea. Some fish that live at the bottom of the ocean know their food by its colour. They will eat only red fungus' (see p. 127). Here the detection of the contradiction presupposes that the subject infers from the last two sentences that the fish can see the colour of their food, which contradicts the information given in the first sentence. Whatever age was examined (8–9, 10–11 and 11–12), virtually none of the subjects spontaneously detected this contradiction, while this was the case in only about half the subjects when the contradiction was explicit (see above). However, unlike the 8-to-9-year-olds, the 11-to-12-year-old subjects spotted implicit contradictions just as easily as explicit contradictions, however little warning they had of the possibility of contradictory sentences appearing in the text.

In fact, it would seem that even the processing of information revealed in the text differs with age and this has consequences for the subjects' control of their own comprehension. Schmidt *et al.* (1984) presented children with stories containing two sentences capable of provoking the same inference (for example, 'Mary covered her eyes and counted to ten' and 'Mary looked behind the bushes but no one was there', presented together, permit the inference that Mary is playing hide-and-seek). The stories also contained another sentence which was incompatible with this inference and was placed either before or after the two compatible sentences. The children then had to reply to an inferential question ('What is Mary doing?'). Whatever the position of the incompatible sentence, about a third of 4-to-5-year-olds and two-thirds of 7-to-8-year-olds responded correctly. In contrast, 6-year-olds were less successful when this sentence was positioned in front of the two compatible sentences (37 per cent success rate) than when it was positioned after them (60 per cent success rate). The authors interpret this result by postulating three levels of development in the process of integration of information:

1. At age 4–5, each of the sentences is processed independently and/or there is an idiosyncratic integration of the information given in the sentences with extratextual data. Success rates for inferential questions are therefore low.
2. At age 6, the child integrates the sequence of information given in the text but cannot use new information to revise an inference which has already been made. Hence the problems caused when the deviant sentence is in initial position. This leads to the forming of an inference with which the convergent sentences encountered later were incompatible.
3. Finally, at age 7–8, the possibility emerges of revising initial inferences when incompatible information is presented.

The above experiment concerns a particular case in which one interpretation of the text is doubly validated (on the strength of the two convergent sentences) while the alternative interpretation is supported only by a single piece of information and is thus less plausible than the former. The case of simple contradiction is different. Here each piece of information is equally likely to be erroneous (providing neither of them contradicts prior knowledge). Using a simple task of retelling stories containing contradictions, Mosenthal (1979) found that 12-year-olds – unlike children of 8–9, who have the opposite tendency – have a tendency to manipulate the last piece of information presented in order to make it compatible with its contradictory antecedent. Markman (1985) used this result to propose the hypothesis that older children use the prior context in order to set up the expectations which will guide their later processing of the text, while younger children tend to alter what they remember of the old information in order to make it compatible with the new information.

The cognitive work which would be performed by older children on the second of a pair of contradictory sentences seems to be confirmed by studies of on-line processing in adults. Greeno and Noreen (1974) show that the adult reads sentences which agree with information already presented in the text faster than those which are not linked in this way. This would suggest that subjects possess expectations based on the information they read and that these expectations guide their processing of the text. However, there is nothing to establish that the subjects control the forming of these inferences;

in consequence, there can be no evidence that they are aware of such control. On the contrary, there is a great deal of literature, based mainly on experiments using tasks of retelling or recognition, which demonstrates that some of these inferential processes seem to be carried out automatically. For example, Bransford *et al.* (1972) found that after hearing 'Three turtles rested on a floating log and a fish swam beneath them', adults believe they have heard 'Three turtles rested on a floating log and a fish swam beneath it'. The representation of the situation is enough to activate an inference without the subject even knowing it. The information extracted from the text is reconsidered in the light of prior knowledge stored in long-term memory.

Here again, memory appears to play a central role. The tasks of retelling show that neither the exact wording nor the distinction between what is explicit and what is implicit in the text is stored in long-term memory. However, at the precise moment the information is absorbed the characteristics of the text do exist in working memory, but this literal memory is very short.

In a study conducted by Sachs (1974), adult subjects were asked to perform a recognition task between one and twenty-three seconds after hearing or reading short passages. Some of the sentences presented were simple paraphrases of elements in the text (the only modifications being of a lexical or syntactic order), others were semantically different, and yet others were taken directly from the initial text. Beyond a four-second delay for reading, and a seven-second delay for oral presentation, the rejection of paraphrases was rare.

Thus the subject has only a very short time to make effective comparisons, since searching the long-term memory for old information does not permit the reactivation of its mode of presentation in the text. In any case, as has already been pointed out, it would seem that this searching of the long-term memory does not occur spontaneously and that incitements to activate it are effective only after a certain age. This seems to be confirmed by the results of Johnson and Smith (1981), who demonstrate that while 10-to-11-year-olds give correct responses to inferential questions, whether the premises for the required inferences are close to each other or situated in different paragraphs, it is only in the first case that correct answers are provided by 8-to-9-year-olds.

The mnemonic factor is likely to play an absolutely central role in the detection of contradictions. If, as has been suggested, certain subjects tend to resolve contradictions by hypothesizing an overall meaning for the text, they have to remember this attempted resolution in order to reevaluate it should it be contradicted by what follows. This also requires the subject to remember that the attempt at interpretation was only an attempt. Otherwise it would be difficult to revise this interpretation should it be contradicted by later information.

To sum up, as Fayol recalls (1985*b*), it appears that even if relatively young children are capable of going beyond explicit information in order to establish relationships between the items of information carried by a text, they do not do so spontaneously: 'We would thus appear to be dealing with a very early skill whose systematic implementation would be slow to develop and would follow the development of the metacognitive procedures which bear not only on the information itself but also on its internal representation' (Fayol, 1985*b*, p. 86).

Conclusion

As Fayol's statement makes clear, the management and monitoring of coherence operate essentially on the conceptual level. We must now ask whether the functioning described above is of a metalinguistic order, which would imply that at least part of the process of monitoring coherence is determined by the linguistic nature of the medium underpinning the information which triggers this conceptual work. To date, we have found nothing which permits us to affirm that this is indeed the case, or to suppose that things would be very different if the information were conveyed by the medium of silent film, for example. Although important to the analysis of metatextual functioning, the data reported above are doubtlessly no less so in a nonmetalinguistic but nevertheless metacognitive context, possessing in particular numerous elements which are of significance for the fields of metamemory and meta-attention.

Quite different from this, however, is the control exercised by the subject over the processing of the surface markers which assure textual cohesion.

The monitoring of cohesion

A text is distinguished from a simple set of sentences by the relationships which exist between its various constituent clauses. These relationships, which assure the cohesion of the text, are realized on the surface by a certain number of markers such as anaphoric pronouns, definite articles and conjunctions. In writing, these are supplemented by the punctuation system (see the next chapter). In production, as in comprehension, we must address the problem of the subject's knowledge of the markers of cohesion and thus the way their use can be manipulated.

The metalinguistic management of anaphora

Anaphora corresponds to the marking of a reference to something mentioned earlier in the text, the anaphor having an antecedent in the text itself. On-line studies of the activity of reading in the adult have revealed that when the subject encounters an anaphoric pronoun while reading, the period of ocular fixation is longer than that usually observed for a word of the same size. Subjects also frequently look back to the antecedent of the pronoun (see, for example, Carpenter and Just, 1977). Similarly, it would appear that the time required for comprehension of a definite reference (generally marked by the presence of a definite article) is affected by the distance between the reference and its antecedent (see, for example, H. H. Clark and Sengul, 1979), and that the presence of definite articles in a series of sentences facilitates its integration into memory (P. A. de Villiers, 1974). These experimental data suggest that at the time the text is processed, the anaphoric marks of cohesion are detected, at least functionally, by the adult. On the other hand, they establish nothing about the level of monitoring exercised by the subject, or about the way this monitoring is implemented during development.

Baker (1979) asked adult subjects to read expository texts containing anaphoric ambiguities. In a subsequent retelling task, numerous subjects did not seem to have noticed these ambiguities. Nevertheless, when advised of the presence of ambiguities and asked to reread the text in order to identify them, 93 per cent of the subjects were successful. This first result gives the impression that the conscious identification of ambiguities associated with cohesion, like that concerned with coherence, is not carried out spontaneously. However, this type of deliberate monitoring does appear to form part of the abilities of the adult. Except under particular circumstances (for example, difficulty in understanding), adults are not generally aware of the cognitive work they are producing in order to establish textual cohesion ('automatically' attributing a single co-reference to a potentially ambiguous pronoun at the time of perception; see Ségui and Kail, 1984). However, the existence of this cognitive work is confirmed by the modifications which occur in on-line processing.

Children, sometimes as young as 2, have been observed to exhibit an astonishingly well adapted use of pronouns and articles in order to differentiate the introduction of a new reference from a simple repetition (for a review of this question, see Hickmann, 1984, 1987a). However, it is not until the age of 8 or 10 that the use of anaphora becomes comparable with that of an adult. Thus Karmiloff-Smith (1979a) shows that (English and French) children initially use and interpret referential expressions, both in production and comprehension, in relation to the extralinguistic context, and only much later in relation to the linguistic context of production.

Moreover, tasks of judgement which use noncontextualized utterances give rise to very low performance levels. Bearison and Levey (1977) asked children to assess (as 'good' or 'bad') questions which referred to previous utterances. Some questions contained ambiguous anaphoric pronouns (e.g. 'Jane got a bicycle for Christmas and Mary got a new coat.' 'What did she get for Christmas, a bicycle or a new coat?'). The ambiguous questions were generally accepted by the children of 5–6 (28 per cent rejection). At age 7–8 the rejection level was approximately the same as that of random choice (58 per cent). It was not until age 9–10 that such questions were rejected by a significant number of subjects (85 per cent). Results obtained by M. W. Pratt and Bates (1982) show that the presence of pictorial assistance helps the 5-to-6-year-old subjects very little in this type of test. This suggests that the inadequacy in evaluation is not linked to a memory problem.

In fact, it appears that young children do not use the linguistic context to understand referential questions, even when the co-reference is explicit (Karmiloff-Smith, 1977, 1979*a*). If asked to act out the sentence 'The boy hit the car and the girl hit the same car' the youngest children will, unlike older children, use two cars.

Although it is predominant for an extended period, this mode of behaviour is not general. Thus Wykes (1981, 1983) found that in a task of comprehension, certain children are able at age 4 to make the correct inferences needed to assign pronouns to their co-references (in sentences of the type 'Jane needed Susan's pencil. She gave it to her.'). However, many children seem to employ a strategy of taking the first substantive as the antecedent, and they continue to do this at a later age even though they realize that making such an attribution contradicts the inference they have made.

While the process of attribution is functionally effective at an early age, it does not seem that children are able to control it deliberately. This agrees with Hickmann's results (1987*a*), which reveal that while children of 5 automatically correct the wrong articles in tasks of repetition, it is not until the age of 10 that they are able to detect errors in the use of anaphora in tasks of judgement.

While it is clear that, in production, young children often do not introduce new referents, or that they introduce them in deictic constructions designed to draw the addressee's attention to them ('it's an X'), it is often difficult to tell whether these apparently anaphoric constructions are truly so. Hickmann (1987*b*) points out the difference between anaphora and co-reference, giving the following two examples:

1. A: 'Look at that!'
   B: 'Yea, it's flying really fast.'
2. All of a sudden a bird appeared in the sky. It was flying really fast.

In (1) *that* and *it* stand in a relationship of co-reference (they refer to the same referent) and each is used in a deictic way. In (2) *it* has an antecedent, the noun *bird*, and this therefore constitutes an intralinguistic reference – in other words, an anaphora. Let us now suppose that in (1) the two statements are produced by the same speaker. What, now, would be the nature of *it*? Would this pronoun refer to *that*, of which it would be an anaphoric repetition, or would it refer to the bird designated by the deictic *that*, with which it would then stand in a relationship of co-reference? In such a case the study of the production alone cannot provide us with an answer. It is the underlying psycholinguistic processes which are the determining factors here. In fact, as Lyons (1975) has proposed, it is quite possible that the differentiation between anaphora and deixis emerges gradually. Deixis comes first, and anaphora appears progressively through the process of designating linguistic items. There would thus seem to be a transitional stage between deixis and anaphora which Lyons supposes to be textual deixis, of which he gives the following example for *it*: A – 'That's a ptarmigan, isn't it?' B – 'A what? Spell it for me.'

Karmiloff-Smith (1977, 1979a, 1981, 1985, 1986, 1987) has attempted to construct a model of the stages leading to the functional implementation of intratextual determiners. In the initial period, before the age of 6, children do not try to establish a cohesion between sentences and use pronouns in an exclusively deictic manner. In the next stage, the use of anaphoric pronouns becomes established. This is a manifestation of the subjects' ability to monitor the cohesion of the texts they produce. However, it is not until the age of 9–10 that this functioning is generalized. In fact it should be possible to observe this growing awareness in the children's U-shaped development curves. The young child should begin to use the nominal determiners relatively quickly in similar ways to those observed in adults. Nevertheless, these high levels of performance at an early age are merely the result of the simple, uncontrolled reproduction of certain phonological forms in the contexts where they most frequently occur. Later, the organization in memory of these verbal schemata, which are gradually acquired through the manipulation of language, should be accompanied by the appearance of applications which deviate from the norm, but nevertheless reveal an increasing awareness of the system. For example, it is during this period that we should observe French children trying to mark the numeral function of the French article 'un' ('un de N' – used to imply 'one N') differently from its referential function ('un N' – 'an N'). Finally, in a third stage, the subject should be aware of the system and able to control it deliberately.

This general model does not permit the appearance of different levels of awareness to be dated to an exact age; the same subject produces differing performances in different situations. Thus Espéret and Charier (1985) show that in 4-to-5-year-olds there is an awareness of the function of 'actualization' of the articles (indefinite article for a new referent; definite article for anaphoric usage) in situations of referential communication, while it is not until age 7–8 that the same level of performance can be observed in the production of narrative (awareness of the quantification function coming later, but with a similar *décalage*). Once again, subjects' performances are less successful when they are not able to rely on the extralinguistic elements of context. This suggests that even at the age of 6 the correct usage of anaphora is at least partially dependent on contextual factors.

The metalinguistic management of connectives

Even if they do sometimes have an undeniable organizational function in relation to the macrostructure of the text (Bronckart and Schneuwly, 1984; Fayol, 1985*b*), it is nevertheless true that connectives are essentially markers of cohesion which link adjacent clauses while indicating the relationships existing between them. Thus it would seem crucial to take account of this type of function word if the general argument of a text is to be grasped. In fact, several studies suggest that connectives are often neglected in attempts at comprehension.

In a passage that dealt with topics in world history, Baker (1979) replaced the original connectives with other, inappropriate ones. College students who were then asked to read the text identified on average only 14 per cent of the incorrect connectives, even though they had been warned of their presence. In fact, it would appear that success in this type of metalinguistic task requires a high level of expertise. Baker (1985) records an experiment in which the subjects had to reinsert connectives into a text from which they had been removed. College students attained only a 58 per cent success rate, while postgraduates and teaching staff enjoyed almost total success.

In contrast, Fayol (1982) demonstrates that causal connectives (like 'because') are used almost systematically by adults when they are asked to reconstruct a narrative containing a causal sequence in an order which does not correspond to the sequence of action.

The lack of an ability to exercise intentional control over the connections between clauses does not imply that they are neglected by subjects when processing texts. Thus by asking children of 9–10 to read and retell sentences in which the causal connectives were either present or omitted, Pearson (1975) was able to show that, on the one hand, the subjects had a tendency to reinsert the missing connectives in their retelling while, on the other hand, when they did not do this there was a 50 per cent chance that their retelling would be incomplete. Likewise, in a longitudinal study, Espéret and Gaonac'h (1986) demonstrate that between the ages of 5 and 8 children have an increasing tendency to augment the cohesion of stories in tasks of retelling by adding connectives which were not present in the original.

One of the most remarkable aspects of this subject, constantly confirmed in the scientific literature, is the sizeable time interval between children's early spontaneous production of the different connectives and their later awareness of them in experimental tasks of either comprehension or production. Kail and Weissenborn (1984) attribute this interval to the fact that the experimental tasks in question essentially require metalinguistic aptitudes which the youngest children do not seem to possess. As these authors point out, such metalinguistic tasks pose particular difficulties for children since, as we have already noted, it is not until a relatively late age that children recognize that connectives are words. This fact on its own can explain why it is not until the age of 11–12 that children become capable of establishing a hierarchy of connectives (Florès d'Arcais, 1978). This late awareness is, in fact, consistent with observations generally obtained in complex metalinguistic tasks.

Conclusion

To sum up, the above-mentioned studies show the importance of cohesion in the processing of texts, in particular for facilitating comprehension. However, the ability for metalinguistic management of anaphora and connectives appears to be very limited. In the child this ability is nonexistent as far as connectives are concerned, and unstable for a long period in the case of anaphora. Indeed, even in adults this ability is fully utilized only by experts in text manipulation.

Nevertheless, it remains the case that it is difficult to consider the phenomena of cohesion, by definition limited to relationships between clauses, without taking account of the overall structural characteristics of the texts within which these phenomena arise. With regard to the use of anaphoric pronouns in narratives, Fayol (1985*b*) emphasizes the particular importance which may be attached to awareness of 'the macrostructure which gives narrative a unity which is marked at the surface level by, among other things, the recourse to anaphoric pronouns' (Fayol, 1985*b*, p. 114).

The monitoring of textual structure

We have deliberately avoided using the terms 'macrostructure' and 'superstructure' in the title of this subsection. In the first place, these concepts are used essentially with regard to narrative, so that the implications of their use might restrict the scope of our argument. In the second place, the term macrostructure, as well as indicating the minimal semantic framework of the text, also points towards the conceptual, and thus 'pre-linguistic', level, while superstructure refers to a basic textual organization which is likewise situated at a representative level. Since we wish to deal primarily with the surface markers, we prefer to speak in terms of the overall structure or organization of the text, which does not exclude the use of the above-mentioned concepts, in particular in addressing the degree of correspondence between the surface form of the text and the organization of the cognitive representation which underlies it.

For Fayol (1985*b*), the relationships between sentences are not limited to the methods of assuring cohesion. They also play a role in linking groups of clauses within the text, and thus contribute to the structuring of the text and help to distinguish it from a simple collection of concatenated sentences. In both comprehension and production, awareness – or at least functional awareness – of the general organization of the text is a competence necessary for effective communication which cannot remain limited to the simple exchange of deictic utterances for very long. Beyond the general issue of textual organization, there is also the question of the diversity of text types and the differentiation which the subject needs to operate between them. This will provide the general framework of this subsection.

The monitoring of the general organization of the text

As Markman (1981) points out, understanding a text composed of several sentences demands more than comprehension of the sentences taken individually. Espéret (1984) shows that at age 5 children begin to show signs of the ability to distinguish explicitly between text and 'nontext' (sequences of sentences without semantic links or markers of cohesion). However, it is not until age 9 that this distinction is clearly established. Awareness of the internal characteristics of texts would appear to be even more problematic.

Garner *et al.* (1986) asked their subjects to look at expository texts, and then (1) to circle those sentences which, in their opinion, constituted a paragraph, and to justify their choice; (2) to join together those sentences which were linked by a common theme from a set of sentences presented separately; (3) to insert sentences between others which already constituted a paragraph. The children of 8–9 and 10–11 did not succeed in any of these tasks, which require reflection on the structural parameters of the texts. The oldest subjects (12–13) were able to explain what constitutes a paragraph, remove the non-thematically linked sentences from a short text, and arrange sentences into coherent groups. However, they experienced difficulty in structuring the texts in such a way that the principal ideas were in modal position.

Evidence of success at an earlier age was obtained in another type of task conducted by Williams *et al.* (1981). Here, the subjects (aged 9–10, 10–11, 11–12, and adults) had to identify those sentences which did not match the others in expository texts. Some of these sentences were not linked to the theme of the text, others violated the canonical theme–commentary format (new information being introduced in the subject when it should be positioned in the predicate). Although their performances were worse than those of the adults, a sizeable proportion of the children succeeded in detecting the abnormal sentences. Three other variables were manipulated in this experiment: (1) some of the deviant sentences, although not linked to the theme, were nevertheless semantically associated with other sentences; (2) some deviant sentences appeared early in the text and others later; (3) some of the texts began with a sentence specifying the theme. As the authors expected, the first two of these factors did influence performance, the semantic links making identification more difficult and the deviant sentences being much better identified the later they appeared in the text (according to the authors, this is because of the progressive construction of the macrostructure). On the other hand, only the adults benefited from the presence of an explicit theme sentence. However, by making the theme sentence more obvious, the authors were able to observe the effect of this factor on the children, with no age-dependent differences appearing. This last point is contradicted by Harris *et al.* (1981), who found that between the ages of 8 and 11 there was an improvement in children's ability to detect sentences not associated with the theme indicated by the title of the text.

There are numerous works studying how the processing of text is affected by the presence of a title indicating its theme. Thus Harris *et al.* show, in the experiment cited above, that at ages 8 and 11 such a title reduces the time taken to read the text, irrespective of whether the title helps the subject to identify those sentences which are not associated with the theme it indicates. The authors infer from this observation that reading time cannot be used as an indication of the subjects' monitoring of their own comprehension. In all cases, at the time of reading, the incongruity between the information provided in the text and the theme indicated by the title affected the on-line processing. Some subjects, however, did not seem capable of interpreting the signal emitted by the processes involved in the reception of information. Other studies show that the presentation of a title improves performance as much in retelling as in comprehension. Bransford and Johnson (1972) asked adults to read the following text:

> The procedure is actually quite simple. First you arrange things into different groups. Of course, one pile may be sufficient depending on how much there is to do. If you have to go somewhere else due to lack of facilities, that is the next step; otherwise, you are pretty well set. It is important not to overdo things. That is, it is better to do a few things at once than too many. In the short run this may not seem important, but complications can easily arise. A mistake can be expensive as well ... (p. 400)

One group of subjects obtained very low levels of performance in a recall test, while the other group attained a much higher success level. The only difference between the two groups was that the second had been given the title: 'Washing clothes'. This result suggests that the conceptual framework provided by knowledge of the theme allowed the subjects to situate each item of new information in relation to this theme. This then provided them with a guide for the interpretation of the text. Such a framework would also permit subjects to complement the meaning of the text by adding those details which are not explicitly mentioned – inferences which, according to Markman (1981), are made automatically. The effect of the title on recall undoubtedly reflects an influence on the actual comprehension of the text.

Capelli and Markman (1982, cited by Markman, 1985) asked children of 8–9 and 11–12 to read stories containing a sentence which was sometimes acceptable and sometimes unrelated to the theme, depending on the title given:

Janet decides to play some music. She looks through all her songs and picks her favourite. It is a song called 'As Time Goes By'.

'I haven't played this one in a long time,' she says to herself.

She plays it quietly so that she won't disturb her family. *She is out of practice, so it sounds funny sometimes.*

Janet likes to sing along with the music. She knows some of the words and she hums the rest. The last verse of the song is the part she likes best. After that song is finished she plays another.

The sentence in italics is acceptable when the title given is 'Playing the piano', but not when it is 'Playing a record'. The subjects had to identify any incongruous sentences. At age 8–9 the reading time increased for the incongruous sentences, but only the 11-to-12-year-olds actually pointed them out explicitly. Here again there is an interval between the functional marking of an obstacle to comprehension and its conscious identification by the child. All the same, it is not impossible that 8-to-9-year-old children notice the problem but do not point it out – either because, being confronted by more comprehension problems than their elders, they are less readily inclined to attribute the problem to the text itself, or because they attribute a different meaning to the text from that intended by the experimenter.

The title is only one specific way of indicating *a priori* the theme of a text. In general, studies of reading indicate that when the theme of a text is revealed at the beginning (for example, in the first sentence), its principal idea is more easily identified (Kieras, 1980). Baker (1985) points out that in such a case, the reader's task is simplified: as the macrostructure has been provided by the initial theme sentence, the sentences which follow can be evaluated during reading in accordance with their relationship to the theme. A similar effect is obtained when the reading of the text is preceded by questions which allow the subjects to process the text in a selective fashion, omitting any information which is secondary to the previously assigned objective. This phenomenon, which is observed in adolescents and adults (see Rickards, 1980), has also been found in children of 9–10, both good and average readers (Goelman, 1982). Fayol *et al.* (1987*a*) also show that when such questions are posed before the wording of an arithmetical problem there is a clear influence on the levels of success attained by children of 6, 8 and 10. Generally the success rate is lower by a quarter when the question is placed at the end of the presentation than when it precedes it. Here too, the most probable hypothesis is that there is an increase in the ability to distinguish between the various pieces of information carried by the text, an ability which not only leads to a better understanding of the whole but also permits a more economical management of all the information in working memory (see also Fayol and Abdi, 1986).

As these last-mentioned studies suggest, it is one thing to identify whether each statement relates to the theme of the text or not, and another to construct a hierarchy for the relative importance of the different statements in relation to that theme. In this regard, several studies appear to indicate that many children do not accord a privileged status to the principal ideas of a text, and all the authors assert that the ability to construct a hierarchy ranking the statements in a text according to their degree of importance develops much later than the ability to extract the theme of a text (for a review, see Fayol, 1985*b*).

A. L. Brown and Smiley (1977) presented texts to children aged 8, 10 and 12, and to adults. The subjects had to assess the relative importance of the different sentences, the most important being those most closely related to the principal idea of the text. This task of judgement was completed successfully from the age of 10 onwards, although the attribution of levels of importance was less precise than that specified by the adults. The 8-year-olds were unsuccessful in this task. However, whatever the age of the subjects, the most important sentences were more frequently recalled than the others.

As Fayol writes (1985*b*):

> Everything happens as if, at the age of seven or eight, there is an automatic processing of the narrative thread with the various elements being assigned to their own level of importance. In contrast, awareness, controlled processing, would call on a more abstract meta-knowledge and develop later and more gradually, with considerable differences between individuals. (p. 91)

One of the consequences of children's difficulty in establishing a hierarchy of importance of intratextual information is revealed in the problem they have in accepting that a text can be summarized. In effect, summarizing a text consists, among other things, of eliminating the least important information. Fayol (1978) demonstrates that before the age of 8–9, children cannot accept that a narrative can be summarized. This fact reveals their reluctance to accept that descriptions of events and states may be only slightly affected by a reduction in the information content. In production, the ability to summarize comes even later. Taylor (1984) points to the difficulties experienced by children of 9 and 11, even outstandingly good pupils, in producing acceptable summaries. These difficulties are even greater for older poor readers (Winograd, 1984). Fayol (1985*a*) relates these observations to the fact that when different subjects spontaneously recalled information, only the most important items were common to all of them. Thus a kind of automatic summarizing process is performed during recall, although its deliberate elaboration appears to be extremely difficult.

One aspect of the construction of a hierarchy of intratextual information is the problem of simply distinguishing between different items of information when this is indispensable to comprehension. This is the case in 'reported speech', which requires the ability to make quotations within a text, with the speaker having to report dialogue which has already been listened to. Some observations have revealed the spontaneous use of quotation, sometimes in children as young as 2 (see for example, Bonnet and Tamine-Gardes, 1984). However, it is difficult to interpret these early productions as quotation, since what is interpreted by the adult as a sign of quotation (for example, 'Daddy says . . .') may be only the denomination of an action for the child, the 'quotation' itself thus corresponding to the description of this action. In such cases, the whole would not conform to any decision to mark the different levels of speech.

Things are quite different when quotation is required for the reporting of a scene at which the child has been present. Hickmann (1985) observes that at the age of 4, children do not differentiate between quoted speech and the rest of their verbalization of an occurrence which they are reporting. Furthermore, the emphasis is often placed on the states or events which are mentioned or can be deduced from the dialogue heard by the child without his or her making any reference to the dialogue itself. At this age, therefore, children do not appear to be able (or do not feel any necessity) to mark in their speech a differentiation between information extracted from speech heard previously and information corresponding to the current text creation. In contrast, the productions of 7-year-old children often indicate such a differentiation. However, at this age the direct style is largely predominant, and this might correspond to a difficulty in reformulating the speech of others for integration into the current speech of the child (although the results obtained by Bassano *et al.*, 1988, seem to indicate that the indirect form is used by the child in order to mark the uncertain character of reported speech. It is frequently used from 4 onwards when the speaker who is being reported was not present at the scene to which the speech refers). It is not until the age of 10, therefore, that the majority of children differentiate explicitly between reported speech and reporting speech.

Most of the experiments reported above reveal that metatextual control is acquired late and is limited in nature, but that the textual parameters are *functionally* taken into account at an early age. A certain number of studies further indicate that the violation of conventional rhetorical structure in an expository text has an effect on the reading time, on the one hand, and impairs performance in retelling, on the other, in adults as much as in children of 8 and over (see, for example, Kieras, 1978; Taylor and Samuels, 1983). A similar effect on retelling has been produced in adults and in children of 6 onwards by disturbing the canonical order of narratives, although this factor does not appear to affect the quality of retelling in 4-to-5-year-olds (for a review, see Fayol, 1985*b*). Finally, Kintsch and Yarbrough (1982) have found that 'canonical organization' facilitates the comprehension of different types of text (classification, comparison, description, etc.). Overall,

> each of the types of text studied seems to be able to take on one 'surface form' which is more appropriate than the others. This specific 'rhetorical' organization

is considered to be *canonical* in so far as it is thought to be isomorphic to the underlying superstructure (that is to say, derived from a prelinguistic representational level). Comprehension and retention in memory would then improve the more this isomorphism is respected (Fayol, 1988*b*, p. 9).

The processing of different types of text

While the juxtaposition of different studies reveals the multiplicity of text types studied by various researchers (argumentation, classification, comparison, definition, description, statement of a problem, essay, report, narrative . . .), the majority of comparative studies contrast narrative and 'expository text', a polymorphic category which groups together all non-narrative texts which report the arrangement of the constituent elements of a state or complex process from an explanatory or descriptive angle. Argumentation itself is the object of a large body of work, but it tends to be viewed from the perspective of logic rather than that of linguistics. Furthermore, when the focus is (psycho)linguistic, it generally takes the form of a comparison of the connectives of language and those of logic, the textual dimension being largely neglected.

The differentiation between different types of text

Here again, it would be advisable to distinguish between the differences which appear in the comparison of the processing mechanisms operating when subjects are confronted with various types of text, and those which the subjects themselves are aware of (for a presentation and in-depth discussion see Fayol, 1988*b*).

On a very generalized level, Kozminsky (1977) emphasizes that, in comprehension, the proportion of elements recalled varies according to the type of text (narrative, report, description) and Goelman (1982) points out that 9-to-10-year-old children are better able to remember the important information in a description than in a narrative, while the overall volume of information remembered is greater for narrative than for description (this is even more true when the presentation of the text has been preceded by questions on the text, and when the mode of presentation is oral). These experimental findings are compatible with the hypothesis of Olson *et al.* (1981) that there is a difference in the actual processing of texts: while narratives give rise to a *prospective* approach, the subject anticipating how the text will continue, expository texts are approached in a *retrospective* way, each piece of new information being related to the information given earlier in the text. This hypothesis might well help to explain the fact, already indicated, that it appears to be easier to detect violations of prior knowledge in narrative than in expository texts.

Similarly, in production, the syntactic complexity varies according to the type of text, the textual units (*T-units*) being shorter in description or narrative than in argumentation, although the clauses are longer (Crowhurst and Piché, 1979). The mode of connection also varies: either the markers used are different, or the same markers are used, but in different distributions (see Bronckart, 1985). The characteristics specific to each type of text seem to be highly influential. Indeed, when adults are asked to remember a text whose type is well marked (scientific article, legal text, children's story), but rewritten in such a way that the stylistic characteristics of each text type are removed, they have a tendency to reintroduce these characteristics in their productions (Brewer and Hay, 1984).

The ability to classify text consciously corresponds to these differences in processing. However, these classifications remain very crude, and we cannot be certain that they are determined by stylistic criteria. According to Stein and Policastro (1984), children of 7 have a relatively precise idea of what a story is. They are even capable of distinguishing between stories, presented in the past tense, and procedures, presented in the future. Nevertheless, it remains the case that most other studies demonstrate that while children do make such distinctions, these are not performed in accordance with the criteria for textual organization. Thus Langer (1985), who shows that 8-to-9-year-old children distinguish between narratives and reports, finds that at that age it is mainly the criteria of content which are used. It is not until age 14–15 that textual organization is taken into account (11–12 according to Espéret, 1984). Furthermore, even in adults, classification is limited to distinguishing between narrative text and other texts which are not differentiated (Faigley and Meyer, 1983). As Fayol points out (1988*b*), the ability to identify different types of text appears to be late to develop and weak. Furthermore, only narrative seems to constitute a specific type of text for the subjects, and this invites us to look more closely at what they know about narrative.

The metalinguistic management of narrative

Narrative forms the basis of a large number of studies both in the field of linguistics (see Adam, 1984) and of psycholinguistics (for reviews, see Denhière, 1984; Fayol, 1985*b*). The majority of these works agree in assuming the existence in the subject of a pre-linguistic representation of a general organization common to all narrative. Apart from certain variations which depend on the author, this organization comprises a setting ('Once upon a time . . .') and various episodes, each composed of a beginning, a development section and an end. This 'schema' plays a central role in the processing carried out by the subjects. In fact, the closer the structure of the narrative is to this schema, the better the subjects' recall and comprehension. This effect on recall has been identified in children of 6.

Furthermore, analysis of reading time in children from the age of 8 onwards reveals differences which depend on the constituents considered. This has been interpreted as indicating the psychological relevance of the differentiation of these constituents (see Frochot, 1989; Frochot *et al.*, 1987*a*). In general, the reading time required is less when the content is presented in the form of a narrative than when the same content is presented as a list of sentences (Frochot *et al.*, 1987*b*).

Although less well established, the schema also appears to be involved in guiding the production of stories (Espéret, 1984; Espéret and Gaonac'h, 1986). However, an alternative explanation is proposed by McKeough and Case (1985), who interpret the increase in complexity of narrative between the ages of 4 and 12 in terms of the evolution of the processing capacity of working memory, rather than as an increase in knowledge of the organization of stories.

In a discussion of the data gathered together in the literature, Fayol (1985*b*) asks how the schema is taken into account during processing. He insists that the processes at work are automatic in nature, and thus justifies the clear discrepancy observed between the effects reported above and performances in tasks in which the subjects must intentionally categorize or form hierarchies for the various constituents of a narrative. Pollart-Gott *et al.* (1979) find that the majority of educated adults form categories which correspond approximately to the organization of the schema, and Pratt *et al.* (1982, cited by Pratt and Nesdale, 1984) demonstrate the important role of the schema in the judgements made by these adults. However, there are some major differences between individuals which are difficult to interpret. Furthermore, it is only late and gradually that the schema seems to allow children to form correct judgements of the actual narrative character of the texts they are presented with (Espéret, 1984; Espéret and Gaonac'h, 1986).

Olson *et al.*'s hypothesis (1981) of a prospective approach to narrative which contrasts with a retrospective approach to expository text proposes an explanation in terms of the involvement of the schema. When subjects are confronted by a narrative, the schema provokes expectations which permit the structuring of new information as and when it appears. This method of processing, effective in 6-year-olds, is of the top–down type in which cognitive representation directs the structuring of the perceived linguistic information. As the construction of the schema improves with age, so the efficiency of this method of processing should increase (Espéret, 1984; Karmiloff-Smith, 1983, 1985) and would correspond, in production, to the transition from early narrative which is closely linked to the situation of utterance (Karmiloff-Smith, 1985) to later narrative monologues which may be independent of the immediate pragmatic demands of the situation (Stenning and Michell, 1985). However, as Fayol writes (1985*b*), while 'the narrative "schema" appears to be used from the age of 6–7, the conscious establishment of a hierarchy of its components rarely appears before age 9–10, and the use of the latter in the resolution of certain problems – better memorization of a text, for example – is revealed even later' (p. 95).

A final question should be raised. This concerns the metalinguistic nature of the subjective judgements which lead to the components of the narrative being classified in a way which is isomorphic to the classification of the components of the schema. Comparable results have been obtained using film presentations of the constituent events of stories or by means of cartoon strips (Bagget, 1979). From this, Fayol (1985*b*) adduces an argument for considering that the schema goes back to a 'pre-linguistic cognitive representation' rather than a linguistic one. The schema is concerned only with content, and all deliberate cognitive work on this content, if it is to be metacognitive in nature, is not, in the first analysis, subject to the influence of the symbolic nature of the vehicle and is not, therefore, metalinguistic in nature.

The processes at work in the monitoring of the overall organization of text can be related to the metalinguistic field: the differentiation of text from nontext, the recognition of a paragraph, the voluntary summarizing of a text or even noticing the transition to reported speech usually require that the criteria specific to the linguistic vehicle are taken into account (consciously if this is to be metalinguistic in nature). Success is then staggered between the ages of 5 and 12–13, according to the complexity of the tasks given. On the other hand, while identification of the theme of a text, the creation of a hierarchy of information in relation to this theme, the differentiation between various types of text and the differentiated processing of each of them can probably form objects of metalinguistic processing for the expert linguist, for most people they seem to be determined by criteria of content, the details of form being only incidental to conceptual considerations. This is clearly true for narrative but is equally true, as Fayol suggests (1988*b*), for the other types of text which, apart from differing in their rhetorical organization, also vary according to their thematic content. The nondissociation of these variables makes it impossible to form any conclusion as to the nature of the criteria taken into account here. However, the wealth of meanings associated with them probably gives them a high priority in processing.

Conclusion

In the introduction to this chapter we postulated the existence of metalinguistic activity specifically linked to the processing of text – metatextual activity. In fact, on an examination of the data available in the literature, this metatextual activity is shown to relate to a body of behaviour which controls the processing of text, not only with reference to its formal aspects but also with reference to the not strictly linguistic representations of the information carried by the text. It is therefore very difficult, and in general very artificial, to separate that which is metalinguistic in nature from that which, despite being of a metacognitive order, is not.

Moreover, the data concerning deliberate text management in production are few and far between and therefore underrepresented in the preceding discussion. This reflects the imbalance which exists between the number of studies devoted to text comprehension and the number concerned with production.

Given the complexity of the variables involved in the processing of text, it appears difficult to identify here any clearly epilinguistic (or, more generally, epicognitive) functions. What is important seems to be to differentiate between behaviour which is manifested in the activity of subjects, but of which they are unaware, and behaviour which indicates such an awareness. In fact, if we take the detection of contradiction as an example, the available data provide instances of modifications in the activity of subjects (for example, in reading time) prior to the explicit identification of a contradiction. However, the data do not report any intermediary behaviour showing that subjects who reject texts containing contradictions are incapable of identifying these contradictions precisely. Such behaviour, which would clearly be 'epitextual', undoubtedly exists, although the general slant of the studies carried out means that it has not been reported.

In the simplest tasks (distinguishing text from nontext; first identification of contradiction or violation of prior knowledge), metatextual behaviour appears at around the age of 5, but major horizontal *décalages* seem to exist depending on the complexity of the task. In certain studies this same behaviour is not observed before age 10. Although we do not wish to suggest the existence of a horizontal *décalage* or, in contrast, a difference in the cognitive processes involved, other behaviour for deliberately monitoring the text seems to develop later. It is not until the age of 8–9 that children accept that a text can be summarized. At 9–10 they can detect ambiguous anaphora, remove a sentence from a paragraph to which it is not thematically linked, and establish a basic hierarchy for the different information in a text. Only later (age 12–13) are they capable of explaining what a paragraph is, and it is not until later still that they develop a complex hierarchy for the information given in a text. Moreover, in many cases these metatextual activities do not seem to be implemented spontaneously even by the adult. In fact, the mnemonic factor appears to play an important role here. Most of those activities which require a high level of cognitive work are undertaken only if the subject clearly recognizes their usefulness (for example, following an explicit instruction). Furthermore, every factor contributing to better organization of textual information in working memory increases the subjects' ability to control their activity by lessening the cognitive workload required in the processing of the text.

Finally, the results reported in this chapter are as much concerned with the processing of oral text as they are with that of written text, although this variable has not been used in comparing behaviour. The next chapter will focus on the particularities of writing.

Chapter 7

Metalinguistic development and written language

Introduction

Even though some authors present written language as being essentially a recoding of spoken language, it is more common for the associated literature to emphasize the differences between these two systems. Most frequently cited is the fact that whereas the meaning of oral language is dependent on the situation of production and on the shared experience of the interlocutors, the meaning of written language is relatively independent of these factors and thus needs to fulfil higher requirements of explicitness. Furthermore, the pragmatic constraints proper to each of these modes of communication differentiate the possibilities of control both in production and in comprehension. Thus, while the person to whom oral speech is addressed can interrupt the speaker to ask for clarification, the reader is obliged to rely on reference to the text alone, and this does not necessarily result in an improvement of comprehension. Similarly, when the addressee misinterprets a spoken production the speaker is in a position to deny the interpretation and, if necessary, to correct the production. Students will know all too well that the same is not true in the case of written productions. The more exacting demands placed on writing are the price of its usefulness, which results from its permanence, a quality which is justified only when there is a temporal distance between the emission and reception of the message (for more detailed discussions of the difference between spoken and written language, see Biber, 1986; Gombert, 1988b; Schneuwly, 1989).

The cognitive consequence of the difference outlined above is the higher level of abstraction and elaboration required in the processing of written language. This strong affirmation of Vygotsky's ideas (for detailed presentations, see Schneuwly, 1989; Schneuwly and Bronckart, 1985) has since been repeated and refined by several authors, increasing numbers of whom have been ready to assert that the manipulation of written language necessitates conscious reflection. This is evident not only at the level of the word and smaller units – as has been demonstrated by studies of the relationship between metaphonological awareness and learning to read (see Chapter 2 above) – but also at the level of larger units, for it is at this level that written language and spoken language are most clearly differentiated (Barton, 1985). Metalinguistic development thus appears to be of primary importance in the acquisition of writing.

The first subsection will deal with the idea of writing in pre-literate children and children who are just starting to learn to read and write. This is intended to demonstrate the links between metalinguistic development and the start of the writing acquisition process. We shall then turn our attention to the metalinguistic aspects involved first in the activities and the learning of reading and then in the activities of writing. In the conclusion we shall turn to a more global approach to the idea of literacy, as well as outlining the pedagogic implications of the data reported in this chapter.

The early conceptions of written language

In an environment in which written language is omnipresent, it is probable that children are aware of writing before they are able to manipulate its production or comprehension. It is also probable that even before entering primary school they have worked out a representation of this particular object. A number of researchers have focused on these early conceptions of writing. Some have interested themselves in the way children apprehend their written environment. Others have attempted to describe the performances of young children in play tasks of writing and reading. All have frequently attempted to establish a link between early attitudes and performances and the level of success the subjects enjoy when subsequently learning to read.

An increasing volume of study has been dedicated to demonstrating that even before learning to read, children have a certain awareness of the objectives of reading and the main conventions applying to the manipulation of the written word, such as directionality (shown at its clearest by the ability to hold a book correctly and by a differentiation between the written and the pictorial). They also know certain characteristics of the letters, and are able to name some of them. They can tell the difference between a word, a letter and a written number. Finally, they are able to recognize certain words when they appear in familiar contexts such as on food packets or in children's books (for a review, see Gombert, 1989). This knowledge of the general traits of writing and the beginnings of an awareness of its graphemic characteristics have often been considered to be factors which later make it easier for the child to learn to read.

Lomax and McGee (1987) have concentrated on the emergence of this early knowledge and attempted to detect whether it obeys any hierarchical organization. Eighty-one child subjects, aged between 3 and 7, were faced with eighteen tasks subdivided into the following five categories:

1. *Knowledge of the general characteristics of writing* (objectives of writing; distinction between writing and drawing and between reading and seeing distinction between a letter, a word and a sentence; directionality; recognition of words common in the environment when presented in context).
2. *Graphemic awareness* (recognition of a visually presented letter, either in a group of other letters or in a group where it is depicted in four different positions; recognition of a word in a written list).
3. *Phonemic awareness* (matching pictures on the basis of the initial or final phoneme of the names of the depicted objects; discrimination between words which differ in only one phoneme).
4. *Knowledge of grapho-phonemic correspondence* (reading of lower- and uppercase letters; matching of pictures with letters on the basis of the first letter of the names of the depicted objects; reading of words after the oral presentation of words differing by only a single consonant and the visible substitution of a letter).
5. *Reading of words*.

The most interesting result to emerge from this study was given by a structural analysis which revealed that the performances in the tasks of the first category explained 91 per cent of the observed variance in the tasks of the second category, which itself explained 99 per cent of the variance observed in the tasks of the third category. This points to the existence of a rigid hierarchy: *knowledge of the general characteristics of writing seems to occur before the onset of graphemic awareness, which itself occurs before the emergence of phonemic awareness.* In contrast, knowledge of grapho-phonemic correspondence does not seem to depend on phonemic awareness alone but on the combination of knowledge of the general characteristics of writing and phonemic awareness (96 per cent of variance). However, it is this knowledge of grapho-phonemic correspondence which explains most of the variance in the word-reading tasks (61 per cent of variance). In fact, this research does not clearly establish whether the knowledge of grapho-phonemic correspondence and phonemic awareness are distinct skills. Thus, the grouping together of these two categories into one single category has very little effect on the explanatory value of the overall model. As the authors themselves say, long-term studies need to be carried out to resolve this issue.

Speaking more generally, this study shows that certain skills emerge at an early age (categories 1 and 2), while others do not appear until the age of 5–6. Nevertheless, at this age the earliest abilities are still not fully established and continue to develop in parallel with the emergence of the later skills. For example, in connection with category 1, even if the majority of 3-to-4-year-olds recognize a large number of environmentally common words, it is still necessary to wait until the age of 5–6 for mastery of the directionality of writing to be established and the general function of the aids to writing to be known. Early contact with writing thus stimulates an incidental learning process which precedes the explicit learning which commences at primary school (or sometimes at nursery school). This observation increases the relevance of the attempt to determine the abilities of young children in the classic tasks of manipulating the comprehension (reading) or production (writing) of written language.

Ferreiro and Teberosky (1979) have conducted a study in Spanish among Argentinian children aged between 4 and 6 who had not yet formally started to learn to read. The method used was very simple. A sentence was read to the children, with the reader following the words with his finger. The children were then asked to identify the position of the different words on the paper and to say what was written at the points not spontaneously pointed out. The responses were grouped into six categories, depending on the degree of development:

1: In the first category, only the nouns are written. They are at the position indicated by the experimenter's finger when read. If the children are asked what is written at the positions not pointed out – for example, words corresponding to verbs – they generally name other nouns which have not been read out but are related to the sense of the sentence. For example, in the sentence 'Daddy throws the ball' (*'Papà patea la pelota'*) the child will say that what is written at the position of the verb is 'Mummy', because if Daddy is present, there is no reason why Mummy should not be present as well. In fact, this suggests that the written text is considered as a representation of the objects (including the people) mentioned, and not as a representation of the phonological sequence. There is thus nothing strange about the addition of details which do not distort the meaning but actually complement it.

2: In another category, the entire sentence is written in a single fragment of text. When asked about the remainder of the text, the child proposes other sentences which are compatible with the first. For example, in the case of the sentence 'Daddy throws the ball', a child asserted that the entire sentence was written at the position of 'Daddy'; 'Daddy is ill' at the position of 'throws'; 'Daddy writes the date' at the position of 'the'; and finally 'Daddy goes to bed' at the position of 'ball'. The entire sentence is thus seen as being contained in one element of the written text, the other elements corresponding to sentences which are semantically related to the first. This behaviour might result from an inability to segment the phonological sequence in a way which corresponds to the evident graphic sequence.

3: This inability in the children to divide up the spoken sentence in a way which corresponds to the fragments of text may also underlie the responses in the following category. 'When the experimenter asks if a particular word is written somewhere in the sentence, the child points to the text in an imprecise and irregular fashion (indicating either the entire text, one or more fragments of it, or simply a single letter). Moreover, if the same question is posed a number of times, the child provides different answers and sees no contradiction in indicating different positions for the same word' (Teberosky and Ferreiro, 1980, p. 163).

4: The fourth category covers the responses which relate to a conception according to which the two nouns in the sentence are written separately, but not the verb. The verb cannot be considered as a part of the written text until it is linked to its object. For example, in the sentence 'The girl buys a sweet' (*'La nene compro un caramelo'*), two children associated 'sweet' with the written word 'girl', 'girl' with 'buys', and the entire sentence with 'a sweet'.

5: The fifth category contains the responses which seem to indicate that the child thinks everything is written apart from the articles. The simple presence of letters does not necessarily mean that something is there to be read. Instead a minimum number of letters is required (three for the majority of the children). There are thus two difficulties connected with articles which, on the one hand, are not considered to be words (see Chapter 4 above) and some of which, on the other hand, are thought to be too short to be read when they are written down.

6: In the final category, the responses affirm that everything is written, including the articles. Furthermore, the word order of both written sentence and spoken sentence correspond.

One item presented to the children is particularly interesting. This is an unsegmented written sentence (*'elosocomemiel'* – thebeareatshoney). Fewer than one child in five disagreed with this mode of writing, and those who did could not agree about the number of segments it should be divided into. (Only one 6-year-old child proposed the four conventional parts, and another suggested three parts with the verb separated in the middle). Even in the face of the experimenter's insistence, the majority of the children aged 4–5 rejected any segmentation, and the suggestions of the few who did accept it revealed their reificatory conception of writing: one child proposed a division into three parts and was then perplexed by the result: 'the bear . . . the bear eats honey . . . Ah, I know! there are two bears and the honey.'

Each of these developmental stages is represented in the first year of primary school in the underprivileged population studied by Ferreiro and Gomez Palacio (1982). This development can be broadly summarized in three main stages (this general model differs from the one proposed by Ferreiro and Teberosky):

1. *Narrow reificatory conception*, which imposes a correspondence between the objects referred to and the written materialization of language. Predication may or may not be represented. When it is, it is indissociably linked

with the object. This type of conception must be allowed to include the behaviour, widely identified in the literature, by which children establish a correspondence between the size of the object and the length of the written word, the longest words corresponding to the biggest objects (Ferreiro *et al.*, 1979, 1982 in Spanish; Lundberg and Tornéus, 1978 in Swedish; Rozin *et al.*, 1974 in English; Kolinsky *et al.*, 1987, also identify similar responses among illiterate Portuguese adults).

2. *Broad reificatory conception*, which authorizes the graphic symbolization not only of objects but also of actions (and therefore also of verbs). These are not then considered as predicates but as facts which have an autonomous reality that can be graphically materialized independently of the materialization of the objects. This conception does not exclude the search for a physical correspondence between signifier and signified which is at work in all reificatory conceptions.

3. *Grapho-phonological conception*, which sees the graphic sign as the translation of a phonological sign: a conception which authorizes the graphic materialization of function words. This conception can be seen to evolve, with the materialization of the syllable preceding that of the phoneme, an element which is not identified until later.

The results which have been obtained in tasks of production are perfectly compatible with this model. De Góes and Martlew (1983) have studied the awareness of written language in English-speaking children aged between 3 and 6 who have not yet formally started to learn to read or write. The experiment consisted of a dictation task and a task in which words were copied from a printed model and then recopied after the original had been removed but the copy made by the child retained. In the final double task, the words were read twice to the children, who had to repeat them and then write them down. The authors identified seven levels of response:

Level 1: The marks resemble neither the words nor the objects referred to. Writing is action, the graphic gesture.

Level 2: In response to dictation, the child produces an approximate pictorial representation of the object referred to. In the copying exercise it is possible to identify some letters of the model. No 'second copy' is made.

Level 3: Whereas dictation and the recopying task still lead to pictorial representations, the model-copying exercise produces a clumsy (for example, nonlinear) reproduction of the original. The written model here seems to be a drawing model, a set of shapes to be reproduced.

Level 4: The only difference from the preceding level is in the second copy. Here the child takes the first copy as a model. At this stage it is only in response to dictation that the child produces a drawing of the referent.

Level 5: Dictation leads to the production of a sequence of letters which in general bear no relation to those of which the dictated words are composed. As of this level, the copies and second copies are faithful reproductions of the model.

Level 6: Despite the similarity between the productions obtained at this level and those obtained at level 4 (drawing in response to dictation, faithful copies and second copies) there are now indications of metalinguistic reflection which were absent before. In fact, these children refuse to write as a response to dictation, using the argument that they do not know how to write.

Level 7: The final level gives rise to the production of identifiable words in response to the dictation exercise.

Taken in their entirety, these productions – in particular the frequency of pictorial productions – demonstrate the importance of the signified objects in the manipulation of the signifiers. This phenomenon has also been detected in a study conducted in Hebrew by Tolchinsky-Landsmann and Levin (1985), who obtained results similar to those of de Góes and Martlew.

In this study, the children could use colouring crayons which they chose themselves in order to draw and write. The authors reported the case of a girl, aged 5½, who drew a flower: the soil was brown, the stem and the leaves were green and the flower itself was red. The researchers then asked her to write 'a red flower', in response to which the child inscribed a sequence of three signs which were, in fact, Hebraic letters which form part of her own name (this is probably the only alphabetic sequence which many children of this age possess. In fact, a large body of research, including that currently under discussion, has established that at the age of 4–5 a far from negligible proportion of children known how to write their own first names). The first letter was written in green, the second in red and the last in brown. The child then looked at her work, burst out laughing and said: 'I haven't written a red flower at all, I'm going to write a red flower now.' The girl then wrote the same letters again, this time using the red crayon for them all. In fact, in the productions observed during this research it is possible to see referential elements in 27 per cent of the 'writings' of children aged 3–4, 50 per cent of those produced by children aged 4–5, and 20 per cent of those produced by children aged 5–6 years.

Beyond these results – which confirm those obtained among English children and the related results of Ferreiro and Teberosky, 1979 – the data reported by Tolchinsky-Landsmann and Levin also provide specific information on these results. They thus show that the characteristics of writing (linearity, unidirectionality, the presence of distinct units and regular white spaces, the small size of the graphic signs) are massively represented at the age of 4–5, even if at the age of 5–6 letters adapted to the dictated sentence appear in less than a quarter of productions. As far as directionality is concerned, unidirectional writing going from left to right appears before the right-to-left writing of Hebrew. Further, better-controlled research conducted by the same authors (Tolchinsky-Landsmann and Levin, 1987) has clearly shown that, while they are no longer pictorial representations, the number of graphic characters contained in the child's early writings corresponds first to the objects referred to and then later to the objects *and* events referred to. Only later still does it begin to correspond to the phonological models. Finally, according to a study conducted by Ferreiro and Gomez Palacio (1982) amongst a thousand Mexican children from underprivileged backgrounds who had just started their first year in primary school, less than 10 per cent of these children constructed their writing (asked of them within the experiment) on the basis of an analysis of the spoken sounds presented to them. Twelve per cent of them still did not do this by the end of the school year.

It is important to emphasize that *all these observations do not concern the child's manipulation of conventional writing but the manipulation of an invented writing*. Initially, this 'invention' bears on many aspects of writing, including the shape of the characters. Later, when the child starts to become aware of grapho-phonemic correspondence, the letters increasingly resemble the norm. However, before formal teaching starts to place serious constraints on the learner's productions, pre-conventional spellings appear which reflect the child's ability to accede to the phonological structure of the word (Mann *et al.*, 1987; Read, 1986). Children are then seen to write the word 'people' in the form 'ppl' (where a simple spoken enumeration of the names of the letters more or less restores the sound configuration of the entire word), or the word 'name' in the form 'nam' (the silent vowel, which does not exist phonologically, not appearing in this written version). Some researchers have shown that the manifestation of this type of orthographic behaviour in kindergarten is, in so far as it indicates an early capacity for phonemic analysis, a reliable indicator of the child's later performances during the explicit learning of reading (see, for example, Mann *et al.*, 1987).

More anecdotal, but no less interesting, are the small number of observations of early manipulations of two subsystems which are specific to writing: punctuation and the use of written numbers.

In research conducted in 1979, Ferreiro *et al.* showed that between the ages of 4 and 6 children progress from a period in which they do not distinguish between punctuation marks and letters to a period in which effective discrimination (although exclamation and question marks are often taken to be letters) goes hand in hand with an inability to specify the function of the different types of symbol. In the case of older children (6–6½), de Góes and Martlew (1983) have shown that once their existence is realized, punctuation marks are either related to the contents of the story (in the same way, Tolchinsky-Landsmann and Levin, 1985, reported the case of a child who insisted that the full stop he had inserted into a sentence about a ball represented the ball), or attributed the role of separating words (to avoid them getting 'jumbled up') or, in the case of the full stop, of marking the end of the story. However, despite thinking that punctuation marks should not be read like words, the majority of children did not know what their purpose was.

This development is particularly interesting. The early lack of discrimination between letters and punctuation marks shows that in the first 'writings' the choice of the shape of the characters used is a matter of preference and motor skills. The only determinism possible, whatever the category of symbol, is the similarity between the configuration of the graphic sign and the extralinguistic reality to which it refers. With the emergence of a grapho-phonological conception of the written word, the punctuation mark becomes differentiated from the letter. Its spatial position between words or at the end of the entire text (the only comprehensible realities for a child who still has no idea of intermediate textual units) leads the child to interpret it in terms of a simplification of the management of the read text.

Like punctuation marks, figures are not initially distinguished from letters (Sinclair and Sinclair, 1984). Moreover, they frequently appear in the 'invented writings' observed in all the research mentioned above. Only very gradually are they attributed a specific function.

Sinclair *et al.* (1983) asked children aged between 4 and 6 to represent different quantities of objects in writing (<9). After a period during which the child represents neither the cardinal amount nor the type of object, the earliest productions consist of a representation of either one or the other of these two elements, but never of both (at this time the type of object is most often represented in pictorial fashion and the cardinality by a sequence of identical characters). Later – but before the appearance of conventional markers of cardinal value and the type of object (for example, '4 pencil') – it is possible to observe productions which, despite revealing an awareness of written numbers, seem to indicate that for the child each object must have its graphic correspondent (for example, '5 houses' is written '12345').

It is interesting to note that very young children treat these numerical ideograms in the same way as alphabetical letters. This is probably due to the fact that these ideograms materialize abstract units of meaning. In fact, it seems that when the child has reached a certain level of writing ability, every written sign is understood as an ideogram (after a pictographic period during which certain physical characteristics of the referents are found in the mode of inscription), but that only the referents form the object of a written materialization. This is probably also the case when the child uses an ordered sequence of figures to materialize a first object, a second, a third, etc., cardinality in this case being specified only indirectly because it corresponds to the ideography of the last element in the series.

This last set of results, which again shows that considerations of meaning long persist in making it impossible for children to understand the formal aspects of language (although this effect is more evident in written than in spoken language), allows us to provide the detail for the developmental model proposed above (for a more detailed discussion of the experimental results, see Gombert, 1989).

The narrow reificatory conception of writing would seem to start with a *pictographic* functioning (the most elementary modality of which is simple pictorial representation, writing and drawing not being distinguished at this level) which is later transformed into an *ideographic* functioning. The fact that this latter type of functioning is not constrained by any similarity of configuration between referents and signifiers makes possible the graphic materialization of actions, and thus the progression to a broad reificatory conception of writing. The first attempts at reading and writing, which banish the early conceptions, lead to the idea that it is the utterance which is directly materialized by writing and, at the same time, permit the appearance of a grapho-phonological conception of writing. It is at this point, at the start of the formal learning process, that a distinction between the processes of comprehension (reading) and the processes of production (writing) becomes relevant.

Metalinguistic development and reading

Before we discuss the metalinguistic dimension of the activity and learning of reading, it is important to present at least a brief summary of the cognitive processes which constitute this activity. Here, the differences between novice or poor readers and expert readers can be particularly illuminating for our attempt to determine the characteristics of efficient reading.

Processes leading to reading comprehension

There are two opposed conceptions concerning the processes at work in the recognition of written words. Some researchers hold that this recognition is performed directly through matching the graphemic configuration of the word with its visual representation in memory. This is the *direct-access procedure*. The opposing view is that this recognition is based on the application of rules of grapho-phonological correspondence in which visual information is transformed into phonological information before the process of lexical retrieval. This is the *indirect-access procedure* (for a more detailed discussion, see Barron, 1986; Content *et al.*, 1986*b*; for a presentation of the study methods, see Zagar, 1988). The ability of all good readers to recognize words which they have never previously seen in their written form suggests, at the very least, that the possibility of indirect access exists. However, the (variable) orthographic irregularity of alphabetical languages means that simple decoding would not be sufficient to give access to phonologically correct information (see Juel *et al.*, 1986). This type of argument has caused some authors to postulate the existence of two procedures for word recognition, the direct-access procedure being at work in the identification of familiar words, and that of indirect access being mobilized when other words have to be recognized (McCusker *et al.*, 1981). Moreover, a certain amount of data seems to demonstrate that the indirect-access procedure is particularly dominant among those starting to read (see Waters *et al.*, 1984) but that very soon (as of the second year of learning) direct access becomes possible (Backman *et al.*, 1984). Here again we find Vygotsky's conception of an automation which would enable direct access to meaning without requiring the establishment of a correspondence between the spoken and the written (Vygotsky, 1935).

It has often been shown that bad readers generally produce poor performances in recoding tasks which require the application of the rules of grapho-phonemic correspondence (see Stanovich *et al.*, 1988). They also seem to be less skilful in using compensatory strategies on the nonidentification of a word. We have stated above that the pre-reading child is very soon able to recognize written words when these are presented in a familiar context. In fact, it appears that in this case it is solely the context, and not the writing itself, which determines the young child's interpretation, and this can lead to incorrect recognitions when a word is presented in a position usually occupied by another word (Goodall, 1984). In the case of written texts, the context is the text itself, and this context can be used by the reader to compensate for difficulties experienced in the comprehension of a particular word or passage. Tunmer *et al.* (1987) have suggested that the development of grammatical skills plays a central role in increasing the child's sensitivity to the 'predictability' of the text. Beginners and poor readers who already have problems decoding words rapidly would thus experience further difficulties, associated with their poor awareness of syntax, in making use of the context in their reading (see Siegel and Ryan, 1988), especially when such action would require them to return to a preceding body of text in order to complete an interpretation left temporarily unresolved (di Vesta *et al.*, 1979).

In fact, because it precedes comprehension, the recognition of words conditions all reading activities. Furthermore, it is not enough that this recognition should be performed correctly. The cognitive effort it involves must also be low enough for the reader to be able to attend to higher-level activities of comprehension. It would thus seem that such a recognition process should be at least partially automated (Juel *et al.*, 1986), and this generally appears to be the case after the second or third year of learning.

The skills of good readers are not limited to the ability to recognize written words. They must also be able to understand the messages they read and this demands, at the very least, an awareness of the grammatical structure which governs the organization of the words in the sentence (Siegel and Ryan, 1988) and the processing of the marks of textual cohesion (see the preceding chapter). Beyond this linguistic processing, understanding depends on the formation of a conceptual representation which corresponds to that desired by the author of the written message. On this subject, a number of studies have shown that beginners and poor readers tend to prefer to process texts at a lexical level. Thus, when they are required to detect anomalies in written texts, the only problems they mention concern the meanings of individual words (Baker, 1984*b*). According to Baker (1985), this constitutes one of the major causes of their comprehension problems. Moreover, their performances lag behind those of good readers in a whole series of metacognitive tasks which relate to written texts: the detection of contradictions and violations of previous knowledge (Baker, 1984*b*); the identification of the main idea of a text (Smiley *et al.*, 1977). In a more general sense, they seem to be largely unaware of their own problems of comprehension (see Forrest-Pressley and Waller, 1984).

Criticizing the tendency of many researchers to concentrate only on recoding or only on comprehension, Forrest-Pressley and Waller (1984) have insisted on the fact that reading does not consist simply of one or the other, or even of a combination of the two. According to them, it is necessary to add a third element: the ability to adapt one's reading strategy to the required objective. For example, the most effective strategy is not the same when looking for a definition in a dictionary or reading a text in order to understand it, to comment critically on it, or simply for pleasure. This, again, is a skill which the young or poor reader seems to lack.

In this rapid overview of the processes involved in reading we have seen the importance of a knowledge of the phonological code, the identification of words, grammatical skills, awareness of textual parameters and adaptation to the aim of the activity. It would thus appear that the majority of the metalinguistic skills discussed in the preceding chapters can be mobilized in connection with reading. This is what is suggested by Forrest-Pressley and Waller (1984), who hold that skilful reading does not imply simply recoding, comprehension and an adaptation of strategy in accordance with the aim of the activity, but also knowledge about each of these skills and the ability to control them.

The metalinguistic competences associated with learning to read

We do not intend to discuss the numerous studies which have now established beyond doubt the importance of metaphonological awareness for children who are starting to learn to read (for a detailed discussion, see Chapter 2 above). The essential point to emerge from this fact is that the metacognitive abilities which underlie metaphonological behaviour seem to be a prerequisite for the successful learning of reading. In the same way, the use, pointed out above, of grapho-phonological correspondence in the identification of written words supposes an ability to identify phonemic units within the word (see Content *et al.*, 1986*b*; Juel *et al.*, 1986).

The usefulness of an awareness of grapho-phonological correspondence is closely linked to the ability to detect lexical units in both the written and the spoken language. In fact, the importance of the role played by this awareness in the recognition of words presupposes that these have a reality for the individual. Evidence of the interdependence of the two abilities is provided by research carried out by Ehri and Robert (1979) which shows that the awareness of grapho-phonological correspondence in the recoding of words is more closely correlated with the recognition of written words than is the case when meaningless graphemic sequences are to be decoded.

In itself, the simple ability of children who are starting to learn to read to break down spoken sentences into words is correlated with reading performance and provides an indicator of their later development (Evans *et al.*, 1979). In fact, it has been shown that before the teaching of reading starts, this ability is generally missing both in children (see Chapter 4 above) and in illiterate adults (Cary *et al.*, cited by Morais, 1987*b*). As was the case with the capacity for phonological segmentation, opinions are divided as to the significance of the link between lexical segmentation and reading. For some researchers, segmentation is a consequence (Ehri, 1979), whereas for others it is a prerequisite (Ryan, 1980). In fact, the first thing children have to know when they start to learn to read is that a specific written word corresponds to one, and only one, spoken word (Biemiller, 1970). A tendency towards metalexical awareness thus appears to be necessary from the very start, even if the visible segmentation of writing then later intervenes to favour the actualization of this preexisting competence. The same reasoning can be applied to the metasemantic awareness of the word. In their judgements of spoken words, illiterate adults (Kolinsky *et al.*, 1987) and children of pre-school age (see Chapter 4 above) both seem to pay more attention to the characteristics of the signified than to those of the signifier. This awareness, which determines the ability to access a concept from a graphemic configuration to which it is arbitrarily bound, can be consolidated only by the materialization of the words in the written language (see Kolinsky, 1986).

Comparing the reading level of good readers in their first learning year (6-to-7-year-olds) with that of poor readers in their third year (8-to-9-year-olds), Tunmer *et al.* (1987) found that the former outperform the latter in two oral metasyntactic tasks: a sentence-completing task and a task in which the subjects were asked to correct ungrammatical sentences (identical to that used by Pratt *et al.*, 1984; see Chapter 3 above). This study confirmed the large body of data already available, and established a link between syntactic awareness and reading performances. Furthermore, it provided a clue about the nature of this link. In effect, the method of comparing good young readers and poor older readers invalidates any interpretation of the observed differences in terms of the effect of a more prolonged experience of reading. This gives weight to the hypothesis that there is a causal link between metasyntactic deficiency (or a factor connected with it) and backwardness in reading, and thus emphasizes the importance of this factor in reading acquisition.

At the metapragmatic level, Ferreiro (1977) has pointed out that a number of child learner-readers find it difficult to distinguish between what the written sentence explicitly says and what it means (a meaning which can, for example, be inferred from an illustration accompanying the sentence). However, Bell *et al.* (1987, cited in Torrance and Olson, 1987) found no correlation between the first performances in reading and the ability to distinguish in oral speech between what is said and what the speaker actually means. In contrast, such a correlation is observed as of the third learning year. This ability does not therefore appear to be a prerequisite for all types of reading. In particular, it is left inactivated in the reading of the simple, explicit texts given to beginners. The problem is quite different with the more complex and less transparent texts with which the reader has to deal later.

Metatextual awareness also seems to be involved in the strategies of reading. Thus Forrest-Pressley and Waller (1984) have shown that unskilful or inexperienced readers are generally unable to focus their attention on important information or to explain their attempts to adapt their reading strategy to the demands of the situation. They thus appear to be deficient in two metatextual domains whose importance for reading has been stressed by Perfetti (1985): the awareness of the levels of textual structuring and the awareness of strategies of comprehension. It is perhaps this same link which explains the relationship between the early ability to recount stories and later success in the acquisition of reading (Tinzmann *et al.*, 1983) and the fact that encouragement to use a schema before the reading of a story improves the level of comprehension attained by young readers (see, for example, Paris and Oka, 1986).

The effect of other factors on reading has been studied by a number of researchers. The capacity for visual discrimination, long the subject of attention, is no longer considered to play a central role in reading acquisition (see Bryant and Bradley, 1985). The memory span and metamemory abilities are also poor indicators of reading performance. In contrast, for the poor reader, problems of short-term memory retention of verbal items often seem to play a role (see Siegel and Ryan, 1988). The poor reader is also less skilful in the use of spoken language (Forrest-Pressley and Waller, 1984) and has a more restricted vocabulary (Stanovich *et al.*, 1988). More curious is the observation that knowledge of the written alphabet before entry into primary school is a very good, if isolated, indicator of future reading level

(Calfee, 1977). Of course, we can see the usefulness of this knowledge for decoding, but taken alone (i.e. without a metaphonological ability) it is unlikely to lead even to the phonological breakdown of words. In fact, the children who are able to name letters doubtlessly come from a more privileged sociocultural background of the type which generally produces better readers.

The majority of the abilities associated with reading are thus metalinguistic in nature. The skills connected with the spoken language also seem to play a part, but the relative importance of this is disputed. Of primary importance for Forrest-Pressley and Waller (1984), it is considered to be less important than the ability to control language by Wallach and Wallach (1976). In fact, everything depends on the level of investigation. Of course, an adequate level of linguistic skill in the spoken language is often a precondition for starting to write. However, once this minimum level has been attained, it is the metalinguistic abilities which seem to play the dominant role. Moreover, language performances can be linked to the family environment, whose influence on learning is not inconsiderable. As for the problems of memory, it is possible that they are linked to reading difficulties in various ways: they may sometimes be the direct cause of these difficulties when the problem is strictly one of memory; they may also themselves be a result of a larger dysfunctioning which is then manifested in other cognitive dimensions, including the metalinguistic abilities; finally, if they are limited to verbal material, these problems can be the manifestations of a basic difficulty in the mental manipulation of language, the metalinguistic dysfunctioning here lying at the root of the problem.

A review of the various studies which attempt to determine the relative importance of the various factors associated with comprehension in reading (see, for example, Forrest-Pressley and Waller, 1984; Juel *et al.*, 1986; Stanovich *et al.*, 1986, 1988; Torrance and Olson, 1987; Tunmer and Bowey, 1984) suggests that *the hierarchy varies as a function of the learning level.* The only not directly metalinguistic factor which is correlated with reading performances at all levels is the importance of lexical knowledge, which seems to us to be a sociological rather than a cognitive indicator. The chronological order in which the abilities are mobilized sees knowledge of what reading is playing the leading role at the start of the learning process. Next to be mobilized are the metalexical and metasemantic abilities, followed by the metaphonological and then, finally, the metasyntactic abilities. After a few years, the predominant factor becomes the automation of the basic abilities (measured in terms of recognition times, for example). It is at this point that the importance of the metapragmatic and metatextual abilities, which are essential at the later level of reading expertise, appears. As we have already argued a number of times in connection with particular metalinguistic abilities, it is probable that there is an interaction between the various metalinguistic abilities and reading at the different levels of acquisition. A specific metalinguistic deficiency would prevent the reader's skills developing beyond the level at which the corresponding metalinguistic ability is predominant. In contrast, in the absence of such a deficiency, the practice of increasingly complex reading tasks would continuously actualize and develop the different preexisting metalinguistic competences.

Metalinguistic development and written production

The process of written composition, classically described in three stages (planning, transcription, revision – see, for example, Flower and Hayes, 1981) is very complex. This is all the more so because these stages do not appear to be organized in a linear way (see, for example, Sommers, 1980). It is thus inconceivable that everything performed by an expert writer should be managed in a conscious and deliberate fashion. The details of the processes as they are revealed by an overview of the results and analyses of different researchers and theorists bear witness to this (the references are given in Fayol and Gombert, 1987; Gombert, 1988*b*).

The writing process

Before all writing, it is necessary to select a theme or determine its objectives and anticipate what is to be communicated to the reader for whom the text is intended. It is then necessary to find, in long-term memory or in external sources, the ideas which are to be put into words. These ideas must be organized in such a way that they link up with the prior knowledge expected in the reader and possess a coherent overall configuration. This overall plan must be retained in working memory until execution, at the same time as: a more restricted plan of the start of the written document; the transcription of this start; subsequent local plans.

Planning is then joined by the process of transcription, which supposes a putting into words (lexical choice and anticipation of the conventions of writing at the level of orthography, syntax and punctuation – all this as a function of the capacity for comprehension expected of the intended readers, and possibly also of aesthetic considerations – the whole then constituting what some authors have called microplanning: see Fayol and Schneuwly, 1988) and extends as far as the management and realization of the grapho-motive activity.

The final revision stage (for a review, see Fayol and Gombert, 1987) implies an evaluation, itself dependent on a rereading, a comparison between the produced text and the planned text, and the implementation of the necessary corrections. To this stage of revision – which may take place at the end of the writing stage or, indeed, at various points within this – we can add a rewriting activity which is more than a simple step within the overall process of composing, constituting rather a modified retranscription of the text which has already been produced (certain authors have called this process 'reviewing' – see, for example, Nold, 1981).

While the production of a high-quality text demands the performance of all these activities (consciously or not), some seem to be less effective than others in less expert writers.

The production of low-quality texts

The following is an overall presentation of the characteristics of low-quality writers. The data concerning young writers and those obtained for poor older writers are similar in many respects (for each characteristic, a single bibliographical reference out of many is given).

The first differences between the expert and the inexperienced writer are manifested in the scope of the planning stage. In the beginner or poor writer, this is more local (sentential or intersentential) (Matsuhashi, 1981) and occupies a lower proportion of the overall composing time (Foulin, 1989). In general, these writers seem to find it difficult to explain their objectives (Humes, 1983) and to anticipate the needs of their readers (Martlew, 1983). At the level of transcription, such writers seem to experience difficulty in applying the conventions of writing (de Góes and Martlew, 1983) and controlling their implementation (Pintrich *et al.*, 1986), with poor syntax, spelling and punctuation (Grundlach, 1981).

Inexperienced writers review their texts less thoroughly than the expert (Nold, 1981) and, in contrast to the latter, they are more interested in the detection of surface errors (grammar, spelling, punctuation) than in checking the meaning and communicative adequacy of their productions (Humes, 1983; Piolat, 1988). One of the problems of detection is that when they reread their texts, such writers see in them what they believe they have written rather than what they have actually written (Fayol *et al.*, 1987*b*). This makes them better able to correct other people's texts than their own (Bartlett, 1982). Finally, the modifications which they introduce do not generally improve the initial production and can even have the opposite effect (Fabre, 1986; Perl, 1980).

Generally speaking, such writers appear to suffer from a lack of knowledge (Pintrich *et al.*, 1986) and a difficulty in knowing when to apply the knowledge they do possess (Bryant and Bradley, 1980). There also appear to be problems connected with the processing capacity of working memory (Scardamalia and Bereiter, 1983). The produced texts are short (Deno *et al.*, 1982), contain shorter and syntactically less complex sentences (Morris and Crump, 1982), use more common words (Deno *et al.*, 1982) and are insufficiently explicit (Kroll, 1986) – as if the reader, in the writer's absence, ought to know what was passing through his head at the moment of production. The overall impression (but it is only an impression) is that inexpert writers write as they speak (Chafe, 1982). Among the least experienced writers, this includes orthography which reflects the application of phonological rules (Goodman *et al.*, 1987). In fact, a more detailed study which differentiates between various levels of expertise reveals a gradual transition from a conversational style to a written style (Bereiter and Scardamalia, 1981), with the productions becoming more independent of their context of emission, increasingly coherent and organized (Van Wijk, 1987).

As Bereiter and Scardamalia (1986) have written with some humour, good writers are, all in all, better than bad writers. These authors have declared themselves willing to bet that if enough cases were tested, we would find that the former are better at tying their shoelaces than the latter. If we look beyond this joke, the systematic character of the differences suggests that as none of the high-level activities is satisfactorily implemented by inexperienced writers, their processing abilities are entirely mobilized by the implementation of the basic activities.

The importance of automation

If we examine the behaviour of experts (see, in particular, Berkenkotter, 1983) or if, just for once, we allow ourselves the luxury of introspection, we soon realize that not all the activities listed above are monitored at a conscious level during writing.

First of all, the graphic act itself, the choice of words, the spelling, the grammatical agreements, the punctuation, are often performed automatically. In the same way, the striving for textual coherence and cohesion, the adaptation of the text to the potential reader and the attempt to be explicit are not always the focus of any particular attention, even though the produced text satisfies all these criteria. Finally, Bartlett (1982) has pointed out that numerous corrections are carried out so quickly that the subjects who perform them cannot reflect on the nature of the problem. Everything leads us to believe that we are in the presence of automated processes. This automation allows the bulk of the cognitive effort to be directed at the elaboration of content.

However, it is noteworthy that each of these activities can be intentionally monitored if the situation calls for it or if a problem arises during writing. This suggests that during the learning process, automation follows the conscious awareness and the subsequent exercise of these different components (this is somewhat akin to the case of certain subactivities of driving). This type of automatic process is very different from the epiprocesses at work in novices who are unable to direct certain elements of their activity consciously (see the next chapter for a discussion of this distinction).

These epiprocesses are at work, for example, when beginners or poor reader-writers 'correct' their texts during the course of a rereading in which they read what they believe they have written rather than the actual letter of their texts. They are also often responsible for punctuation, even among many experienced writers, a reflection of the fact that this skill is only infrequently taught at school. This makes it difficult to substitute a reflected punctuation for an automatic (epiprocedural) punctuation (see Fayol, 1989; Fayol and Abdi, 1988; Fayol and Lété, 1987).

Numerous authors have pointed out the deficient automation of certain activities in the beginner or in poor writers, who consequently find themselves in a permanent state of cognitive overload. The areas designated most frequently are planning and its grapho-motive and orthographic realization (Foulin, 1989), the application of the rules of grammar and conventions of usage (Flower and Hayes, 1980) and these are joined by the generation of content, which is necessarily a focus of the writer's attention. This is what led Yde and Spoelders (1985) to consider written production as an activity in which numerous different subprocesses are competing for a limited capacity for attention (Yde and Spoelders refer to this as the 'cognitive balance' model of the writing process).

This is confirmed by the improvements brought about by procedures designed to reduce the workload. Such attempts generally concern the final revision of the produced texts. Thus Scardamalia and Bereiter (1983) have helped children aged between 9 and 14 in the revision of their texts. They asked them questions concerned with the characteristics of the production and then suggested a range of correction strategies from which the subjects were allowed to choose. However, although such assistance increased the level and effectiveness of spontaneously produced local corrections, it failed to bring about any notable changes at the higher structural levels.

A number of researchers have indicated the existence of similar improvements when texts are processed on a microcomputer (Bridwell *et al.*, 1985; Daiute, 1983, 1985, 1986; Levin *et al.*, 1985; Morocco, 1986; Pearson and Wilkinson, 1986; Rosegrant, 1984; Selfe, 1985; Womble, 1985).

In fact, neither assistance nor encouragement in revision provokes the appearance of any high-level strategies. They simply act as simplifiers and motivators which increase the efficiency of spontaneously mobilized strategies. This not only confirms the handicap imposed by the cognitive overload but also suggests that, rather than being obscured by lower-level activities, certain activities necessary for expert production are not available to inexperienced writers. Case studies conducted by Pearson and Wilkinson (1986) seem to show that the assistance provided by such things as word processors are in fact 'catalysts of progress' which do not allow the subject to implement new procedures unless these are already on the point of being adopted.

The metalinguistic activities mobilized during the activity of writing

Here and there the literature notes or postulates the conscious character of certain subprocesses of writing. Moreover, many of the activities described above have been brought to light by the 'protocol method', which consists of asking writers to describe what they think about while they are writing (see, in particular, the initial study carried out by Flower and Hayes, 1981). Those activities which are capable of verbalization are thus necessarily conscious in nature or can, at the very least, be consciously accessed (see Foulin and Fayol, 1988)

In fact, if we take account of the totality of the data, we see that *most of the components of the activity of writing are consciously monitored by the subject at some stage during the learning process, from first acquaintance with the activity of writing to expertise in the production of the written text.* We also see that the various aspects of metalinguistic awareness are mobilized, with the metaphonological, metasyntactic and metasemantic abilities which are necessary at the beginning of the learning process gradually giving way to the metapragmatic and, most importantly, metatextual abilities. This observation validates the position held by Daiute (1985), who sees 'self-monitoring' as a central factor in the development of writing.

Conclusion

Even though the data reported in this chapter establish that metalinguistic development plays a crucial role in the development of literacy, there is nothing to establish any strict parallelism between the acquisition of reading and writing.

Some researchers who have concentrated on the basic abilities of recoding and orthography think that the beginnings of reading are based on a visual strategy, while the first attempts at spelling seem to point to the use of phonological indications. This specialization is then thought to diminish in the later stages of acquisition (see Bryant and Bradley, 1983; Frith, 1980). This point of view is less at odds than it might appear with the large volume of data reported above, which establishes that at the start of acquisition the procedure for recognizing written words makes use of the subject's knowledge of grapho-phonological correspondences. In fact, the subjects studied by Bryant and Bradley were not absolute beginners, and it has been suggested that direct access procedures for recognizing words seem to appear as of the second learning year. However, we do not find it improbable that the direct-access procedure should be the earliest to develop, as Ferreiro and Gomez Palacio (1982) have suggested.

Before absolute beginners are able to use their knowledge of grapho-phonological correspondence, it is necessary for them to possess this knowledge. Studies involving subjects who have not yet commenced formal tuition have shown that many of them are able to recognize a certain number of words, although they are not yet able to determine the phonological correspondents of the letters which form them. At the current level of knowledge, it seems that directly before any formal learning process (recognition at this point being based on the awareness of clues, the recognition of a name, for example, being based simply on its initial letter), the learner-readers' procedure for recognition must become indirect (so that they can decode words which they have never encountered in the written form) before later becoming direct again when the procedure for accessing meaning becomes automated. The indirect method then remains available for the ever-decreasing number of unfamiliar words. 'Whole-word writing' (the production of which would presuppose that a graphemic sequence is understood as a complete configuration) is more difficult to conceive of (except perhaps in the cursive writing of the first name) because the writer necessarily has to draw each of the letters in sequence. The activity of writing recognizable words thus seems to us to necessitate at least the beginnings of formal training, an important factor of which is grapho-phonological correspondence (whether explicit or not). The subsequent development does not so much appear to reveal the adoption of a visual strategy as an automation (and thus the apparent disappearance) of the phono-graphemic strategy.

Knowledge of grapho-phonological correspondence and the metaphono-logical awareness which is associated with it appear to be particularly important in learning to write, in terms of both the recognition and the writing of words. These two developments would thus appear to be linked, since they both depend on the same sources of knowledge (Juel *et al.*, 1986). This argument is not intended to reduce reading to recoding or written composition to orthography, but rather to emphasize that reading and writing are these things as well. Comprehension in reading and the elaboration of meaning in writing are here dimensions of the utmost importance, as is the adoption of different strategies in accordance with the particular objective of each act of comprehension or written production.

Mitterer (1982) – followed by Bialystok and Mitterer (1987) – has identified two types of poor reader who can be observed from the second year of learning onwards: there are the 'recoders', who concentrate too much on grapho-phonological correspondence in both reading and writing, and the 'whole-worders', who apprehend too many words as complete visual configurations and are thus broadly unable to read or write words which are unfamiliar to them. The metasyntactic tasks given to these subjects reveal that the 'recoders' are able to pay conscious attention to the linguistic form but find it difficult to monitor the processing they perform, and that this leads them to interpret problems of meaning in terms of form. The whole-worders, for their part, are no better at analyzing linguistic forms than they are at monitoring the processing they apply. This leads the authors to predict a more pessimistic long-term development for the latter. In fact, given the framework of the model proposed above, everything suggests that the whole-worders have remained at the initial stage of the visual processing of written words, whereas the recoders would appear to have attained the subsequent stage of phonological processing but not the final stage of direct processing.

All these considerations invite us to reject any theory which holds that learning to read is based solely on the exercise of recoding or solely on the association between word configurations and their meaning, and this irrespective of the learning period.

As Tunmer and Bowey (1984) have suggested, it is probably useful to prepare for formal learning by encouraging the child to recognize whole words and to become aware of their reality as distinct from the objects or actions to which they refer. This exercise – which, we think, could take place at nursery school after the child has been initiated into what writing and the activity of reading are – would make possible the acquisition of the minimum of metalexical and metasemantic awareness which is necessary if the child is to be able to identify the words to be analyzed by means of the application of the knowledge of grapho-phonological correspondence. Certainly, those beginning formal learning should not forgo the systematic training of recoding, followed by written syntax and exercises designed to assist in the automation of these basic activities (without work on meaning being abandoned). The later step of becoming a skilful reader presupposes that the subject is confronted with a variety of texts and is trained in the different strategies of reading, which vary with the desired objective.

Shanahan and Lomax (1986) have compared three alternative theoretical models of the reading–writing relationship. These are: a model which postulates a transfer of knowledge from reading to writing; a second one which postulates a transfer of knowledge in the opposite direction; and a third, interactive, model which permits knowledge gathered in either field to be used in the other. Gathering together a large volume of data concerning knowledge of reading and writing, these authors have shown that the interactive model comes closest to what is actually observed both in children in their second year of primary education and those in their fifth year. More precisely, at any given linguistic level reading seems to exert a greater influence on writing than the other way round. For example, the ability to analyze words seems to influence spelling, whereas orthographic knowledge exerts less of an influence on the recognition of words. The result is that pupils are able to recognize a word before they are able to represent it in writing. When writing influences reading, this influence seems to be exerted from a given linguistic level of writing to the linguistic reading level immediately above it. Thus knowledge of spelling should have an effect on the breadth of vocabulary identified in reading, and on the child's knowledge of the meaning of words. This effect increases as children become more advanced in their learning. The authors explain this by the fact that during the learning process the orthographic structure of learned words increasingly reflects the relationship between the meanings of semantically related words rather than simple grapho-phonological correspondences. The overall model is consistent with the descriptions which show that reading abilities precede the corresponding writing abilities, but that writing is a source of information for reading (Freedman and Calfee, 1984; Goodman and Goodman, 1983).

Taken together with research results which have brought to light the usefulness for spelling of the knowledge gained from reading words (see, for example, Goswami, 1988), this analysis suggests that these two areas of learning must necessarily be initially linked, *writing simultaneously constituting an extended field for the knowledge gained in reading and a tool for the consolidation of this knowledge.* Although these two activities are similar where basic skills are concerned, they are later essentially differentiated by the higher degree of expertise which is required in the activity of writing. In writing, as in reading, one of the essential points seems to be the requirement for exercises to automate low-level processes. The ability, which emerges at an advanced stage, to plan one's text may doubtlessly be prepared for by training focused on entirely explicit spoken discourse (situations of referential communication) and the adaptation of the message to the addressee. The development of the ability to revise the produced texts must be founded on the training in differentiated reading which is suggested above, rereading for revision purposes simply being one particular type of reading among others. An important point here is to teach the subject to distinguish between the intention of the author and the meaning of the message. Throughout this learning process, feedback constitutes one of the most important vectors for progress (Faigley *et al.*, 1985).

As we have specified elsewhere (Gombert, 1988*a*), these suggestions, which have arisen from research into underlying processes, must be evaluated in real-life situations before being pressed into premature service. Such research remains sterile until the ecological validity of its results has been established by vigorous, applied research which goes beyond the bristling defence of pedago-ideological points of view to examine the potential for the reinvestment and pedagogic adaptation of scientifically attested facts.

Chapter 8

The dynamics of metalinguistic development

Introduction

The six preceding chapters have listed and attempted to link the majority of the data concerning metalinguistic development currently available in the associated scientific literature. A simple concern with differentiating the behaviour which reveals a *reflection* on or *intentional monitoring* of language (*metalinguistic behaviour*) from that – earlier – behaviour which, despite manifesting a cognitive activity of monitoring of linguistic representations, lacks any kind of conscious management (*epilinguistic behaviour*) would not in itself constitute a model of metalinguistic development, any more than the simple affirmation of the late emergence of reflection on language when compared with the effective use of language in production and/or comprehension.

The variable nature of this field of study, as well as its relatively recent emergence, mean that the number of models of metalinguistic development which have so far been proposed is low. If we except the outline worked out by Marshall and Morton (1978, see below), then only Karmiloff-Smith (1986, 1987) has risked elaborating a formal model – one, moreover, with a scope which covers the entire field of metacognition. Together with the results examined in the preceding chapters, it is this model which will provide our mainstay when, at the conclusion of this chapter, we, too, attempt this risky enterprise. Before this we shall discuss – or recall – the theoretical positions of various authors and examine the developmental scheme proposed by Karmiloff-Smith in greater detail.

The different conceptions of metalinguistic development

In the overview presented in their 1984 article, Tunmer and Herriman contrasted three points of view concerning the relationship between metalinguistic development and language acquisition. These were the points of view of contemporaneity; the conception of metalinguistic awareness as reflecting, at the level of language, the acquisition of operational thought; and the affirmation of the simple effect of school education.

Early metalinguistic competence

For Clark and Andersen (1979, cited by Tunmer and Grieve, 1984), from the very start of language acquisition, linguistic development requires children to realize that their first productions are inadequate. They must therefore become conscious of their own language errors. This system is thus essentially based on the effect of negative feedback and would therefore both explain linguistic development and make conscious monitoring an indissociable part of this development. The first metalinguistic behaviour would be contemporaneous with the emergence of language and constitute an intentional management component within it (this point of view is shared by E. V. Clark, 1978; Horgan, 1981; Slobin, 1978). In their formalization of this type of system, Marshall and Morton (1978) postulated the existence of a faculty which controls the primary mechanisms of comprehension and production of language. This control module (which Marshall and Morton called EMMA, 'Even More Mysterious Apparatus', and Karmiloff-Smith, 1986, could not resist renaming the 'Eloquent Marshall Morton Aberration'), which is specialized in the detection of errors (a detection which is a prerequisite for their identification and correction), would constitute a true control centre for language activity.

The exercise of this type of control over language does not seem to demand a very high level of reflection. Moreover, the conscious character of the corrective activities is not directly discussed by those who believe in the early existence of metalinguistic activities, but is rather evoked as evidence for this belief. In fact, formal errors, as well as pragmatic inadequacies (Tunmer and Herriman, 1984), are no doubt corrected quasi-automatically when the productions of young speakers do not correspond to what they are trying to say or are not adapted to their context of utterance. This undeniable early language-monitoring behaviour, which is dependent on nonexplicit 'feelings' concerning the inadequacy of the production, does not seem to be of a metalinguistic nature but rather appears to correspond to an epilinguistic functioning which has a very different cognitive status (see below).

Operational reflection on language

Herriman (1986) considers that metalinguistic behaviour is characteristic of a stage of general linguistic development. In this theory, the first stage, that of one- or two-word productions, is thought to last from the age of 8 months to the age of 3. This would be followed by a stage of simple subject-verb-object constructions, which continues until the age of 5–6. Finally, from the age of about 6 onwards, the ability to reflect on language appears, together with the production and comprehension of more complicated syntactic constructions. This type of description is consistent with the conception which sees a relationship between the emergence of metalinguistic competence and the attainment of the stage of concrete operations, both of which reveal the child's new-found ability to monitor its own thought (within this same conceptual framework, J. W. Smith, 1976, links the appearance of more elaborate metalinguistic behaviour, such as the full comprehension of metaphors, to the attainment of formal thought). This analysis is sometimes supported by the identification of statistical correlations between performances in metalinguistic tasks and those corresponding to Piagetian tasks testing the attainment of concrete operations (Hakes, 1980; Tunmer and Fletcher, 1981).

Simple correlations are not sufficient for the affirmation of a causal link between operational and metalinguistic functionings. However, Van Kleeck (1982, 1984) has taken the observation of this contemporaneity as lending support to the hypothesis that it is the ability for decentration and the awareness of reversibility (characteristic of operational functioning) that, on the one hand, permit children to consider language both as a means of conveying meaning and as a separate object and, on the other, allow them to perform comparisons of meanings. The same reasoning has led Flavell (1977, 1978, 1981) to suggest that both metalinguistic awareness and concrete operational thought reflect a more general change in the cognitive abilities: the development of metacognition.

This type of global explanation, which reduces the appearance of a monolithic metalinguistic ability (with the exception of horizontal *décalages*) to a simple manifestation within linguistic processing of the general evolution of thought, now seems obsolete. In effect, even if such a conception does not neglect the facts, its excessive generality strips it of any real explanatory force and thus impairs its heuristic scope.

The effect of learning

Donaldson (1978) thinks that metalinguistic awareness is an effect of learning acquired at school, particularly learning to read. In the preceding chapters we have frequently reported data which show the trigger effect of learning to read on certain metalinguistic functions. However, other data seem to indicate that the chain of causality is, in fact, the other way round. This suggests that an explanation in terms of strictly unidirectional causal links is insufficient to account for the complexity of the facts.

This is not a question of models of development but of general conceptions reflecting different viewpoints. Even if none of these perspectives appears to be acceptable in its entirety, each of them concentrates on an important characteristic which we must take into account in our attempt to develop a model. Unlike the conceptions themselves, these characteristics are not incompatible:

1. *on the appearance of language, or very shortly afterwards, second-level behaviour emerges whose object is, at least in part, the linguistic behaviour belonging to the first level (both in comprehension and production)*;
2. *the majority of the activities which reveal an awareness or intentional monitoring of language first manifest themselves during 'middle childhood', at approximately 6–7 years of age*;
3. *learning at school, in particular the learning of reading, plays a trigger role for certain manifestations of metalinguistic competence.*

As well as these general conceptions, the literature contains an important theoretical analysis which attempts to distinguish between different types of behaviour within the framework of metalinguistic activity. Bialystok (1978, 1979, 1981, 1982, 1986*a*, *b*; Bialystok and Ryan, 1985*a*, *b*), referring primarily to the study of second-language acquisition, has established a distinction between *types of knowledge* and *control of this knowledge*. As far as types of knowledge are concerned, she makes an initial distinction between *implicit knowledge*, which is not available for conscious analysis, and *explicit knowledge*, which can be verbally defended and transmitted. In 1982, Bialystok got rid of the terms 'implicit' and 'explicit' and introduced a description in terms of the *unanalyzed* and the *analyzed* dimensions of knowledge. What we see here, described by means of a new terminology, is the difference between epilinguistic and metalinguistic knowledge. From 1985 onwards (see, in particular, Bialystok and Ryan, 1985*a*), Bialystok insists on the differentiation within the metalinguistic ability of, on the one hand, *the analysis of linguistic knowledge into explicitly structured categories*, and on the other, *the cognitive control of the attentive procedures of selection and processing of specific linguistic information*. She holds that these two aspects are implied in the development of language, from the earliest stage to the most advanced, but that the metalinguistic ability refers solely to a high-level awareness of both of them.

For Bialystok, 'analysis of knowledge' designates the gradual process of structuring linguistic knowledge and the organization which results from it at any period of development. This process is responsible for the transformation of representations which are initially implicit or intuitive into explicit representations. The 'cognitive control of linguistic processing', for its part, refers to the deliberate ability to consider the aspects of language which are relevant for the resolution of a given problem. A high level of intentionality is considered to be an essential factor in the resolution of complicated tasks.

In this model Bialystok assigns the declarative and procedural aspects of metalinguistic awareness to different levels. Moreover, she postulates a relative independence between these two aspects. The analysis of knowledge would be required when the situation of linguistic processing is devoid of the extralinguistic signs which usually make unreflected comprehension or production possible. Control would be necessary when the situation demands that the formal aspects of language are taken into consideration at the expense of its meaning. Menyuk's (1985) commentary on this model emphasizes that the two dimensions differentiated by Bialystok cannot be independent of each other. The analysis of knowledge must necessarily occur at an earlier level of development than the aspect of control, since the awareness of the structural characteristics of language is a prerequisite for their deliberate integration into the subject's control of his or her activities of linguistic processing. Moreover, we consider that a general model should specify the relationship between its components, which does not appear to be the case here. Finally, when we are speaking about development, it is not possible, as Bialystok does, to ignore those elements which are capable of explaining the dynamic of the development itself. If *the reality of two complementary aspects, declarative and procedural, has to be taken into account in the model which we shall propose, then it must also account for the linkage between these two aspects and the evolutionary 'motor'.*

The final theoretical considerations which are relevant to us here are those which address the *décalages* which exist in the field of metalinguistic development between very early behaviour and behaviour which does not appear until later, at school age. Thus Content (1985) has emphasized that although certain judgements of grammaticality, the understanding of metaphors or the detection of semantic ambiguity seem to be late to develop, there is still, at 2 years of age, a certain amount of behaviour which indicates a reflection on language. Van Kleeck (1982) has explained this discontinuity by differentiating between early metalinguistic activity which simply requires the child to focus on a single component of language at any one time (the form or, more often, the content, but never both at the same time) and a more complex, but also later, metalinguistic activity in which both components can be manipulated simultaneously. In other words, young children are very quickly able to focus on language, but either as a communicative tool intended to convey information or as a play object detached from its use in a meaningful communicative context, the two aspects never being considered together in the same activity (Van Kleeck, 1984). In fact, however interesting it might be, this attempted explanation is not supported by the data reported in the preceding chapters. More than just a difference in scope, what distinguishes the early from the later behaviour is the level of conscious control which they require on the part of the subject.

As Pratt and Grieve (1984*a*) have noted, it is necessary for authors to agree on the scope of the term 'metalinguistic awareness' before the debate about the age of emergence of the behaviour designated by it can be productive. We have tried to be clear on this point, proposing, by definition, that the conscious and/or intentional character of the knowledge and/or the control determines whether or not they belong to the field of metalinguistics. As we have tried to show throughout this volume, *the décalage which interests us here is not a horizontal* décalage *between early metalinguistic manifestations in simple tasks and manifestations which appear later because they are oriented towards the comprehension of more complex or more abstract linguistic material. We are interested in the vertical* décalage *between, on the one hand, an intuitive knowledge and functional control of linguistic processing, and, on the other, a reflection and an intentional control.* What characterizes so-called 'early metalinguistic' (for us: *epilinguistic*) behaviour is: the low, and often not specifically linguistic, level of the knowledge it supposes (Kolinsky, 1986); the lack of intentionality (Hakes, 1980); and its interweaving in rich situational contexts (Boutet *et al.*, 1983; Hickmann, 1985; Lefebvre-Pinard, 1985; Vygotsky, 1934).

This last point makes conscious management on the part of the young child implausible. The situations in which epilinguistic behaviour is manifested are richer, and thus more complex, than the experimental situations under which later metalinguistic behaviour is observed. *Simplification through decontextualization, far from advancing the age of success in metalinguistic tasks, makes it impossible for young children to succeed. This suggests that early successes are essentially dependent on a regulation exerted by the situation itself* (this is consistent with Vygotsky's 1934 viewpoint). If this type of behaviour, which is directed by external factors, continues to exist in older children and in adults, then it is augmented by an ability to reflect on language and control its processing (Hakes, 1980).

Of course, this intentional control is necessarily limited to certain aspects of processing. For example, as Levelt *et al.* (1978) have pointed out, neither children nor adults are able to take account of the biological mechanisms at work in their use of language.

According to Vygotsky (1934), language is learned automatically and unconsciously. It is not until a later period that conscious, active control appears. Children

> do not learn new grammatical or syntactic forms at school but, as a result of the teaching of grammar and writing, become conscious of what they are doing and learn to use these skills intentionally. In the same way that children, through learning how to write, realize for the first time that the word *Moscow* is composed of the sounds m-o-s-c-o-w and learn to pronounce them separately, they also learn to construct sentences, to do consciously what they have already done unconsciously when speaking. (Vygotsky, 1934/1962, p. 101)

In this passage, Vygotsky deals with the *décalage* between the automatic application of rules of production and the relatively late consciousness of these rules. It seems possible to see the same type of *décalage* between epilinguistic and metalinguistic behaviour. For example, at a very early age children repair certain grammatical utterances when they repeat them, but it is not until later – probably in part due to explicit tuition – that they become conscious of the rules which they previously respected automatically when making their early repairs (see Chapter 3 above). A frequently cited characteristic of the automatic cognitive processes is their inaccessibility to consciousness (for a detailed discussion of automatic processes v. controlled processes in the treatment of language, see Fayol, 1988*a*). If we transpose what Hakes (1980) has said about comprehension, the inaccessibility of the epilinguistic processes might be seen as a characteristic which differentiates them from the *automated processes*: those which are the result of an automation of intentionally controlled processes (i.e. the metaprocesses) which is effected by means of practice. In contrast to what happens with the epiprocesses, a conscious control can always interrupt these automated processes if an obstacle is encountered during the performance of the activity, or if the subject decides to pay particular attention to the task which has to be accomplished. We shall return to this difference later.

The seemingly undeniable existence of vertical *décalages* does not exclude the possibility of horizontal *décalages*. Flavell and Wellman (1977) think it possible that abilities might emerge successively within the framework of metacognition, the meta-abilities related to easily perceived external objects being the earliest to appear. Thus the appearance of metalanguage would precede that of metamemory. In the same way – although they disagree about the order of emergence – Rozin and Gleitman (1977) and Nesdale and Tunmer (1984) think that although most of the metalinguistic competences (metaphonological, metalexical, metasyntactic, metasemantic, metapragmatic) are acquired between the ages of 4 and 8, some of them appear at an earlier age than others. This seems to be a very speculative affirmation. In fact, the existence of *décalages* between the different subfields of the metalinguistic competence supposes that each of these subfields is homogeneous, both in so far as the cognitive processes at work are concerned and in the factors bearing on the complexity of the tasks which derive from them. We consider that this is far from being proved. In contrast, much of the data reported in the preceding chapters points to the existence of horizontal *décalages* at the very heart of the metalinguistic subfields themselves. The complexity and level of abstraction of the tasks sometimes causes discontinuities of several years between the ages at which success is first achieved.

The existence of vertical and horizontal décalages *must therefore be integrated into the model, along with a clear differentiation between the early epiprocesses and the late automated processes.*

We thus possess a set of anchor points for the elaboration of a model of metalinguistic development. What is lacking is a guiding thread and an explanation of what it is that determines the dynamics of this development. These central elements may be found in the model gradually developed since 1979 by Karmiloff-Smith.

The Karmiloff-Smith model

The model elaborated by Karmiloff-Smith has appeared in a number of publications (Karmiloff-Smith, 1979*a*, *b*, 1983, 1985, 1986, 1987). However, the final two accounts are the most detailed, and these will serve as the principal basis for *our reading* of this model.

Taking as her target the Marshall and Morton model (1978; see above), Karmiloff-Smith criticized the explanations of development which see the child's attempt to get beyond the errors it has made as being the principal motor of evolution ('failure-driven' models: Karmiloff-Smith, 1986). These conceptions assign a principal role to negative feedback, which stimulates the subject to a more elaborate functioning that brings with it a higher level of success. Even though this type of explanation can be used to describe the temporary, local rearrangements which are effected during the course of an activity, the author considers that it cannot under any circumstances be applied to macrodevelopmental change. The main argument used by Karmiloff-Smith is based on the observation that *the progression from a level of cognitive functioning to a more elaborate level takes place when the child, who has become skilful in the control of the cognitive tools of the initial level, encounters only a low failure rate in its cognitive undertakings*. This argument makes it difficult to attribute a determining role to negative feedback. At a simpler level, it can also be argued that if it were failure alone that determined cognitive progress, then the influence of the attempts at comprehension intended to bring about success would mean that we would be most 'knowledgeable' about the fields in which we are the least skilful (and thus most often confronted with failure) – which, to say the least, is at odds with the facts.

Arguing against the conceptions presented above, Karmiloff-Smith asserted that the fundamental prerequisite for macrodevelopmental change is success – that is to say, the confirmation of the success of the actions undertaken, communicated by means of positive feedback. The behavioural changes relating to one particular activity within one level of development would be determined by both positive and negative feedback. A link between the processes which consolidate current functioning and those which motivate the progression to increasingly elaborate functions is proposed by the author, who first describes the types of cognitive representations which characterize successive levels of functioning. Karmiloff-Smith has identified four of these:

1. *Implicit knowledge*: This knowledge underlies the young child's first linguistic competences. It is the cognitive correspondent of early linguistic actions. The items composing this knowledge, which can be inferred from the totality of procedures in which they are involved, are juxtaposed despite the possible presence of common elements – elements which cannot under any circumstances be activated in isolation.

2. *Primary explicit knowledge*: The result of an internal reorganization of

implicit knowledge. The items of knowledge are no longer simply juxtaposed but are interlinked around their shared elements. This knowledge, which is not accessible to conscious analysis, is structured in terms of the same representational code (kinaesthetic, spatial, temporal, linguistic . . .) as the implicit knowledge from which it derives.

3. *Secondary explicit knowledge*: While perpetuating the same representational code as the primary knowledge which it succeeds, this knowledge is accessible to the subject's consciousness.

4. *Tertiary explicit knowledge*: This knowledge results from the recoding of secondary knowledge in a more abstract code. Whatever the initial mode of coding, it is generally possible for this knowledge to be encoded linguistically, and it is thus capable of verbalization.

If we restrict the discussion to metalinguistic development, then, in the vocabulary we have been using, implicit knowledge is characteristic of the first linguistic skills, primary knowledge underlies epilinguistic activity and secondary and tertiary knowledge are implicated in metalinguistic activity in the strict sense of the term. Our general conception thus corresponds, apart from differences of terminology, to that of Karmiloff-Smith. In fact, this author does not restrict the notion of 'meta' to acts of conscious access, and this leads her to consider that primary knowledge is available for metaprocedural functioning without – in contrast to secondary and tertiary knowledge – being accessible to the subject's consciousness. As Karmiloff-Smith has been careful to define her terms clearly, the use to which she puts them is perfectly legitimate. However, our own choice of concepts (differentiation between 'epi' and 'meta') seems to us to have the advantage of allowing us to distinguish better between functionings whose cognitive determinants are different both in nature and in level of elaboration.

To describe the dynamics of development, Karmiloff-Smith has proposed a three-phase recursive model but has specified that there is not necessarily any contemporaneity between the various aspects of the awareness of language. Thus a given child might be at phase 1 for certain syntactic aspects but at phase 2 or 3 for certain phonological aspects or other syntactic aspects.

1. The first phase is seen as having two main characteristics:

(a) The production of a particular linguistic form is essentially dependent on external factors.

(b) The different representations (implicit knowledge) corresponding to the different linguistic forms are stored in memory independently of one another.

In fact, the child establishes a one-to-one correspondence between each of the particular linguistic forms and certain of their extralinguistic contexts of use (the existence of multiple functions for the same form leads to the storage of multiple pairs independently of one another), the reference model being that provided by the adult. The successful establishment of a correspondence between condition and action leads to its storage in memory. The development of the linguistic system during this phase is thus motivated by the aims of behavioural success (not the objective of economy in the use of cognitive tools). The end of this phase is characterized by a procedural success. From then on, the child's productions are similar to those of the adult and thus provoke no further negative feedback. The stability of the system, demonstrated by the continual positive feedback, gives the signal for the representational change which is characteristic of phase 2 and makes possible an internal monitoring of potential inconsistencies, redundancies or conflicts amongst the representations stored in memory.

2. In the second phase, the motor for development is the search for a control of the internal organization of the implicit knowledge accumulated during phase 1. A translation of this implicit knowledge into primary explicit knowledge ensues. This organization, which is conducted under the influence of endogenous factors, makes it possible to substitute multifunctional forms for the initial mass of unifunctional form–function pairs. The end of this phase, which is characterized by the low level of influence exerted by external factors, is revealed by 'unconscious metaprocedural' successes ('epiprocedural' in our terminology). However, because the progression to explicit knowledge is accompanied by a loss of information, and because metaprocedural management can prove a greater cognitive burden than the automatic activation of a form when the context strictly associated with it arises, errors and approximations are more common during this phase than during the preceding one. It is in this way that Karmiloff-Smith explains the U-curves frequently observed in the evolution of linguistic and other performances in children (see, for example, Bowerman, 1982*a*, *b*; Karmiloff-Smith, 1979*a*, *b*).

3. During the third phase, the links established during the second phase are reconsidered in the light of external stimuli. It is at this point that conscious access becomes possible (appearance of secondary and tertiary explicit knowledge). However, Karmiloff-Smith does not make any pronouncements as to the obligatory or optional character of access in this phase.

One of the examples given by Karmiloff-Smith (1985, 1986) is that of the acquisition of the indefinite article in French. During phase 1, children store a large number of form–function pairs in memory, the correct usage being reinforced by positive feedback. In phase 2 the links between the different pairs are constructed in such a way that the same form (indefinite article) is brought into a relationship with its different functions (in particular, the function of nonspecific reference and the function of numeration). This organization can lead to certain errors. For example, children continue to use the indefinite article for a nonspecific reference, but add a partitive to indicate the function of numeration (*'un de mouchoir'* – 'one of handkerchief'). This type of error disappears during phase 3, at the end of which the articles form a system which can be progressively linked with the other noun determiners, the speaker then being able to choose from the entire selection.

One of Karmiloff-Smith's objectives was to go beyond the classical dichotomies (implicit/explicit, procedural/declarative, unconscious/conscious, etc.) which have proved inadequate to account for the complexity of the processes leading to conscious access. However, for her it is not a question of simply replacing a redundant general developmental model with a Piagetian description of structural development. The three phases described above are not general stages of cognitive development, nor are they levels within the evolution of specific fields. *They are recursive cycles of processes which repeat themselves for each aspect of the linguistic system during overall development* (it is thus pointless to try to find an age corresponding to each of these phases) and whose effect is augmented, according to Karmiloff-Smith, by the constraints which innate linguistic universals exert on processing at the beginning of language acquisition. Finally, the author predicts the possibility of automating certain linguistic choices by postulating, in addition to the existence of innate modules (see Fodor, 1983), the existence of a late modularization of certain aspects of language which have attained the level of explicit representation. These aspects correspond to the obligatory choices which follow the initial choice of a discursive marker (for example, the various morpho-syntactic components of the passive form). This late modularization would explain the (in our opinion, relative) unavailability of these choices for conscious analysis.

Even though we are convinced of the very great explanatory power of this model – it will constitute the framework of our explanation of metalinguistic development – we have rather more reservations concerning two points: on the one hand, its recursive character; on the other, the strict alternation it postulates between the awareness of exogenous and endogenous factors.

To postulate the recursive nature of developmental cycles is to impose the determination of laws which preside over the chaining of successive cycles or, at least, the linking of partly contemporaneous cycles. In fact, rather than recursive cycles, Karmiloff-Smith seems to be talking about isomorphic, but mutually independent, cycles. More precisely – seeing that a strict independence in the evolution of the control of adjoining microaspects of language (for example, systems of definite and indefinite noun determiners) is very unlikely – the model just presented must be considered as a stage in the construction of a more elaborate model which presents a more integrated analysis of language development. We are not yet in a position to engage in this type of heuristic progression. In fact, Karmiloff-Smith seems to have undertaken a bottom–up construction which starts with the cell in order to try to explain the system, whereas we have set out in the opposite direction, starting with a global view in order to come to an ever more detailed analysis. Although they are complementary, these two types of approach still have a long way to go before they are reconciled.

Furthermore, the strict succession of periods during which external factors are fundamental and others in which they are largely ineffective also raises problems. In fact, this type of model makes it necessary to postulate the existence in the subject of a specialized stability detector for every microaspect of language which would, when activated at the end of the first phase, trigger the translation of implicit knowledge into explicit knowledge and thus open the way for 'metaprocedural' organization (to remain faithful to Karmiloff-Smith's terminology). Perhaps such detectors do exist, but this is (and will doubtless remain) difficult to establish. It is possible to propose another hypothesis that envisages the interaction of the developmental cycles which, with the exception of any *décalage*, coexist at any given moment.

When, at the end of the first phase, a particular linguistic subsystem is operative and functioning efficiently, its functioning remains stable as long as the child's productions remain unchanged. A simple increase in the length of the produced utterances necessitates an organization of the representations to ensure the possibility of interaction with related linguistic subsystems which are now increasingly likely to co-occur with the first. For example, good, early functional awareness of the deictic use of the articles will be called into question, as the length of the produced utterances increases, by the encoding of new form–function pairs which correspond to the anaphoric uses. Thus the triggering of the second phase for a particular subsystem might be provoked by a destabilization of the responses automated during the first phase. Even if the ensuing reorganization is essentially endogenous in nature, it is still subject to the influence of exogenous factors involved in the triggering of a new cycle for a related subsystem which is complementary to the first.

Lastly, knowledge of whether final access to consciousness is obligatory or optional is an important point which, in our view, should not be relegated to the background.

A 'model' of metalinguistic development in the child

Using the Karmiloff-Smith model as a basis, and taking account of the other ideas and data reported throughout this volume, we postulate a metalinguistic development over four successive phases. Each aspect of language (aspects whose scope we are currently unable to specify) is affected by this development in a way which is *initially* independent of (and not necessarily contemporaneous with) the other aspects. Finally, only the first two phases are obligatory in nature. The first phase corresponds to *the acquisition of the first linguistic skills*, the second to *the acquisition of epilinguistic control*, the third to *the acquisition of metalinguistic awareness*, and the last to *the automation of the metaprocesses*.

1. The acquisition of the first linguistic skills

This first phase is identical on all points with the first phase of the Karmiloff-Smith model. The first linguistic skills are established on the basis of the model provided by the adult, with negative and positive feedback allowing inadequate productions to be eliminated and the others reinforced. This leads to the storage in memory of a multiplicity of unifunctional pairs which establish a correspondence between a particular linguistic form and each of the pragmatic contexts in which it has consistently been positively reinforced. At the end of this phase, the uses to which the linguistic form concerned is put are thus close to those of the adult (although simplified in conformity with the characteristics of the models presented; compare the idea of 'format': Bruner, 1983). This constitutes an initial level of automation of linguistic behaviour. However, two points need to be dealt with in greater detail.

First of all, this acquisition of the first skills does not concern production only but processing in its entirety, both in production and in comprehension. The feedback relating to production concerns the utterances' conformity to the model provided by the adult. As far as comprehension is concerned, it is the adequacy of the child's response that gives rise to positive or negative reinforcement. *This response is never interpretative but simply an action* (behavioural and/or linguistic). In comprehension, as in production, the implicit knowledge used by the child at this level is thus always procedural in nature. The dichotomy between declarative and procedural is therefore irrelevant here.

Next, it is in a metaphorical sense that we can affirm that each of the particular linguistic forms is associated with its context of occurrence. What the child stores in memory is a sound configuration which probably embraces a number of linguistic forms and meanings which frequently coexist in a short segment of the speech chain.

It is when the stability gained in the first phase is cast into doubt by the increased length and complexity of the models provided by the adult and the length of the child's own productions that the reorganization which is characteristic of the second phase is triggered. The simple increase in the size of the segments of the speech chain which have to be taken into account has two consequences. In the first place, this increase makes possible the appearance of new functions for the forms previously associated with certain contexts (in particular, the appearance of discursive functions). In the second place, as the new functions generally interact with the first, the number of bi–univocal form–function pairs – or, more precisely, of sound configuration-context pairs – increases to such an extent that it threatens the simple 'practicality' of the initial functioning.

On this point, our model differs from the one proposed by Karmiloff-Smith. Although behavioural success and the ensuing repetition of positive feedback mark the end of the first phase, they are not sufficient to trigger the start of the second. In fact, the determining factor here is the reappearance of negative feedback (which may be implicit and simply consist of failures of or difficulties in communication).

We share Karmiloff-Smith's opinion that macrodevelopmental change cannot be adequately explained by the simple effect of the child's attempts to get beyond the failures experienced in its successive modes of functioning. A determining role here is played by success. However, we think that at the time of the transition from the first to the second phase, this role is concerned not with stimulating progress to a higher level of functioning but with consolidating the current level. This consolidation is a prerequisite for the appearance of a destabilization (which supposes a prior stability), and it is this which determines the increasing reorganization of knowledge. Seen from this perspective, the reappearance of errors where previous linguistic behaviour was always correctly adapted is thus not (*or at least not solely*) the consequence of the progression to a higher level of cognitive functioning but is rather partly the cause of it. These errors occur because, *in contrast to what an overly local analysis seems to suggest, the child is required to resolve increasingly complex problems of communication* as the model with which it is provided increasingly requires the interaction of different linguistic forms.

2. The acquisition of epilinguistic control

As in the Karmiloff-Smith model, this second phase corresponds to an organization of the implicit knowledge accumulated during the initial period. It reveals itself as a substitution of multifunctional forms for the initial multitude of form–function pairs. However, our conception differs from the Karmiloff-Smith model on a number of points.

First of all, in our model the motor of development is not just the control of the internal organization of knowledge acquired during phase 1 but also, because of this organization, the creation of a possibility of linking this knowledge to other, new knowledge concerning the same forms or forms frequently associated with those which are in the course of being organized. This new knowledge is acquired as a result of the enrichment of the models provided by the adult and the increase in the scope of the speech chain taken into account by the child (or the precision of the analysis applied by the child to the verbal segments it considers).

Secondly, the extralinguistic context of the linguistic processing performed by the child has a very important role to play here. The general process at work during this phase is an internal linking of the implicit knowledge which leads to a functional (i.e. unreflected) awareness of a system. Nevertheless, the construction of the rules for the use of the linguistic form concerned is determined by, and affects, the real and thus contextualized uses of these forms.

Thus, for instance, the epilinguistic detection of ungrammatical utterances may be dependent on two factors. The child may be alerted by the dissonance of the utterance, a dissonance which is not absolute but relative to the context of utterance. The control process here is partly dependent on the contexts which have already been encountered by the child, and particularly on those contexts to which the current situation is functionally assimilated. The second possibility is the child's inability to understand the perceived utterance. This equates to the impossibility of retrieving from memory a linguistic organization which is capable of activating a representation in a context comparable to the present one.

In the same way, epilinguistic other-repairs and self-repairs are incidental to the wording (or rewording) of the meaning perceived (or desired) by the child. This process leads to a verbal production adapted to the current context and is identical to the process which determines the adaptation of the young child's productions to the characteristics of their context of utterance (for example, the characteristics of the interlocutor).

With the establishment of a system of rules of use for the linguistic form concerned, the child gradually acquires the ability to refer implicitly to a prototypical context as this phase progresses. This context, which corresponds to the common denominator of the real contexts which occur most frequently (or are most striking) in connection with this form, can serve as a reference point when the current context is unfamiliar (in particular, in formal experimental situations). This elaboration of a stable pragmatic reference point for each linguistic form is the principal characteristic of the second phase of our model. This stability marks the end of the second phase and allows subjects a type of top–down control of the linguistic processing they apply. However, consciousness of the system of rules constructed in this way is not gained automatically and becomes effective only after a metacognitive effort which is not manifested until it becomes required. As epilinguistic control is stable and effective in the management of everyday verbal exchanges, fresh external stimuli are necessary if this consciousness is to be gained. The 'metalinguistic competence' of which we have occasionally spoken as a prerequisite for the learning of certain abilities (see Chapters 2 and 7) corresponds to this *stable epilinguistic control*. This functional control marks the end of the second phase, during which the epilinguistic behaviour which controls language activities applies rules which become increasingly general in scope and which progressively constitute a system.

As 'unconscious declarative knowledge' can manifest itself only in the subject's actions (it cannot be described verbally), the distinction between declarative and procedural knowledge again seems to be irrelevant at this level.

3. The acquisition of metalinguistic awareness

In contrast to what happens at the end of the first phase, the progression to this level of functioning is linked not to a questioning of a preexistent stability but to a necessity for an intentional control of the stability acquired at the end of the second phase. This explains the optional character of access to this level of functioning. As much of the research reported in this volume (in particular the research conducted among illiterate adults) has suggested, the subject becomes aware in a 'meta' (i.e. conscious) sense only of those aspects of language which *have to be* apprehended in such a way if the new linguistic tasks demanded of him or her are to be accomplished.

In fact, a command of reading and writing *necessitates* the conscious knowledge and intentional control of numerous aspects of language (see the preceding chapter). In our societies it thus plays a trigger role in the appearance of metalinguistic awareness. However, that there are other factors which can play this role is shown by results obtained following formal metalinguistic training in the spoken language conducted before the subjects had started to learn to read and write. In this case, early metalinguistic awareness seems to facilitate the acquisition of abilities which, being necessary to this awareness, then stimulate it in their turn. This facilitation process probably follows a lightening of the workload during learning. Children who are already able to analyze language consciously can devote their activities to learning the rules for the use of written language.

The absolute prerequisite for this consciousness is epilinguistic control. Only that which has already been mastered at a functional level can be so at a conscious level.

The consequence of the nonobligatory (i.e. determined not by maturational factors but by external factors whose occurrence is not systematic) character of the acquisition of metalinguistic awareness is that certain aspects of language are very probably never submitted to this level of control. To give an example, it is not difficult to imagine that for many individuals, the formal modifications made to productions as a function of the characteristics of the interlocutor are never the object of conscious awareness and thus remain at an epilinguistic level.

As conscious management imposes a high cognitive burden, the subject does not become consciously aware of everything simultaneously. The complexity of the systems in question, their frequency in the language and their usefulness in new tasks which need to be resolved thus give rise to horizontal *décalages* in the appearance of metalinguistic awareness of them.

Finally, at the level of conscious cognitive effort, the distinction between declarative knowledge and procedural knowledge becomes meaningful. It is one thing to know the rules which preside over the formal organization of language, but it is quite another to know how to control their application deliberately. In the light of Menyuk's (1985) common-sense argument ('we cannot use knowledge which we do not have'), we think that declarative metalinguistic knowledge precedes metalinguistic control and the application of this knowledge.

4. The automation of the metaprocesses

It is clear that 'meta' functioning imposes a high cognitive burden, and we know that we do not always control our linguistic processing consciously. To a great extent, this fact is linked to the automation of metalinguistic processes (i.e. the metaprocesses).

In a more general discussion of metacognition, the same point of view is defended by Borkowski *et al.* (1987), who consider automation to be the final state in the repeated use of metacognitive strategies. In the same way, Sternberg (1986) thinks that, for the expert confronted with familiar tasks, the role of the executive system is limited to the recognition of the automatic processes which are likely to be required. In fact, the metalinguistic functions which are automated are those whose use has frequently been seen to be effective.

In contrast to what Karmiloff-Smith says about 'belated encapsulated modules', it is possible to think of automated metaprocesses as always being available to conscious access (which differentiates them from the – equally automatic – epiprocesses). But this (more or less straightforward) return to a 'meta' functioning is not effected unless an obstacle is encountered while the activity is being performed or the subject decides to pay particular attention to the task which is to be accomplished.

There are therefore two types of automatic process: the epiprocesses and the automated processes. In both cases the cognitive effort is applied unconsciously, but the automated processes, in contrast to the epiprocesses, can always be replaced by metaprocesses if an obstacle impairs the automatic functioning of linguistic processing.

Even if the four-phase cycle proposed here does not constitute a system of general stages, the studies reported in the preceding chapters nevertheless allow us to make some observations concerning the age of access. Whatever the subfield of metalinguistic development concerned, it is at about 6–7 years of age that the first 'meta' functionings are generally identified, and it is only rarely that the various types of training can provoke such functioning before the age of 5. We therefore think that the first stable epilinguistic controls do not appear before the end of the fifth year. The majority of these controls are acquired at between 5 and 6 years of age, and starting to learn to read is the factor which triggers the progression to metalinguistic functioning. Although the first epilinguistic functionings (at the start of phase 2) are not contemporaneous with the start of language acquisition, they emerge very soon after its appearance, as soon as the first stabilized linguistic skills are called into question by the awareness of longer and more complex adult models.

Chapter 9

Conclusion

The radical empirical reductionism of the behaviourists, which considers that all behaviour can be analyzed as a set of reflexes, holds the concept of *consciousness* to be scientifically useless. Very early in its development, this conception was denounced by psychologists such as Janet or Vygotsky, for whom consciousness constituted an object of research as a particular item of behaviour which, during development, is progressively superimposed on elementary behaviour. In contrast to what might be thought, this debate is not obsolete and, as may be imagined, is of interest to the researcher who uses the conscious character of behaviour as a criterion for the differentiation between behaviour of the type 'meta' and that of the type 'epi'.

For us there is much at stake here. What we want to know is no more and no less than whether metalinguistic development is a legitimate object of study for the cognitive psychologist. More than simply a question of principle, the reluctance of numerous cognitivists to recognize the relevance of identifying a conscious level in processing is linked to concerns of a methodological order. In fact, as Fowler (1986) has indicated, despite being a fundamental fact of human nature which psychologists must try to understand, consciousness does not offer itself readily to experimental study. This is also the position of Fodor (1983), who has suggested that consciousness might be associated with a central processor whose nonmodular nature makes scientific investigation impossible. In fact, proof of subjects' consciousness of the cognitive operations which they perform in order to attain a particular goal has classically been seen in their ability to report these operations verbally. This is clearly a weak indication of consciousness since, on the one hand, nonverbalization constitutes insufficient grounds to establish lack of consciousness and, on the other, the possibility of reconstructing a plausible behavioural sequence *a posteriori* makes it possible to give a subsequent verbal rendition of processing which was performed unconsciously. However, that this indication still retains a certain level of validity is suggested by a variety of studies which point to a correspondence between verbalizations at the end of an activity and the modifications observed during processing by the subject (see, in particular, some of the experiments cited in Chapters 6 and 7). Moreover, as we have tried to do ourselves (Gombert and Boudinet, 1988), it is possible to establish the probability that the processing is unconscious in nature by showing that the behaviour observed in the resolution of a task thought to require conscious control (for example, a task of grammatical correction) does not differ from the behaviour caused by related tasks which prescribe a control whose expected behavioural effect is the opposite of that predicted for the first task (for example, a task requiring the literal repetition of the same ungrammatical sentences used in the first task; see Chapter 3).

As Latto and Campion (1986) have suggested, it is necessary to distinguish between theoretical and experimental levels of discourse. For reasons of psychological validity, it is necessary to incorporate consciousness into certain models of information processing. However, at the experimental level we have to rely on observable behaviour, of which verbalizations form a part.

Beyond the practicability of the study of consciousness, there is also the problem of its usefulness. Behaviourist thinking, which sees consciousness as an epiphenomenon, denies that it has any. While recognizing that certain mental processes and contents are accessible to consciousness, the authors who have pursued this line of thinking consider that the conscious nature of processes does not affect their execution, which would be identical whether the processes are conscious or not. No one should be surprised to learn that we do not share this point of view. In particular, it seems to us to be difficult not to recognize the possibility of modifying the course of an activity in response to the conscious monitoring of the different stages of the resolution of a problem, and the possibility of deliberate choices being made before and during resolution as a result of reflection. This leads us to believe in the functions of direction and selection which can be exercised by consciousness (see Johnson-Laird, 1983).

It is probably best to follow Piaget (see, in particular, 1974*a*, *b*) and pose the question in terms of degrees or levels of consciousness rather than address it as a dichotomy. The lowest level would then be that of the automatic processes, with the higher levels corresponding to an ever greater measure of control. Moreover, this makes it possible for processes occupying different levels of consciousness to coexist within the same activity (see Fraisse, 1987). Here again, the affirmation risks having only a theoretical validity. In fact, although it is dangerous to try to demonstrate the conscious character of an activity, it is even more so to try to establish experimentally either the degree of consciousness which it implies or the transient nature of this consciousness. However, affirming the existence of degrees of consciousness does have the merit of directly raising the question of how this consciousness is acquired. We agree with Levelt *et al.* (1978) in thinking that consciousness is implicit knowledge which has become explicit. This is the case with the difference between knowledge which is 'epi' and knowledge which is 'meta', the former clearly being a prerequisite for the latter.

One of the principal justifications for our affirmation of the existence of a vertical *décalage* between early epilinguistic control and later metalinguistic control is the usefulness of this distinction for the learner. In support of the position held by Mandler and Nakumura (1987), we are convinced that consciousness is frequently involved in learning and that although not all learning is necessarily conscious in nature (cf. the classical distinction between intentional and incidental learning), the acquisition and restructuring of knowledge generally requires the conscious participation of the subject. The explanation of procedures, an approach often used by teachers, can be useful for learning only if the child is capable of a conscious management of its attempts to complete tasks. Such explanations would be useless if they concerned knowledge which had not yet attained the level of stable epicognitive control and could not therefore under any circumstances attain metacognitive status. In such a case, the teacher's action must aim at the establishment and stabilization of the corresponding epicognitive knowledge. This is essentially performed by means of the manipulation of objects (linguistic objects being the ones which interest us here) whose rules of functioning correspond to the rules which will later have to be mastered at a conscious level. It is by means of these manipulations that the child is brought to a functional awareness which is indispensable for the effectiveness of the efforts which will later focus on comprehension.

Undoubtedly these general principles correspond to a number of effective intuitive practices. Moreover, they are currently insufficiently operationalized to be always taken into account in a considered way which is adapted to individual situations. These insufficiencies indicate the direction our research must take. Fundamental research must validate models of metalinguistic functioning and metalinguistic development rather than accumulate isolated data whose significance is difficult to measure. It is the task of applied research to gauge the pedagogic consequences of the functioning which has been brought to light, and to evaluate its potential applications.

Bibliography

Ackerman, B.P. (1986), 'Children's sensitivity to comprehension failure in interpreting a nonliteral use of an utterance', *Child Development*, *57*, 485–97.

^Adam, J.-M. (1984), *Le récit*, Paris: PUF.

Alegria, J., Morais, J. (1979), 'Le développement de l'habileté d'analyse phonétique consciente de la parole et l'apprentissage de la lecture', *Archives de Psychologie*, *47*, 251–70.

Alegria, J., Pignot, E., Morais, J. (1982), 'Phonetic analysis of speech and memory codes in beginning readers', *Memory and Cognition*, *10*, 451–6.

Ammon, P. (1981), 'Communication skills and communicative competence: A neoPiagetian process-structural view', *in* W.P. Dickson (ed.), *Children's Oral Communication Skills*, New York: Academic Press.

Andersen, E. (1977), 'Young children's knowledge of role-related speech differences: A mommy is not a daddy is not a baby', *Papers and Reports on Child Language Development*, *13*, 83–90.

Asch, S., Nerlove, H. (1960), 'The development of double function terms in children', *in* B. Kaplan and W. Warpner (eds), *Perspective in Psychological Theory*, New York: International Universities Press.

Asher, S.R. (1978), 'Referential communication', *in* C.J. Whitehurst and B.J. Zimmerman (eds), *The Functions of Language and Cognition*, New York: Academic Press.

Axia, G., Baroni, M.R. (1985), 'Linguistic politeness at different age levels', *Child Development*, *56*, 918–27.

Backman, J., Bruck, M., Hebert, M., Seidenberg, M.S. (1984), 'Acquisition and use of spelling–sound correspondences in reading', *Journal of Experimental Child Psychology*, *38*, 114–33.

Bagget, P. (1979), 'Structurally equivalent stories in movie and text and the effect of the medium on recall', *Journal of Vergal Learning and Verbal Behavior*, *18*, 333–56.

Baker, L. (1979), 'Comprehension monitoring: Identifying and coping with text confusions', *Journal of Reading Behavior*, *11*, 365–74.

Baker, L. (1984a), 'Children's effective use of multiple standards for evaluating their comprehension', *Journal of Educational Psychology*, *76*, 588–97.

Baker, L. (1984b), 'Spontaneous versus instructed use of multiple standards for evaluating comprehension: Effects of age, reading proficiency, and type of standard', *Journal of Experimental Child Psychology*, *38*, 289–311.

Baker, L. (1985), 'How do we know when we don't understand? Standards for evaluating text comprehension', *in* D.L. Forrest-Pressley, G.E. MacKinnon and T.G. Waller (eds), *Metacognition, Cognition, and Human Performance*, vol. 1, New York: Academic Press.

Baker, L., Anderson, R.I. (1982), 'Effects of inconsistent information on text processing: Evidence for comprehension monitoring', *Reading Research Quarterly*, *17*, 281–94.

Barret, M.D. (1983), 'The early acquisition and development of the meanings of action-related words', *in* T.B. Seilers and W. Wannenmacher (eds), *Concept Development and the Development of Word Meaning*, Berlin: Springer-Verlag.

Barrie-Blackley, S. (1973), 'Six-year-old children's understanding of sentences adjoined with time adverbs', *Journal of Psychological Research*, *2*, 153–65.

Barron, R.W. (1986), 'Word recognition in early reading: A review of the direct and indirect access hypotheses', *Cognition*, *24*, 93–119.

Bartlett, E.J. (1982), 'Learning to revise: Some component processes', *in* M. Nystrand (ed.), *What Writers Know: The language, process, and structure of written discourse*, New York: Academic Press.

Barton, D. (1985), 'Awareness of language units in adults and children', *in* A.W. Ellis (ed.), *Progress in the Psychology of Language*, vol. 1, Hillsdale, NJ: Erlbaum.

Bassano, D., Champaud, C., Hickmann, M. (1988), *Statement Modalities in Reported Speech by French Children*, 3rd ISSBD European Conference on Developmental Psychology, Budapest.

Bates, E. (1976), *Language and Context: The acquisition of pragmatics*, New York: Academic Press.

Bates, E. (1979), *The Emergence of Symbols: Cognition and communication in infancy*, New York: Academic Press.

Beal, C.R., Flavell, J.H. (1982), 'Effect of increasing the salience of message ambiguities on kindergarteners' evaluations of communicative success and message adequacy', *Developmental Psychology*, *18*, 43–8.

Beal, C.R., Flavell, J.H. (1983), 'Comprehension in a referential communication task', *Child Development*, *54*, 148–53.

Beal, C.R., Flavell, J.H. (1984), 'Development of the ability to distinguish communicative intention and literal message meaning', *Child Development*, *55*, 920–8.

Bearison, D.J., Levey, L.M. (1977), 'Children's comprehension of referential communication: Decoding ambiguous messages', *Child Development*, *48*, 716–20.

Beaudichon, J. (1982), *La communication sociale chez l'enfant*, Paris: PUF.

Beaudichon, J., Sirgurdsson, T., Trelles, C. (1978), 'Etude chez l'enfant de l'adaptation verbale à l'interlocuteur lors de la communication', *Psychologie française*, *23*, 213–20.

Becker, J.A., Smenner, P.C. (1986), 'The spontaneous use of *thank you* by preschoolers as a function of sex, socioeconomic status, and listener status', *Language in Society*, *15*, 537–46.

Beilin, H. (1975), *Studies in the Cognitive Basis of Language Development*, New York: Academic Press.

Benveniste, E. (1974), *Problèmes de linguistique générale*, vol. 2, Paris: Gallimard.

Bereiter, C., Scardamalia, M. (1986), 'Levels of inquiry into the nature of expertise in writing', *in* E.Z. Rothkopf (ed.), *Review of Research in Education*, vol. 13, Washington, DC: American Educational Research Association.

Berger, C. (1980), 'Self-consciousness and the study of interpersonal attraction', *in* H. Gites, P. Robinson and P. Smith (eds), *Language: Social psychological perspectives*, Oxford: Pergamon Press.

Berkenkotter, C. (1983), 'Decisions and revisions: The planning strategies of a publishing writer', *College Composition and Communication*, *34*, 156–69.

Berko, J. (1958), 'The child learning of English morphology', *Word*, *14*, 150–77.

Bernicot, J. (1988), *Linguistic Forms of Request: Children's metapragmatic knowledge*, Université Paris 5, internally circulated document, personal communication.

Bernicot, J., Legros, S. (1987*a*), 'Direct and indirect derectives: What do young children understand?', *Journal of Experimental Child Psychology*, *43*, 346–58.

Bernicot, J., Legros, S. (1987*b*), 'La compréhension des demandes par les enfants de 3 à 8 ans: les demandes directes et les demandes indirectes non conventionnelles', *Cahiers de Psychologie cognitive*, *7*, 267–93.

Bernstein, D.K. (1986), 'The development of humor: Implications for assessment and intervention', *Topics in Language Disorders*, *6*, 65–71.

Bertelson, P. (1986), 'The onset of literacy: Liminal remarks', *Cognition*, *24*, 1–30.

Berthoud, I., Sinclair, H. (1978), 'L'expression d'éventualités et de conditions chez l'enfant', *Archives de Psychologie*, *46*, 205–33.

Berthoud-Papandropoulou, I. (1978), 'An experimental study of children's ideas about language', *in* A. Sinclair, R.J. Jarvella and W.J.M. Levelt (eds), *The Child's Conception of Language*, Berlin: Springer-Verlag.

Berthoud-Papandropoulou, I. (1980), *La réflexion métalinguistique chez l'enfant*, Geneva: Imprimerie Nationale.

Berthoud-Papandropoulou, I., Sinclair, A. (1983), 'Meaningful or meaningless: Children's judgments', *in* T.B. Seilers and W. Wannenmacher (eds), *Concept Development and the Development of Word Meaning*, Berlin: Springer-Verlag.

Bertoncini, J. (1984), 'L'équipement initial pour la perception de la parole', *in* M. Moscato and G. Piéraut-Le Bonniec (eds), *Le langage, construction et actualisation*, Rouen: Publications de l'Université de Rouen.

Bertoncini, J., Mehler, J. (1981), 'Syllables as units in infants' speech perception', *Infant Behavior and Development*, *4*, 247–60.

Bialystok, E. (1978), 'A theoretical model of second language learning', *Language Learning*, *28*, 69–83.

Bialystok, E. (1979), 'Explicit and implicit judgements of L2 grammaticality', *Language Learning*, *29*, 81–103.

Bialystok, E. (1981), 'The role of linguistic knowledge in second language use', *Studies in Second Language Acquisition*, *4*, 31–45.

Bialystok, E. (1982), 'On the relationship between knowing and using linguistic forms', *Applied Linguistics*, *3*, 181–206.

Bialystok, E. (1986*a*), 'Children's concept of word', *Journal of Psycholinguistic Research*, *15*, 13–32.

Bilaystok, E. (1986*b*), 'Factors in the growth of linguistic awareness', *Child Development*, *57*, 498–510.

Bialystok, E., Mitterer, J. (1987), 'Metalinguistic differences among three kinds of readers', *Journal of Educational Psychology*, *79*, 147–53.

Bialystok, E., Ryan, E.B. (1985*a*), 'A metacognitive framework for the development of first and second language skills', *in* D.L. Forrest-Pressley, G.E. MacKinnon and T.G. Waller (eds), *Metacognition, Cognition and Human Performance*, vol. 1, New York: Academic Press.

Bialystok, E., Ryan, E.B. (1985*b*), 'Toward a definition of metalinguistic skill', *Merrill-Palmer Quarterly*, *31*, 229–51.

Biber, D. (1986), 'Spoken and written textual dimensions in English: Resolving the contradictory findings', *Language*, *62*, 384–414.

Biemiller, A. (1970), 'The development of the use of graphic and contextual information as children learn to read', *Reading Research Quarterly*, *6*, 75–96.

Billow, R.A. (1975), 'A cognitive developmental study of metaphor comprehension', *Developmental Psychology*, *11*, 415–23.

Billow, R.A. (1981), 'Observing spontaneous metaphor in children', *Journal of Experimental Psychology*, *31*, 430–45.

Blum-Kulka, S. (1987), 'Indirectness and politeness in requests: Same or different?', *Journal of Pragmatics*, *11*, 131–46.

Bohannon, J.N. (1975), 'The relationship between syntax discrimination and sentence imitation in children', *Child Development*, *46*, 444–51.

Bohannon, J.N. (1976), 'Normal and scrambled grammar in discrimination, imitation and comprehension', *Child Development*, *47*, 669–81.

Bohn, W.E. (1914), 'First steps in verbal expression', *Pedagogical Seminary*, *21*, 278–95.

Bonitatibus, G. (1988), 'Comprehension monitoring and the apprehension of literal meaning', *Child Development*, *59*, 60–70.

Bonnet, C. (1986), 'Définitions et conscience du signe chez l'enfant', *Revue suisse de Psychologie pure et appliquée*, *45*, 29–53.

Bonnet, C., Tamine-Gardes, J. (1984), *Quand l'enfant parle du langage*, Brussels: Mardaga.

Borkowski, J.G., Carr, M., Pressley, M. (1987), ' "Spontaneous" strategy use: Perspectives from metacognitive theory', *Intelligence*, *11*, 61–75.

Boutet, J., Gauthier, F., Saint-Pierre, M. (1983), 'Savoir dire sur la phrase', *Archives de Psychologie*, *51*, 205–28.

Bowerman, M. (1978), *Word, Object and Conceptual Development*, New York: Norton.

Bowerman, M. (1982*a*), 'Reorganizational processes in lexical and syntactic development', *in* E. Wanner and L.R. Gleitman (eds), *Language Acquisition: The state of the art*, London: Cambridge University Press.

Bowerman, M. (1982*b*), 'Starting to talk worse: Clues to language acquisition from children's late speech errors', *in* S. Strauss (ed.), *U-shaped Behavior Growth*, New York: Academic Press.

Bowey, J.A. (1986), 'Syntactic awareness and verbal performance from preschool to fifth grade', *Journal of Psycholinguistic Research*, *15*, 285–308.

Bowey, J.A., Tunmer, W.E. (1984), 'Word awareness in children', *in* W.E. Tunmer, C. Pratt and M.L. Herriman (eds), *Metalinguistic Awareness in Children*, Berlin: Springer-Verlag.

Bowey, J.A., Tunmer, W.E., Pratt, C. (1984), 'Development of children's understanding of the metalinguistic term *word*', *Journal of Educational Psychology*, 76, 500–12.

Boysson-Bardies, B. de, Sagart, L., Durand, C. (1984), 'Discernible differences in the babbles of infants according to target language', *Journal of Child Language*, 11, 1–15.

Bradley, L., Bryant, P.E. (1978), 'Difficulties in auditory organization as a possible cause of reading backwardness', *Nature*, 271, 746–7.

Bradley, L., Bryant, P.E. (1983), 'Categorizing sounds and learning to read: A causal connection', *Nature*, 301, 419–21.

Bradley, L., Bryant, P.E. (1985), *Rhyme and Reason in Reading and Spelling*, Ann Arbor: University of Michigan Press.

Brami-Mouling, M.-A. (1977), 'Notes sur l'adaptation de l'expression verbale de l'enfant en fonction de l'âge de son interlocuteur', *Archives de Psychologie*, 45, 225–34.

Bransford, J.D., Barclay, J.R., Franks, J.J. (1972), 'Sentence memory: A constructive versus interpretive approach', *Cognitive Psychology*, 3, 193–209.

Bransford, J.D., Johnson, M.K. (1972), 'Contextual prerequisites for understanding: Some investigations of comprehension and recall', *Journal of Verbal Learning and Verbal Behavior*, 11, 717–26.

Bredart, S. (1980), 'Un problème de métalinguistique: l'expression des échecs de communication chez l'enfant de huit á douze ans', *Archives de Psychologie*, 48, 303–21.

Bredart, S., Rondal, J.-A. (1982), *L'analyse du langage chez l'enfant: les activités métalinguistiques*, Brussels: Mardaga.

Brewer, W.F., Hay, A.E. (1984), 'Reconstructive recall of linguistic style', *Journal of Verbal Learning and Verbal Behavior*, 23, 237–49.

Bridwell, L., Sirc, G., Brooke, R. (1985), 'Revising and computing: Case studies of student writers', *in* S.W. Freedman (ed.), *The Acquisition of Written Language: Response and revision*, Norwood, MA: Ablex.

Bronckart, J.-P. (1985), 'Les opérations temporelles dans deux types de textes d'enfants', *Bulletins de Psychologie*, 38, 653–66.

Bronckart, J.-P., Schneuwly, B. (1984), 'La production des organisateurs textuels chez l'enfant', *in* M. Moscato and G. Piéraut-Le Bonniec (eds), *Le langage, construction et actualisation*, Rouen: Publications de l'Université de Rouen.

Brown, A.L. (1978), 'Knowing when, where, and how to remember: A problem of metacognition', *in* R. Glaser (ed.), *Advances in Instructional Psychology*, vol. 1, Hillsdale, NJ: Erlbaum.

Brown, A.L., Smiley, S.S. (1977), 'Rating the importance of structural units of prose passages: A problem of metacognitive development', *Child Development*, 48, 1–8.

Brown, G.D.A., Sharkey, A.J.C., Brown, G. (1987), 'Factors affecting the success of referential communication', *Journal of Psycholinguistic Research*, 16, 535–49.

Brown, R.W. (1973), *A First Language: The early stages*, Cambridge, MA: Harvard University Press.

Brown, R.W., McNeill, D. (1966), 'The "tip of the tongue" phenomenon', *Journal of Verbal Learning and Verbal Behavior*, 5, 325–37.

Bruce, D.J. (1964), 'The analysis of word sounds by young children', *British Journal of Educational Psychology*, 34, 158–70.

Bruner, J. (1983), *Le développement de l'enfant: savoir faire, savoir dire*, Paris: PUF.

Bruner, J., Hickmann, M. (1983), 'La conscience, la parole et la "zone proximale": réflexions sur la théorie de Vygotsky', *in* J.S. Bruner (ed.), *Le développement de l'enfant: savoir faire, savoir dire*, Paris: PUF.

Bryant, P.E., Bradley, L. (1980), 'Why children sometimes write words which they do not read', *in* U. Frith (ed.), *Cognitive Processes in Spelling*, London: Academic Press.

Bryant, P.E., Bradley, L. (1983), 'Psychological strategies and the development of reading and writing', *in* M. Martlew (ed.), *The Psychology of Written Language*, Sussex: Wiley.

Bryant, P.E., Bradley, L. (1985), *Children's Reading Problems*, Oxford: Blackwell.

Bryant, P.E., Goswami, U. (1987), 'Beyond grapheme–phoneme correspondence', *European Bulletin of Cognitive Psychology*, 7, 439–43.

Caffi, C. (1984), 'Some remarks on illocution and metacommunication', *Journal of Pragmatics*, 8, 449–67.

Calfee, R.C. (1977), 'Assessment of independent reading skills: Basic research and practical applications', *in* A.S. Reber and D.L. Scarborough (eds), *Toward a Psychology of Reading*, Hillsdale, NJ: Erlbaum.

Calfee, R.C., Lindamood, P., Lindamood, C. (1973), 'Acoustic-phonetic skills and reading–kindergarten through twelfth grade', *Journal of Educational Psychology*, 64, 293–8.

Campbell, R., Butterworth, B. (1985), 'Phonological dyslexia and dysgraphia in a highly literate subject: A developmental case with associated deficits of phonemic processing and awareness', *The Quarterly Journal of Experimental Psychology*, 37A, 435–75.

Carlson, P., Anisfeld, M. (1969), 'Some observations on the linguistic competence of a two-year-old child', *Child Development*, 40, 565–75.

Caron, J. (1983), *Les régulations du discours*, Paris: PUF.

Carpenter, P.A., Just, M. (1977), 'Reading comprehension as eyes see it', *in* M. Just and P.A. Carpenter (eds), *Cognitive Processes in Comprehension*, Hillsdale, NJ: Erlbaum.

Carr, D. (1979), 'The development of young children's capacity to judge anomalous sentences', *Journal of Child Language*, 6, 227–41.

Cazden, C.B. (1976), 'Play with language and metalinguistic awareness: One dimension of language experience', *in* J.S. Bruner, A. Jolly and K. Silva (eds), *Play: Its role in development and evolution*, New York: Basic Books.

Ceci, S.J., Caves, R.D., Howe, M.J.A. (1981), 'Children's long-term memory for information that is incongruous with their prior knowledge', *British Journal of Psychology*, 72, 443–50.

Chafe, W.L. (1982), 'Integration and involvement in speaking, writing, and oral literature', *in* D. Tannen (ed.), *Spoken and Written Language: Exploring orality and literacy*, Norwood, MA: Ablex.

Chaudron, C. (1983), 'Research on metalinguistic judgements: A review of theory, methods, and results', *Language Learning*, 33, 343–77.

Chomsky, C. (1979), *The Acquisition of Syntax in Children from 5 to 10*, Cambridge, MA: MIT Press.

Chomsky, N. (1965), *Aspects of the Theory of Syntax*, Cambridge, MA: MIT Press.

Chomsky, N., Halle, M. (1968), *The Sound Pattern of English*, New York: Harper & Row.

Christinat-Tièche, C. (1982), 'Segmentation d'énoncés et construction d'une histoire par de jeunes enfants: une approche de l'analyse des segments constitutifs du récit', *Archives de Psychologie*, *50*, 251–60.

Chukowsky, K. (1968), *From Two to Five*, Berkeley: University of California Press (1st edn in Russian, 1927).

Clark, E.V. (1970), 'How young children describe events in time', *in* G.B. Flores d'Arcais and W.J.M. Levelt (eds), *Advances in Psycholinguistics*, Amsterdam: North-Holland Publishing Co.

Clark, E.V. (1971), 'On the acquisition of meaning of before and after', *Journal of Verbal Learning and Verbal Behavior*, *10*, 266–75.

Clark, E.V. (1978), 'Awareness of language: Some evidence from what children say and do', *in* A. Sinclair, R.J. Jarvella and W.J.M. Levelt (eds), *The Child's Conception of Language*, Berlin: Springer-Verlag.

Clark, E.V., Barron, B.J.S. (1988), 'A thrower-button or a button-thrower? Children's judgments of grammatical and ungrammatical compound nouns', *Linguistics*, *26*, 3–19.

Clark, H.H., Haviland, S.E. (1977), 'Comprehension and the given–new contract', *in* R.O. Freedle (ed.), *Discourse Production and Comprehension*, Norwood, MA: Ablex.

Clark, H.H., Sengul, C.J. (1979), 'In search of referents for nouns and pronouns', *Memory and Cognition*, *7*, 35–41.

Cometa, M.S., Eson, M.E. (1978), 'Logical operations and metaphor interpretation: A Piagetian model, *Child Development*, *49*, 649–59.

Content, A. (1984), 'L'analyse phonétique explicite de la parole et l'acquisition de la lecture', *L'Année psychologique*, *84*, 555–72.

Content, A. (1985), 'Le développement de l'habileté d'analyse phonétique de la parole', *L'Année psychologique*, *85*, 73–99.

Content, A., Kolinsky, R., Morais, J., Bertelson, P. (1986*a*), 'Phonetic segmentation in prereaders: Effect of corrective information', *Journal of Experimental Child Psychology*, *42*, 49–72.

Content, A., Morais, J., Alegria, J., Bertelson, P. (1982). 'Accelerating the development of phonetic segmentation skills in kindergarteners', *Cahiers de Psychologie cognitive*, *2*, 259–69.

Content, A., Morais, J., Alegria, J., Bertelson, P. (1986*b*), 'Acquisition de la lecture et analyse segmentale de la parole', *Psychologica Belgica*, *26*, 1–15.

Content, A., Morais, J., Kolinsky, R., Bertelson, P., Alegria, J. (1986*c*), 'Explicit speech-segmentation ability and susceptibility to phonological similarity in short-term retention: No correlation', *Perceptual and Motor Skills*, *63*, 81–2.

Corrigan, R. (1975), 'A scalogram analysis of the development of the use and comprehension of "because" in children', *Child Development*, *46*, 195–201.

Cossu, G., Marshall, J.C. (1990), 'Are cognitive skills a prerequisite for learning to read and write?', *Cognitive Neuropsychology*, *7*, 21–40.

Costermans, J., Giurgea, D. (1988), 'L'influence du sens sur la segmentation syllabique chez des enfants de trois à sept ans', *Archives de Psychologie*, *56*, 137–49.

Crowhurst, M., Piché, G.L. (1979), 'Audience and mode of discourse effects on syntactic complexity in writing at two grade levels', *Research in the Teaching of English*, *13*, 101–9.

Culioli, A. (1968), 'La formalisation en linguistique', *Cahiers pour l'analyse*, *9*, 106–17.

Daiute, C. (1983), 'The computer as stylus and audience', *College Composition and Communication*, *34*, 134–45.

Daiute, C. (1985), 'Do writers talk to themselves?' *in* S.W. Freedman (ed.), *The Acquisition of Written Language: Response and revision*, Norwood, MA: Ablex.

Daiute, C. (1986), 'Physical and cognitive factors in revising: Insights from studies with computers', *Research in the Teaching of English*, *20*, 141–59.

Dale, P.S. (1976), *Language Development: Structure and function*, 2nd edn, New York: Holt, Rinehart & Winston.

DeCasper, A.J., Prescott, P.A. (1984), 'Human newborns' perception of male voices: Preference, discrimination and reinforcing value', *Developmental Psychobiology*, *17*, 481–91.

DeCasper, A.J., Spence, M.J. (1986), 'Prenatal maternal speech influences newborns' perception of speech sounds', *Infant Behavior and Development*, *9*, 133–50.

De Góes, C., Martlew, M. (1983), 'Young children's approach to literacy', *in* M. Martlew (ed.), *The Psychology of Written Language*, New York: Wiley.

Denhière, G. (1984), *Il était une fois ... Compréhension et souvenir de récits*, Lille: Presses Universitaires de Lille.

Deno, S., Marston, D., Mirkin, P. (1982), 'Valid measurement procedures for continuous evalution of written expression', *Exceptional Children*, *48*, 368–71.

Dent, C.H. (1987), 'Developmental studies of perception and metaphor: The twain shall meet', *Metaphor and Symbolic Activity*, *2*, 53–71.

De Villiers, J.G., de Villiers, P.A. (1974), 'Competence and performances in child language: Are children really competent to judge?', *Journal of Child Language*, *1*, 11–22.

De Villiers, J.G., de Villiers, P.A. (1978), *Language Acquisition*, Cambridge, MA: Harvard University Press.

De Villiers, P.A. (1974), 'Imagery and theme in recall of connected discourse', *Journal of Experimental Psychology*, *103*, 263–8.

De Villiers, P.A., de Villiers, J.G. (1972), 'Early judgments of semantic and syntactic acceptability by children', *Journal of Psycholinguistic Research*, *1*, 299–310.

Ding, G.F., Jersild, A.T. (1932), 'A study of laughing and crying in preschool children', *Journal of Genetic Psychology*, *40*, 452–72.

Di Vesta, F.J., Hayward, K.G., Orlando, V.P. (1979), 'Developmental trends in monitoring text for comprehension', *Child Development*, *50*, 97–105.

Dollaghan, C., Kaston, N. (1986), 'A comprehension monitoring program for language-impaired children', *Journal of Speech and Hearing Disorders*, *51*, 264–71.

Donahue, M. (1984), 'Learning disabled children's conversational competence: An attempt to activate the inactive listener', *Applied Psycholinguistics*, *5*, 21–35.

Donaldson, M. (1978), *Children's Minds*, Glasgow: Collins.

Downing, J. (1969), 'How children think about reading', *The Reading Teacher*, *23*, 217–30.

Downing, J. (1970), 'Children's conceptions of language in learning to read', *Education Research*, *12*, 106–12.

Downing, J. (1972), 'Children's developing concepts of spoken and written language', *Journal of Reading Behavior*, *4*, 1–19.

Downing, J. (1979), *Reading and Reasoning*, Edinburgh: Chambers.

Downing, J., Fijalkow, J. (1984), *Lire et raisonner*, Toulouse: Privat.

Downing, J., Oliver, P. (1974), 'The child's concept of a word', *Reading Research Quarterly*, *9*, 568–82.

Dubois, J. (1968), 'La grammaire générative, sa place dans la linguistique moderne', *Psychologie française*, *13*, 127–36.

Ehri, L.C. (1975), 'Word consciousness in readers and pre-readers', *Journal of Educational Psychology*, *67*, 204–12.

Ehri, L.C. (1979), 'Linguistic insight: Threshold of reading acquisition', *in* T.G. Waller and G.E. MacKinnon (eds), *Reading Research: Advances in theory and practice*, vol. 1, New York: Academic Press.

Ehri, L.C., Robert, K.T. (1979), 'Do beginners learn printed words better in contexts or in isolation?', *Child Development*, *50*, 675–85.

Ehri, L.C., Wilce, L.S., Taylor, B.B. (1987), 'Children's categorization of short vowels in words and the influence of spellings', *Merrill-Palmer Quarterly*, *33*, 393–421.

Eilers, R.E., Gavin, W., Wilson, W.R. (1979), 'Linguistic experience and phonemic perception in infancy: A cross-linguistic study', *Child Development*, *50*, 14–18.

Eimas, P.D. (1985), 'The perception of speech in early infancy', *Scientific American*, *252*, 46–52.

Eimas, P.D., Siqueland, E.R., Jusczyk, P.W., Vigorito, J. (1971), 'Speech perception in infants', *Science*, *171*, 303–6.

Elliot, A.J. (1981), *Child Language*, Cambridge: Cambridge University Press.

Elrod, M.M. (1983), 'Young children's responses to direct and indirect directives', *The Journal of Genetic Psychology*, *143*, 217–27.

Engelkamp, J. (1983), 'Word meaning and word recognition', *in* T.B. Seilers and W. Wannenmacher (eds), *Concept Development and the Development of Word Meaning*, Berlin: Springer-Verlag.

Ervin-Tripp, S. (1977), 'Wait for me, roller skate!', *in* S. Ervin-Tripp and C. Mitchell-Kernan (eds), *Child Discourse*, New York: Academic Press.

Ervin-Tripp, S., Gordon, D. (1985), 'The development of requests', *in* R.L. Schiefelbusch (ed.), *Communicative Competence: Assessment and intervention*, Baltimore, MD: University Park Press.

Espéret, E. (1984), 'Processus de production: genèse et rôle du schéma narratif dans la conduite de récit', *in* M. Moscato and G. Piéraut-Le Bonniec (eds), *Le langage, construction et actualisation*, Rouen: Publications de l'Université de Rouen.

Espéret, E., Charier, D. (1985), *Fonctions actualisation et quantification de l'article entre 4 et 8 ans: analyse en situation de communication et de récit*, 8th ISSBD Biennial Meeting, Tours.

Espéret, E., Gaonac'h, D. (1986), *The Role of Narrative Schema on Story Production and Recall: A longitudinal study*, 2nd ISSBD European Conference on Developmental Psychology, Rome.

Evans, M. (1985), 'Self-initiated speech repairs: A reflection of communicative monitoring in young children', *Developmental Psychology*, *21*, 365–71.

Evans, M., Taylor, N., Blum, I. (1979), 'Children's written language awareness and its relation to reading acquisition', *Journal of Reading Behavior*, *11*, 7–19.

Fabre, C. (1986), *Des variantes de brouillons au cours préparatoire*, Université de Perpignan, internally circulated document, personal communication.

Faigley, L., Cherry, R.D., Jolliffe, D.A., Skinner, A.M. (1985), *Assessing Writers' Knowledge and Processes of Composing*, Norwood, MA: Ablex.

Faigley, L., Meyer, P. (1983), 'Rhetorical theory and readers' classifications of text types', *Text*, *3*, 305–25.

Fayol, M. (1978), 'Les conservations narratives chez l'enfant', *Enfance*, 4–5, 247–59.

Fayol, M. (1982), 'Le plus-que-parfait. Etude génétique en compréhension et en production chez l'enfant de quatre à dix ans', *Archives de Psychologie*, 50, 261–83.

Fayol, M. (1985*a*), 'Analyser et résumer des textes: une perspective génétique', *Etudes de Linguistique appliquée*, 59, 54–64.

Fayol, M. (1985*b*), *Le récit et sa construction. Une approche de psychologie cognitive*, Neuchâtel: Delachaux & Niestlé.

Fayol, M. (1986), 'Cohérence et cohésion: une revue des travaux français de psychologie expérimentale', *in* M. Charolles, J.S. Petofi and E. Sozer (eds), *Research in Text Connexity and Text Coherence: A survey*, Hamburg: Buske.

Fayol, M. (1988*a*), *Compréhension, production et contrôle du langage*, Colloque annuel de la section psychologie expérimentale de la SFP, Dijon.

Fayol, M. (1988*b*), 'Text typologies: A cognitive approach', *in* G. Denhière and J.-P. Rossi (eds), *Text and Text Processing*, Amsterdam: North-Holland Publishing Co.

Fayol, M. (1989), 'Une approche psycholinguistique de la ponctuation. Etude en production et compréhension', *Langue française*, 81, 21–39.

Fayol, M., Abdi, H. (1986), 'Impact des formulations sur la résolution de problèmes additifs chez l'enfant de 6 à 10 ans', *European Journal of Psychology of Education*, 1, 41–58.

Fayol, M., Abdi, H. (1988), 'Influence of script structure on punctuation', *European Bulletin of Cognitive Psychology*, 8, 265–79.

Fayol, M., Abdi, H., Gombert, J.E. (1987*a*), 'Arithmetical problems formulation and working memory load', *Cognition and Instruction*, 4, 183–202.

Fayol, M., Gombert, J.E. (1987), 'Le retour de l'auteur sur son texte: Bilan provisoire des recherches psycholinguistiques', *Repères*, 73, 85–96.

Fayol, M., Gombert, J.E., Baur, V. (1987*b*), 'La révision de textes écrits dans l'activité rédactionnelle précoce', *Revue d'Audio-Phonologie*, 3, 689–701.

Fayol, M., Lété, B. (1987), 'Ponctuation et connecteurs: une approche textuelle et génétique', *European Journal of Psychology of Education*, 2, 57–72.

Fayol, M., Monteil, J.-M. (1988), 'The notion of script: From general to developmental and social psychology', *European Bulletin of Cognitive Psychology*, 8, 335–61.

Fayol, M., Schneuwly, B. (1988), 'Les problèmes de la mise en texte', *in* J.-L. Chiss, J.-P. Laurent, J.-C. Meyer, H. Romian and B. Schneuwly (eds), *Apprendre/ enseigner à produire des textes écrits*, Brussels: Duculot.

Feldman, C., Shen, M. (1971), 'Some language-related cognitive advantages of bilingual five-year-olds', *The Journal of Genetic Psychology*, 118, 235–44.

Ferreiro, E. (1971), *Les relations temporelles dans le langage de l'enfant*, Geneva: Droz.

Ferreiro, E. (1977), 'Vers une théorie génétique de l'apprentissage de la lecture', *Revue suisse de Psychologie pure et appliquée*, 36, 109–30.

Ferreiro, E., Gomez Palacio, M., Guarjago, E., Rodriguez, B., Vega, A., Cantu, R. (1979), *El niño preescolar y su comprensión del sistema de escritura*, Mexico: Organización de los Estados Americanos.

Ferreiro, E., Gomez Palacio, M. (1982), *Analisis de las perturbaciones en el proceso de aprendizaje de la lecto-escritura* (5 fasc.), Mexico: Dirección General de Educación Especial. Traduction française: *Lire-écrire à l'école. Comment s'y apprennent-ils?*, Lyon, CRDP, 1988.

Ferreiro, E., Teberosky, A. (1979), *Los sistema de escritura en el desarrollo del niño*, Mexico: Siglo Vientiuno Editores. English translation: *Literacy Before Schooling*, London: Heinemann, 1982.

Fey, M., Leonard, L. (1984), 'Partner age as a variable, in the conversational performance of specifically language impaired children', *Journal of Speech and Hearing Research, 27*, 413–24.

Flavell, J.H. (1970), 'Developmental studies of mediated memory', *in* H.W. Reese and L.P. Lipsitt (eds), *Advances in Child Development and Behavior*, vol. 5, New York: Academic Press.

Flavell, J.H. (1976), 'Metacognitive aspects of problem solving', *in* B. Resnick (ed.), *The Nature of Intelligence*, Hillsdale, NJ: Erlbaum.

Flavell, J.H. (1977), *Cognitive Development*, Englewood Cliffs, NJ: Prentice-Hall.

Flavell, J.H. (1978), 'Metacognitive development', *in* J.M. Scandura and C.J. Brainerd (eds), *Structural/Process Models of Complex Human Behaviour*, Alphen an den Rijn, The Netherlands: Sijthoff & Noordhoff.

Flavell, J.H. (1981), 'Cognitive monitoring', *in* W.P. Dickson (ed.), *Children's Oral Communication Skills*, New York: Academic Press.

Flavell, J.H., Botkin, P., Fry, C., Wright, J., Jarvis, P. (1968), *The Development of Role-taking and Communication Skills in Children*, New York: Wiley.

Flavell, J.H., Speer, J.R., Green, F.L., August, D.L. (1981), 'The development of comprehension monitoring and knowledge about communication', *Monographs for the Society for Research in Child Development, 46*, 1–65.

Flavell, J.H., Wellman, H.M. (1977), 'Metamemory', *in* R.V. Kail Jr and J.W. Hagen (eds), *Perspectives on the Development of Memory and Cognition*, Hillsdale, NJ: Erlbaum.

Florès d'Arcais, G.B. (1978), 'Levels of semantic knowledge in children's use of connectives', *in* A. Sinclair, R.J. Jarvella and W.J.M. Levelt (eds), *The Child's Conception of Language*, Berlin: Springer-Verlag.

Flower, L.S., Hayes, J.R. (1980), 'The dymamics of composing: Making plans and juggling constraints', *in* L.W. Gregg and E.R. Steinberg (eds), *Cognitive Processes in Writing*, Hillsdale, NJ: Erlbaum.

Flower, L.S., Hayes, J.R. (1981), 'A cognitive process theory of writing', *College Composition and Communication, 32*, 365–87.

Fodor, J.A. (1983), *The Modularity of Mind: An essay on faculty psychology*, Cambridge, MA: MIT Press.

Forrest-Pressley, D.L., Waller, T.G. (1984), *Cognition, Metacognition, and Reading*, Berlin: Springer-Verlag.

Foulin, J.N. (1989), 'La production écrite chez les enfants de CE1 et de CE2: étude en temps réel', *Etudes de Linguistique appliquée, 73*, 35–46.

Foulin, J.-N., Fayol, M. (1988), 'Etude en temps réel de la production écrite chez des enfants de sept et huit ans', *European Journal of Psychology of Education, 3*, 461–75.

Fourment, M.-C., Emmenecker, N., Pantz, V. (1987), 'Etude de la production des métaphores chez des enfants de 3 à 7 ans', *L'Année psychologique, 87*, 535–51.

Fowler, C.A. (1986), 'An operational definition of conscious awareness must be responsible to subjective experience', *Behavioral and Brain Sciences, 9*, 33–5.

Fox, B., Routh, D.K. (1975), 'Analyzing spoken language into words, syllables and phonemes. A developmental study', *Journal of Psycholinguistic Research, 4*, 331–42.

Fox, B., Routh, D.K. (1980), 'Phonemic analysis and severe reading disability in children', *Journal of Psycholinguistic Research*, *9*, 115–19.

Fox, B., Routh, D.K. (1984), 'Phonemic analysis and synthesis as word attack skills: Revisited', *Journal of Educational Psychology*, *76*, 1059–64.

Fraisse, P. (1987), 'Brain and mind', *Bulletin de Psychologie*, *40*, 683–8.

Francis, H. (1973), 'Children's experience of reading and notions of units in language', *British Journal of Educational Psychology*, *43*, 17–23.

Freedman, S.W., Calfee, R.C. (1984), 'Understanding and comprehending', *Written Communication*, *1*, 459–90.

Friederici, A. (1983), 'Children's sensitivity to function words during sentence comprehension', *Linguistics*, *21*, 717–39.

Frith, V. (ed.) (1980), *Cognitive Processes in Spelling*, London: Academic Press.

Frochot, M. (1989), 'Une application de la méthode d'Auto-Présentation Segmentée à l'étude comparée des processus de compréhension du texte narratif chez l'enfant et chez l'adulte', *Etudes de Linguistique appliquée*, *73*, 29–34.

Frochot, M., Fayol, M., Zagar, D. (1987a), 'Lire des histoires: une revue', *Les Sciences de l'Education*, *3*, 5–33.

Frochot, M., Zagar, D., Fayol, M. (1987b), 'Effets de l'organisation narrative sur la lecture de récits. Etude comparée, en temps réel, chez l'enfant et chez l'adulte', *L'Année psychologique*, *87*, 237–52.

Gallagher, T.H. (1977), 'Revision behaviors in the speech of normal children developing language', *Journal of Speech and Hearing Research*, *20*, 303–18.

Gardner, H. (1974), 'Metaphors and modalities: How children project polar adjectives onto diverse domains?', *Child Development*, *45*, 84–91.

Gardner, H. (1980), 'Children's literacy development: The realms of metaphors and stories', *in* P.E. McGhee and A.J. Chapman (eds), *Children's Humor*, New York: Wiley.

Gardner, H., Kircher, M., Winner, E., Perkins, D. (1975), 'Children's metaphoric productions and preferences', *Journal of Child Language*, *2*, 125–41.

Gardner, H., Winner, E. (1979), 'The child is father to the metaphor', *Psychology Today*, May, 81–91.

Garner, R., Alexander, P., Slater, W., Hare, V.C., Smith, T., Reis, R. (1986), 'Children's knowledge of structural properties of expository text', *Journal of Educational Psychology*, *78*, 411–16.

Garner, R., Kraus, C. (1982), 'Good and poor comprehender differences in knowing and regulating reading behaviors', *Educational Research Quarterly*, *6*, 5–12.

Garvey, C., BenDebba, M. (1974), 'Effects of age, sex, and partner on children's dyadic speech', *Child Development*, *45*, 1159–61.

Gentner, D. (1977), 'Children's performance on a spatial analogies task', *Child Development*, *48*, 1034–9.

Gentner, D. (1988), 'Metaphor as structure mapping: The relational shift', *Child Development*, *59*, 47–59.

Gérard, J. (1981), 'La maîtrise du principe de récursivité langagière chez l'enfant', *Archives de Psychologie*, *49*, 95–114.

Ghezzi, P.M., Bijou, S.W., Umbreit, J., Chia-Chen Chao (1987), 'Influence of age of listener on preadolescents' linguistic behavior', *The Psychological Record*, *37*, 109–26.

Gilliéron, C. (1984), 'Réflexions préliminaires à une étude de la négation', *Archives de Psychologie*, *52*, 231–53.

Glass, A.L., Holyak, K.J., Kossan, N.E. (1977), 'Children's ability to detect semantic contradictions', *Child Development*, *48*, 279–83.

Gleason, J.B. (1973), 'Code switching in children's language', *in* T.E. Morre (ed.), *Cognitive Development and the Acquisition of Language*, New York: Academic Press.

Gleason, J.B., Perlmann, R.Y., Greif, E.B. (1984), 'What's the magic word?: Learning language through politeness routines', *Discourse Processes*, *7*, 493–502.

Gleitman, L.R., Gleitman, H. (1970), *Phrase and Paraphrase: Some innovative uses of language*, New York: Norton.

Gleitman, L.R., Gleitman, H., Shipley, E.F. (1972), 'The emergence of the child as grammarian', *Cognition*, *1*, 137–64.

Glucksberg, S., Krauss, R.M., Weisberg, R. (1966), 'Referential communication in nursery school children: Method and some preliminary findings', *Journal of Experimental Child Psychology*, *3*, 333–42.

Goelman, H. (1982), 'Selective attention in language comprehension: Children's processing of expository and narrative discourse', *Discourse Processes*, *5*, 53–72.

Goldstein, D. (1976), 'Cognitive-linguistic functioning and learning to read in pre-schoolers', *Journal of Educational Psychology*, *68*, 680–8.

Golinkoff, R.M. (1978), 'Critique: Phonemic awareness skills and reading achievement', *in* F.B. Murray and J.J. Pikulski (eds), *The Acquisition of Reading: Cognitive, linguistic and perceptual prerequisites*, Baltimore, MD: University Park Press.

Gombert, J.E. (1983*a*), 'La prise en compte de l'ordre d'énonciation par l'enfant d'âge préscolaire', *Archives de Psychologie*, *51*, 327–39.

Gombert, J.E. (1983*b*), 'Un élément important de la signification verbale: l'ordre d'énonciation', *Rééducation orthophonique*, *21*, 505–26.

Gombert, J.E. (1984), 'Processus d'inférence dans le traitement des phrases par l'enfant d'âge préscolaire', *L'Année psychologique*, *84*, 489–506.

Gombert, J.E. (1985), *The Determination of Speech Adaptation of 4-year-old Children to Younger Addressee*, 8th ISSBD Biennial Meeting, Tours.

Gombert, J.E. (1986), 'Le développement métalinguistique: le point de la recherche', *Etudes de Linguistique appliquée*, *62*, 5–25.

Gombert, J.E. (1987), 'Are young children's speech adaptations conscious or automatic? A short theoretical note', *International Journal of Psychology*, *22*, 375–82.

Gombert, J.E. (1988*a*), 'La conscience du langage à l'âge préscolaire', *Revue française de Pédagogie*, *83*, 65–81.

Gombert, J.E. (1988*b*), 'Processus rédactionnels et développement des méta-connaissances dans le domaine langagier', *in* J.-L. Chiss, J.-P. Laurent, J.-C. Meyer, H. Romian and B. Schneuwly (eds), *Apprendre/enseigner à produire des textes écrits*, Brussels: Duculot.

Gombert, J.E. (1989), 'Conceptions de l'écrit chez les enfants pré-lettrés', *Etudes de Linguistique appliquée*, *73*, 97–106.

Gombert, J.E., Boudinet, S. (1988), *Le contrôle de la grammaticalité des phrases par l'enfant de 4–5 ans*, Colloque annuel de la section psychologie expérimentale de la SFP, Dijon.

Gombert, J.E., Fayol, M. (1988), 'Auto-contrôle par l'enfant de ses réalisations dans des tâches cognitives', *Revue française de Pédagogie*, *82*, 47–59.

Goodall, M. (1984), 'Can four year olds "read" words in the environment?', *The Reading Teacher*, *37*, 478–82.

Goodman, K., Goodman, Y. (1983), 'Reading and writing relationships: Pragmatic functions', *Language Arts*, *60*, 590–9.

Goodman, L., Casciato, D., Price, M. (1987), 'LD students' writing: Analysing errors', *Academic Therapy*, *22*, 453–61.

Goswami, U. (1988), 'Children's use of analogy in learning to spell', *British Journal of Developmental Psychology*, *6*, 21–33.

Gréco, P. (1980), 'Comment ça marche? Réflexions préliminaires à quelques questions de méthode et aux problèmes dits "fonctionnels" ', *Bulletin de Psychologie*, *33*, 633–6.

Greeno, J.G., Noreen, D.L. (1974), 'Time to read semantically related sentences', *Memory and Cognition*, *2*, 117–20.

Greif, E.B., Gleason, J.B. (1980), 'Hi, thanks, and goodbye: Some more routine information', *Language and Society*, *9*, 159–66.

Grewendorf, G. (1984), 'On the delimitation of semantics and pragmatics: The case of assertion', *Journal of Pragmatics*, *8*, 517–38.

Grice, H.P. (1975), 'Logic and conversation', *in* P. Cole and J.L. Morgan (eds), *Syntax and Semantics 3: Speech acts*, New York: Academic Press.

Grieve, R., Hoogenrad, R. (1979), 'First words', *in* P. Fletcher and M. Garman (eds), *Language Acquisition*, Cambridge: Cambridge University Press.

Gundlach, R.A. (1981), 'On the nature and development of children's writing', *in* C.H. Frederiksen and J.F. Dominic (eds), *Writing: The nature, development and teaching of written communication*, vol. 2, Hillsdale, NJ: Erlbaum.

Guralnick, J., Paul-Brown, D. (1977), 'The nature of verbal interactions among handicapped and nonhandicapped preschool children', *Child Development*, *48*, 254–60.

Hakes, D.T. (1980), *The Development of Metalinguistic Abilities in Children*, Berlin: Springer-Verlag.

Hakes, D.T. (1982), 'The development of metalinguistic abilities: What develops?', *in* S.A. Kuczaj (ed.), *Language Development: Language thought and culture*, Hillsdale, NJ: Erlbaum.

Hale, C.L., Delia, J.G. (1976), 'Cognitive complexity and social perspective-taking', *Communication Monographs*, *43*, 195–203.

Hall, N.A. (1976), 'Children's awareness of segmentation in speech and print', *Reading*, *10*, 11–19.

Hall, W.S., Cole, M., Reder, S., Dowley, G. (1977), 'Variations in young children's use of language: Some effects of setting and dialect', *in* R.O. Freedle (ed.), *Discourse Processes: Advances in research and 'theory'*, vol. 1, Norwood, MA: Ablex.

Harris, P.L., Kruithof, A., Terwogt, M.M., Visser, T. (1981), 'Children's detection and awareness of textual anomaly', *Journal of Experimental Child Psychology*, *31*, 212–30.

Harvey, N. (1985), 'Sentential synonymity judgment', *Journal of Psycholinguistic Research*, *14*, 219–62.

Herriman, M.L. (1986), 'Metalinguistic awareness and the growth of literacy', *in* S. de Castell, A. Luke and K. Egan (eds), *Literacy, Society, and Schooling: A reader*, Cambridge: Cambridge University Press.

Hickmann, M. (1983), *Le discours rapporté: aspects métapragmatiques du langage et de son développement*, Nijmegen, The Netherlands: Max-Planck-Institut für Psycholinguistik, internally circulated document.

Hickmann, M. (1984), 'Fonction et contexte dans le développement du langage', *in* M. Deleau (ed.), *Langage et communication à l'âge pré-scolaire*, Rennes: Presses Universitaires de Rennes 2.

Hickmann, M. (1985), 'Metapragmatics in child language', *in* E. Mertz and R.J. Parmentier (eds), *Semiotic Mediation: Sociocultural and psychological perspectives*, New York: Academic Press.

Hickmann, M. (1987*a*), *The Developmental Implications of Discourse Cohesion for Discourse Processing: A study of how children repair textual anomalies*, 2nd International Congress of Applied Psycholinguistics, Kassel.

Hickmann, M. (1987*b*), 'The pragmatics of reference in child language: Some issues in developmental theory', *in* M. Hickmann (ed.), *Social and Functional Approaches to Language and Thought*, New York: Academic Press.

Hirsh-Pasek, K., Gleitman, L.R., Gleitman, H. (1978), 'What did the brain say to the mind? A study of the detection and report of ambiguity by young children', *in* A. Sinclair, R.J. Jarvella and W.J.M. Levelt (eds), *The Child's Conception of Language*, Berlin: Springer-Verlag.

Holden, M.H., MacGinitie, W.H. (1972), 'Children's conception of word boundaries in speech and print', *Journal of Educational Psychology*, *63*, 551–7.

Hollos, M. (1977), 'Comprehension and use of social rules in pronoun selection by Hungarian children', *in* S. Ervin-Tripp and C. Mitchell-Kernan (eds), *Child Discourse*, New York: Academic Press.

Horgan, D. (1980), 'Nouns: Love 'em or leave 'em', *Annals of the New York Academy of Sciences*, *345*, 5–26.

Horgan, D. (1981), 'Learning to tell jokes: A case study of metalinguistic abilities', *Journal of Child Language*, *8*, 217–24.

Howe, H.E., Hillman, D. (1973), 'The acquisition of semantic restriction in children', *Journal of Verbal Learning and Verbal Behavior*, *12*, 132–9.

Hudson, J., Nelson, K. (1984), 'Play with language: Overextensions as analogies', *Journal of Child Language*, *11*, 337–46.

Hughes, M., Grieve, R. (1980), 'On asking children bizarre questions', *First Language*, *1*, 149–60.

Humes, A. (1983), 'Research on the composing process', *Review of Educational Research*, *55*, 201–16.

Huttenlocher, J. (1964), 'Children's language: Word–phrase relationship', *Science*, *143*, 264–5.

Ianco-Worrall, A.D. (1972), 'Bilingualism and cognitive development', *Child Development*, *43*, 1390–400.

Jakobson, R. (1963), *Essais de linguistique générale*, Paris: Editions de Minuit.

James, S.L. (1978), 'Effects of listeners' age and situation on the politeness of children's directive', *Journal of Psycholinguistic Research*, *7*, 307–17.

James, S.L., Miller, J.F. (1973), 'Children's awareness of semantic constraints in sentences', *Child Development*, *44*, 69–76.

Johnson, H., Smith, L.B. (1981), 'Children's inferential abilities in the context of reading to understand', *Child Development*, *52*, 1216–23.

Johnson, H.M. (1928), *Children in the 'Nursery School'*, New York: John Day & Co.

Johnson-Laird, P.N. (1983), *Mental Models: Towards a cognitive science of langauge, inference, and consciousness*, Cambridge, MA: Harvard University Press.

Johnston, J.C., MacClelland, J.L. (1980), 'Experimental test of a hierarchical model of word identification', *Journal of Verbal Learning and Verbal Behavior*, *19*, 503–24.

Jorm, A.F., Share, D.L., Maclean, R., Matthews, R. (1984), 'Phonological recoding skills and learning to read: A longitudinal study', *Applied Psycholinguistics*, *5*, 201–7.

Juel, C., Griffith, P.L., Gough, P.B. (1986), 'Acquisition of literacy: A longitudinal study of children in first and second grade', *Journal of Educational Psychology*, *78*, 243–55.

Jusczyk, P.W. (1981), 'Infant speech perception: A critical appraisal', *in* P.D. Eimas and J.L. Miller (eds), *Perspectives on the Study of Speech*, Hillsdale, NJ: Erlbaum.

Kail, M., Weissenborn, J. (1984), 'L'acquisition des connecteurs: critiques et perspectives', *in* M. Moscato and G. Piéraut-Le Bonniec (eds), *Le langage: construction et actualisation*, Rouen: Presses Universitaires de Rouen.

Kamhi, A.G. (1987), 'Metalinguistic abilities in language-impaired children', *Topics in Language Disorders*, *7*, 1–12.

Karabenick, J.D., Miller, S.A. (1977), 'The effects of age, sex, and listener feedback on grade school children's referential communication', *Child Development*, *48*, 678–84.

Karmiloff-Smith, A. (1977), 'Développement cognitif et acquisition de la plurifonctionnalité des déterminants', *in* Symposium de l'APSLF: *La genèse de la parole*, Paris: PUF.

Karmiloff-Smith, A. (1979*a*), *A Functional Approach to Child Language*, London: Cambridge University Press.

Karmiloff-Smith, A. (1979*b*), 'Micro- and macrodevelopmental changes in language acquisition and other representation systems', *Cognitive Science*, *3*, 91–118.

Karmiloff-Smith, A. (1981), 'The grammatical marking of thematic structure in the development of language production', *in* W. Deutsch (ed.), *The Child's Construction of Language*, New York: Academic Press.

Karmiloff-Smith, A. (1983), 'A note on the concept of "metaprocedural processes" in linguistic and non-linguistic development', *Archives de Psychologie*, *51*, 35–40.

Karmiloff-Smith, A. (1985), 'Language and cognitive processes from a developmental perspective', *Language and Cognitive Processes*, *1*, 61–85.

Karmiloff-Smith, A. (1986), 'From meta-processes to conscious access: Evidence from metalinguistic and repair data', *Cognition*, *23*, 95–147.

Karmiloff-Smith, A. (1987), 'Function and process in comparing language and cognition', *in* M. Hickmann (ed.), *Social and Functional Approaches to Language and Thought*, New York: Academic Press.

Karpova, S.N. (1966), 'The preschooler's realization of the lexical structure of speech', summarized by D.I. Slobin *in* F. Smith and G.A. Miller (eds), *The Genesis of Language: A psycholinguistic approach*, Cambridge, MA: MIT Press.

Katz, R.B. (1986), 'Phonological deficiencies in children with reading disability: Evidence from an object-naming task', *Cognition*, *22*, 225–57.

Keil, F.C. (1986), 'Conceptual domains and the acquisition of metaphor', *Cognitive Development*, *1*, 73–96.

Kieras, D.E. (1978), 'Good and bad structure in simple paragraphs: Effect on apparent theme, reading time and recall', *Journal of Verbal Learning and Verbal Behavior*, *17*, 13–28.

Kieras, D.E. (1980), 'Initial mention as a signal to thematic content in technical passages', *Memory and Cognition*, *8*, 345–53.

Kitchener, K.S. (1983), 'Cognition, metacognition, and epistemic cognition: A three-level model of cognitive processing', *Human Development*, *26*, 222–32.

Kleiman, G.M. (1975), 'Speech recording in reading', *Journal of Verbal Learning and Verbal Behavior*, *14*, 323–39.

Kochnower, J., Richardson, E., DiBenedetto, B. (1983), 'A comparison of the phonic decoding ability of normal and learning disabled children', *Journal of Learning Disabilities*, *16*, 348–51.

Kolinsky, R. (1986), 'L'émergence des habiletés métalinguistiques', *Cahiers de Psychologie cognitive*, *6*, 379–404.

Kolinsky, R., Cary, L., Morais, J. (1987), 'Awareness of words as phonological entities: The role of literacy', *Applied Psycholinguistics*, *8*, 223–32.

Kossan, N.E., Markman, E.M. (1981), 'Referential communication: Effects of listener's presence on the performance of young speakers', *Merrill-Palmer Quarterly*, *27*, 307–15.

Kozminsky, E. (1977), 'Altering comprehension: The effect of biasing titles on text comprehension', *Memory and Cognition*, *5*, 482–90.

Kroll, B.M. (1986), 'Explaining how to play a game: The development of informative writing skills', *Written Communication*, *3*, 195–218.

Kuczaj, S.A., Maratsos, M.P. (1975), 'On the acquisition of *front*, *back* and *side*', *Child Development*, *46*, 202–10.

Kuhl, P.K. (1987*a*), 'Perception of speech and sound in early infancy', *in* P. Salapatek and L. Cohen (eds), *Handbook of Infant Perception to Cognition*, vol. 2, New York: Academic Press.

Kuhl, P.K. (1987*b*), 'The special-mechanisms debate in speech research: Categorization tests on animals and infants', *in* S. Harnad (ed.), *Categorical Perception: The ground-work of cognition*, Cambridge: Cambridge University Press.

Lafontaine, D. (1983), 'L'adaptation des enfants à leur interlocuteur lors de la communication', *L'Année psychologique*, *83*, 199–224.

Laguna, G. de (1927), *Speech: Its function and development*, College Park, McGrath, ed. 1970.

Lang, C. (1986), *Les devinettes chez l'enfant*, dissertation, Maîtrise de Lettres, Aix-Marseille 1.

Langer, J.A. (1985), 'Children's sense of genre', *Written Communication*, *2*, 157–87.

Lasky, R.E., Syrdal-Lasky, A., Klein, R.E. (1975), 'VOT discrimination by four-to-six-and-a-half-month-old infants from Spanish environments', *Journal of Experimental Child Psychology*, *20*, 215–25.

Latto, R., Campion, J. (1986), 'Approaches to consciousness: Psychophysics or philosophy?', *Behavioral and Brain Sciences*, *9*, 36–7.

Lefebvre-Pinard, M. (1985), 'La régulation de la communication de l'enfance à l'âge adulte', *in* G. Noizet, Bélanger and F. Bresson (eds), *La communication*, Paris: PUF.

Lenel, J.C., Cantor, J.H. (1981), 'Rhyme recognition and phonemic perception in young children', *Journal of Psycholinguistic Research*, *10*, 57–67.

Levelt, W.J.M., Sinclair, A., Jarvella, R.J. (1978), 'Causes and functions of linguistic awareness in language acquisition: Some introductory remarks', *in* A. Sinclair, R.J. Jarvella and W.J.M. Levelt (eds), *The Child's Conception of Language*, Berlin: Springer-Verlag.

Levin, J.A., Reil, M.M., Rowe, R.D., Boruta, M.J. (1985), 'Muktuk meets Jacuzzi: Computer networks and elementary school writers', *in* S.W. Freedman (ed.), *The Acquisition of Written Langauge: Response and revision*, Norwood, MA: Ablex.

Liberman, I.Y. (1973), 'Segmentation of the spoken word and reading acquisition', *Bulletin of the Orton Society*, *23*, 65–77.

Liberman, I.Y., Shankweiler, D., Fisher, W.F., Carter, B. (1974), 'Explicit syllable and phoneme segmentation in the young child', *Journal of Experimental Child Psychology*, *18*, 201–12.

Lloyd, P. (1985), *The Ability to Communicate Route Directions by Telephone: A comparison of the performance of 7-year-olds and adults*, 8th ISSBD Biennial Meeting, Tours.

Lomax, R.G., McGee, L.M. (1987), 'Young children's concepts about print and reading: Toward a model of word reading acquisition', *Reading Research Quarterly*, *22*, 237–56.

Lundberg, I., Olofsson, A., Wall, S. (1980), 'Reading and spelling skills in the first school years predicted from phonemic awareness skills in kindergarten', *Scandinavian Journal of Psychology*, *21*, 159–73.

Lundberg, I., Tornéus, M. (1978), 'Nonreaders' awareness of the basic relationship between spoken and written words', *Journal of Experimental Child Psychology*, *25*, 404–12.

Lyons, J. (1975), 'Deixis and the source of reference', *in* E.L. Keenan (ed.), *Formal Semantics of Natural Language*, Cambridge: Cambridge University Press.

Maclean, M., Bryant, P., Bradley, L. (1987), 'Rhymes, nursery rhymes, and reading in early childhood', *Merrill-Palmer Quarterly*, *33*, 255–81.

Mandler, G., Nakumura, Y. (1987), 'Aspects of consciousness', *Personality and Social Psychology Bulletin*, *13*, 299–313.

Mann, V.A. (1984), 'Longitudinal prediction and prevention of reading difficulty', *Annals of Dyslexia*, *34*, 117–37.

Mann, V.A. (1986), 'Phonological awareness: The role of reading experience', *Cognition*, *24*, 65–92.

Mann, V.A., Liberman, I.Y. (1984), 'Phonological awareness and verbal short-term memory', *Journal of Learning Disabilities*, *17*, 592–8.

Mann, V.A., Tobin, P., Wilson, R. (1987), 'Measuring phonological awareness through the invented spellings of kindergarten children', *Merrill-Palmer Quarterly*, *33*, 365–91.

Maratsos, M.P. (1973), 'Nonegocentric communication abilities in preschool children', *Child Development*, *44*, 697–700.

Markman, E.M. (1977), 'Realizing that you don't understand: A preliminary investigation', *Child Development*, *48*, 986–92.

Markman, E.M. (1979), 'Realizing that you don't understand: Elementary school children's awareness of inconsistencies', *Child Development*, *50*, 643–55.

Markman, E.M. (1981), 'Comprehension monitoring', *in* W.P. Dickson (ed.), *Children's Oral Communication Skills*, New York: Academic Press.

Markman, E.M. (1985), 'Comprehension monitoring: Developmental and educational issues', *in* S.F. Chipman, J.W. Segal and R. Glaser (eds), *Thinking and Learning Skills*, vol. 2, Hillsdale, NJ: Erlbaum.

Markman, E.M., Gorin, L. (1981), 'Children's ability to adjust their standards for evaluating comprehension', *Journal of Educational Psychology*, *73*, 320–5.

Markman, E.M., Wachtel, G.F. (1988), 'Children's use of exclusivity to constrain the meanings of words', *Cognitive Psychology*, *20*, 121–57.

Marshall, J.C., Morton, J. (1978), 'On the mechanics of EMMA', *in* A. Sinclair, R.J. Jarvella and W.J.M. Levelt (eds), *The Child's Conception of Language*, Berlin: Springer-Verlag.

Marslen-Wilson, W.D. (1973), 'Linguistic structure and speech shadowing at very short latencies', *Nature*, *244*, 522–3.

Marslen-Wilson, W.D., Tyler, L.K. (1975), 'Processing structure of sentence perception', *Nature*, *257*, 784–6.

Marslen-Wilson, W.D., Welsh, A. (1978), 'Processing interactions and lexical access during word recognition in continuous speech', *Cognitive Psychology*, *10*, 29–63.

Martlew, M. (1983), 'Problems and difficulties: Cognitive and communicative aspects of writing', *in* M. Martlew (ed.), *The Psychology of Written Language*, New York: Wiley.

Martlew, M., Connolly, K., McCleod, C. (1978), 'Language use, role and context in a five-year-old', *Journal of Child Language*, *5*, 81–99.

Masur, E.F. (1978), 'Preschool boys' speech modifications: The effect of listeners' linguistic levels and conversational responsiveness', *Child Development*, *49*, 924–7.

Matsuhashi, A. (1981), 'Pausing and planning: The tempo of written discourse production', *Research in the Teaching of English*, *15*, 113–34.

McClelland, J.L., Rumelhart, D.E. (1981), 'An interactive-activation model of context effects in letter perception, part 1: An account of basic findings', *Psychological Review*, *88*, 375–407.

McCusker, L.X., Hillinger, M.L., Bias, R.G. (1981), 'Phonological recoding and reading', *Psychological Bulletin*, *89*, 217–45.

McDevitt, T.M., Carroll, M. (1988), 'Are you trying to trick me? Some social influences on children's responses to problematic messages', *Merrill-Palmer Quarterly*, *34*, 131–45.

McGhee, P.E. (1979), *Humour: Its origin and development*, San Francisco: Freeman.

McKeough, A., Case, R. (1985), *Developmental Stages in Narrative Composition: A neo-Piagetian interpretation*, 8th ISSBD Biennial Meeting, Tours.

Mehler, J. (1976), 'Psycholinguistique et psychanalyse: quelques remarques', *Revue française de Psychanalyse*, *40*, 605–22.

Mehler, J. (1981), 'The role of syllables in speech processing: Infant and adult data', *Philosophical Transactions of the Royal Society*, *B295*, 333–52.

Mehler, J. (1986), *Structure and Function in Development*, 2nd ISSBD European Conference on Developmental Psychology, Rome.

Meline, T.J., Brackin, S.R. (1987), 'Language-impaired children's awareness of inadequate messages', *Journal of Speech and Hearing Disorders*, *52*, 263–70.

Menig-Peterson, C.L. (1975), 'The modification of communicative behavior in preschool-aged children as a function of the listener's perspective', *Child Development*, *46*, 1015–18.

Menyuk, P. (1985), 'Wherefore metalinguistic skills? A commentary on Bialystok and Ryan', *Merrill-Palmer Quarterly*, *31*, 253–9.

Mitterer, J.O. (1982), 'There are at least two kinds of poor readers: Whole-word poor readers and recording poor readers', *Canadian Journal of Psychology*, *36*, 445–61.

Miyawaki, K., Strange, W., Verbrugge, R., Liberman, A.M., Jenkins, J.J., Fujimura, O.

(1975), 'An effect of linguistic experience: The discrimination of /r/ and /l/ by native speakers of Japanese and English', *Perception and Psychophysics*, *18*, 331–40.

Morais, J. (1987*a*), 'Phonetic awareness and reading acquisition', *Psychological Research*, *49*, 147–52.

Morais, J. (1987*b*), 'Segmental analysis of speech and its relation to reading ability', *Annals of Dyslexia*, *37*, 126–41.

Morais, J., Alegria, J., Content, A. (1987*a*), 'The relationship between segmental analysis and alphabetic literacy: An interactive view', *European Bulletin of Cognitive Psychology*, *7*, 415–38.

Morais, J., Alegria, J., Content, A. (1987*b*), 'Segmental awareness: Respectable, useful, and almost always necessary', *European Bulletin of Cognitive Psychology*, *7*, 530–56.

Morais, J., Bertelson, P., Cary, L., Alegria, J. (1986), 'Literacy training and speech segmentation', *Cognition*, *24*, 45–64.

Morais, J., Cary, L., Alegria, J., Bertelson, P. (1979), 'Does awareness of speech as a sequence of phones arise spontaneously?', *Cognition*, *7*, 323–31.

Morais, J., Cluytens, M., Alegria, J. (1984), 'Segmentation abilities of dyslexics and normal readers', *Perceptual and Motor Skills*, *58*, 221–2.

Morocco, C.C. (1986), *'You Changed My Story!' Word processing as an intelligent environment for revision*, AERA Annual Meeting, San Francisco.

Morris, N.T., Crump, D.T. (1982), 'Syntactic and vocabulary development in the written language of learning disabled and non-learning disabled students at four age levels', *Learning Disability Quarterly*, *5*, 163–72.

Morton, J. (1969), 'Interaction of information in word recognition', *Psychological Review*, *76*, 165–78.

Mosenthal, P. (1979), 'Children's strategy preferences for resolving contradictory story information under two social conditions', *Journal of Experimental Child Psychology*, *28*, 323–43.

Nelson, K.E. (1974), 'Concept, word and sentence: Interrelations in acquisition and development', *Psychological Review*, *81*, 267–85.

Nelson, K.E. (1983), 'The conceptual basis of language', *in* T.B. Seilers and W. Wannenmacher (eds), *Concept Development and the Development of Word Meaning*, Berlin: Springer-Verlag.

Nesdale, A.R., Herriman, M.L., Tunmer, W.E. (1984), 'Phonological awareness in children', *in* W.E. Tunmer, C. Pratt and M.L. Herriman (eds), *Metalinguistic Awareness in Children*, Berlin: Springer-Verlag.

Nesdale, A.R., Pratt, C., Tunmer, W.E. (1985), 'Young children's detection of propositional inconsistencies in oral communication', *Australian Journal of Psychology*, *37*, 289–96.

Nesdale, A.R., Tunmer, W.E. (1984), 'The development of metalinguistic awareness: A methodological overview', *in* W.E. Tunmer, C. Pratt and M.L. Herriman (eds), *Metalinguistic Awareness in Children*, Berlin: Springer-Verlag.

Nold, E.W. (1981), 'Revising', *in* C.H. Frederiksen and J.F. Dominic (eds), *Writing: The nature, development, and teaching of written communication*, vol. 2, Hillsdale, NJ: Erlbaum.

Oller, D.K., Eilers, R.E., Bull, D.H., Carney, A.E. (1985), 'Prespeech vocalizations of a deaf infant: A comparison with normal metaphonological development', *Journal of Speech and Hearing Research*, *28*, 47–63.

Olofsson, A., Lundberg, I. (1985), 'Evaluation of long-term effects of phonemic awareness training in kindergarten: Illustrations of some methodological problems in evaluation research', *Scandinavian Journal of Psychology, 26,* 21–34.

Olson, G.M., Mack, R.L., Duffy, S.A. (1981), 'Cognitive aspects of genre', *Poetics, 10,* 283–315.

Osherson, D., Markman, E. (1975), 'Language and the ability to evaluate contradictions and tautologies', *Cognition, 3,* 213–26.

Owings, R.A., Petersen, G.A., Bransford, J.D., Morris, C.D., Stein, B.S. (1980), 'Spontaneous monitoring and regulation of learning: A comparison of successful and less successful fifth graders', *Journal of Educational Psychology, 72,* 250–56.

Papandropoulou, I., Sinclair, H. (1974), 'What is a word? Experimental study of children's ideas on grammar', *Human Development, 17,* 241–58.

Paris, S.G., Oka, E.R. (1986), 'Children's reading strategies, metacognition, and motivation', *Developmental Review, 6,* 25–56.

Patel, P.G., Soper, H.V. (1987), 'Acquisition of reading and spelling in a syllabo-alphabetic writing system', *Langauge and Speech, 30,* 69–81.

Patterson, C.J., Cosgrove, J.M., O'Brien, R.G. (1980), 'Nonverbal indicants of comprehension and noncomprehension in children', *Developmental Psychology, 16,* 38–48.

Patterson, C.J., Kister, M.C. (1981), 'The development of listener skills for referential communication', *in* W.P. Dickson (ed.), *Children's Oral Communication Skills,* New York: Academic Press.

Patterson, C.J., O'Brien, C., Kister, M.C., Carter, D.B., Kotonis, M.E. (1981), 'Development of comprehension monitoring as a function of context', *Developmental Psychology, 17,* 379–89.

Pearson, H., Wilkinson, A. (1986), 'The use of word processors in assisting children's writing development', *Educational Review, 38,* 169–87.

Pearson, P.D. (1975), 'The effect of grammatical complexity on children's comprehension, recall, and conception of certain semantic relations', *Reading Research Quarterly, 10,* 155–92.

Perfetti, C.A. (1985), *Reading Ability,* New York: Oxford University Press.

Perfetti, C.A., Beck, I., Bell, L., Hughes, C. (1987), 'Phonemic knowledge and learning to read are reciprocal: A longitudinal study of first grade children', *Merrill-Palmer Quarterly, 33,* 283–320.

Perl, S. (1980), 'Understanding composing', *College Composition and Communication, 31,* 363–9.

Perner, J., Leekam, S.R. (1986), 'Belief and quantity: Three-year-old's adaptation to listener's knowledge', *Journal of Child Language, 13,* 305–15.

Peterson, C.L., Danner, F.W., Flavell, J.H. (1972), 'Developmental changes in children's response to three indications of communicative failure', *Child Development, 43,* 1463–8.

Piaget, J. (1926), *La représentation du monde chez l'enfant,* Paris: Alcan (new edn, PUF, 1947).

Piaget, J. (1945), *La formation du symbole chez l'enfant,* Neuchâtel: Delachaux & Niestlé.

Piaget, J. (1974*a*), *La prise de conscience,* Paris: PUF.

Piaget, J. (1974*b*), *Réussir et comprendre,* Paris: PUF.

Piaget, J., Inhelder, B. (1966), *La psychologie de l'enfant,* Paris: PUF.

Piché, G.L., Rubin, D.L., Michlin, M.L. (1978), 'Age and social class in children's use of persuasive communicative appeals', *Child Development*, 49, 773–80.

Pintrich, P.R., Cross, D.R., Kozma, R.B., McKeachnie, W.J. (1986), 'Instructional psychology', *Annual Review of Psychology*, 37, 611–51.

Piolat, A. (1988), *Le retour sur le texte dans l'activité rédactionnelle précoce*, Colloque annuel de la section psychologie expérimentale de la SFP, Dijon.

Pisacreta, R., Gough, D., Redwood, E., Goodfellow, L. (1986), 'Auditory word discriminations in the pigeon', *Journal of the Experimental Analysis of Behavior*, 45, 269–82.

Pollart-Gott, L., McCloskey, M., Todres, A.K. (1979), 'Subjective story structure', *Discourse Processes*, 2, 251–81.

Pratt, C., Grieve, R. (1984a), 'Metalinguistic awareness and cognitive development', *in* W.E. Tunmer, C. Pratt and M.L. Herriman (eds), *Metalinguistic Awareness in Children*, Berlin: Springer-Verlag.

Pratt, C., Grieve, R. (1984b), 'The development of metalinguistic awareness: An introduction', *in* W.E. Tunmer, C. Pratt and M.L. Herriman (eds), *Metalinguistic Awareness in Children*, Berlin: Springer-Verlag.

Pratt, C., Nesdale, A.R. (1984), 'Pragmatic awareness in children', *in* W.E. Tunmer, C. Pratt and M.L. Herriman (eds), *Metalinguistic Awareness in Children*, Berlin: Springer-Verlag.

Pratt, C., Tunmer, W.E., Bowey, J.A. (1984), 'Children's capacity to correct grammatical violations in sentences', *Journal of Child Language*, 11, 129–41.

Pratt, M.W., Bates, K.R. (1982), 'Young editors: Preschoolers' evaluation and production of ambiguous messages', *Developmental Psychology*, 18, 30–42.

Prentice, N.M., Fatham, R.E. (1975), 'Joking riddles: A developmental index of children's humor', *Developmental Psychology*, 10, 210–16.

Read, C. (1971), 'Pre-school children's knowledge of English phonology', *Harvard Educational Review*, 41, 1–34.

Read, C. (1978), 'Children's awareness of language, with emphasis on sound system', *in* A. Sinclair, R.J. Jarvella and W.J.M. Levelt (eds), *The Child's Conception of Language*, Berlin: Springer-Verlag.

Read, C., Zhang Yun-Fei, Nie Hong-Yin, Ding Bao-Qing (1986), 'The ability to manipulate speech sounds depends on knowing alphabetic writing', *Cognition*, 24, 31–44.

Reynolds, R.E., Wade, S.I. (1986), 'Thinking about thinking: Reflections on metacognition', *Harvard Educational Review*, 56, 307–16.

Rickards, J.P. (1980), 'Adjunct postquestions in text: A critical review of methods and processes', *Review of Educational Research*, 49, 181–96.

Riesbeck, C.K. (1980), ' "You can't miss it!": Judging the clarity of directions', *Cognitive Science*, 4, 285–303.

Robinson, E.J. (1981), 'The child's understanding of inadequate messages and communication failures: A problem of ignorance or egocentrism?' *in* W.P. Dickson (ed.), *Children's Oral Communication Skills*, New York: Academic Press.

Robinson, E.J., Gœlman, H., Olson, D.R. (1983), 'Children's understanding of the relation between expressions (what was said) and intentions (what was meant)', *British Journal of Developmental Psychology*, 1, 75–86.

Robinson, E.J., Robinson, W.P. (1976), 'Developmental changes in the child's explanation of communication failure', *Australian Journal of Psychology*, 28, 155–65.

Robinson, E.J., Robinson, W.P. (1977), 'Children's explanations of communication failure and the inadequacy of the misunderstood message', *Developmental Psychology*, *13*, 156–61.

Robinson, E.J., Robinson, W.P. (1978), 'The relationship between children's explanations of communication failure and their ability deliberately to give bad messages', *British Journal of Social and Clinical Psychology*, *17*, 219–25.

Robinson, E.J., Robinson, W.P. (1983), 'Children's uncertainty about the interpretation of ambiguous messages', *Journal of Experimental Child Psychology*, *36*, 81–98.

Robinson, E.J., Whittaker, S.J. (1985), 'Children's response to ambiguous messages and their understanding of ambiguity', *Developmental Psychology*, *21*, 446–54.

Robinson, E.J., Whittaker, S.J. (1986), 'Children's conceptions of meaning–message relationships', *Cognition*, *22*, 41–60.

Rogers, S. (1978), 'Self-initiated corrections in the speech of infant-school children', *Journal of Child Language*, *5*, 365–71.

Rosegrant, T. (1984), 'Fostering progress in literacy development: Technology and social interaction', *Seminars in Speech and Language*, *5*, 47–57.

Rosner, J., Simon, D.P. (1971), 'The auditory analysis test: An initial report', *Journal of Learning Disabilities*, *4*, 384–92.

Routh, D.K., Fox, B. (1984), ' "MM ... is a little bit of May": Phonemes, reading, and spelling', *Advances in Learning and Behavioral Disabilities*, *3*, 94–124.

Rozin, P., Bressman, B., Taft, M. (1974), 'Do children understand the basic relationship between speech and writing? The mow-motorcycle test', *Journal of Reading Behavior*, *6*, 327–34.

Rozin, P., Gleitman, L. (1977), 'The structure and acquisition of reading, 2: The reading process and the acquisition of the alphabetic principle of reading', *in* A.S. Reber and D.L. Scarborough (eds), *Towards a Psychology of Reading*, Hillsdale, NJ: Erlbaum.

Ryan, E.B. (1980), 'Metalinguistic development and reading', *in* F.B. Murray (ed.), *Language Awareness and Reading*, Newark, NJ: International Reading Association.

Ryan, E.B., Ledger, G.W. (1979), 'Grammaticality judgments, sentence repetitions, and sentence corrections of children learning to read', *International Journal of Psycholinguistics*, *6*, 23–40.

Sachs, J. (1974), 'Memory in reading and listening to discourse', *Memory and Cognition*, *2*, 95–100.

Sachs, J., Devin, J. (1976), 'Young children's use of age-appropriate speech styles in social interaction and role-playing', *Journal of Child Language*, *3*, 81–98.

Sakata, S. (1987), 'The development of referential communication', *Journal of Human Development*, *23*, 31–41.

Scardamalia, M., Bereiter, C. (1983), 'The development of evaluative, diagnostic, and remedial capabilities in children's composing', *in* M. Martlew (ed.), *The Psychology of Written Language: Developmental and educational perspectives*, Sussex: Wiley.

Schank, R.C., Abelson, R.P. (1977), *Scripts, Plans, Goals, and Understanding*, Hillsdale, NJ: Erlbaum.

Scheerer-Neumann, G. (1981), 'The utilization of intraword structure in poor readers: Experimental evidence and a training program', *Psychological Research*, *43*, 155–78.

Schiff, N., Ventry, I. (1976), 'Communication problems in hearing children of deaf parents', *Journal of Speech and Hearing Disorders*, *41*, 348–58.

Schmidt, C.R., Paris, S.G. (1983), 'Children's use of successive clues to generate and monitor inferences', *Child Development*, 54, 742–59.

Schmidt, C.R., Paris, S.G. (1984), 'The development of verbal communicative skills in children', *Advances in Child Development and Behavior*, 18, 1–47.

Schmidt, C.R., Schmidt, S.R., Tomalis, S.M. (1984), 'Children's constructive processing and monitoring of stories containing anomalous information', *Child Development*, 55, 2056–71.

Schneider, W. (1985), 'Developmental trends in the metamemory–memory behavior relationship: An integrative review', *in* D.L. Forrest-Pressley, G.E. MacKinnon and T.G. Waller (eds), *Metacognition, Cognition and Human Performance*, vol. 1, New York: Academic Press.

Schneuwly, B. (1989), 'La conception vygotskyenne du langage écrit', *Etudes de Linguistique appliquée*, 73, 107–17.

Schneuwly, B., Bronckart, J.-P. (1985), *Vygotsky aujourd'hui*, Neuchâtel: Delachaux & Niestlé.

Scholl, D.M., Ryan, E.B. (1975), 'Child judgements of sentences varying in grammatical complexity', *Journal of Experimental Child Psychology*, 20, 274–85.

Scholl, D.M., Ryan, E.B. (1980), 'Development of metalinguistic performance in the early school years', *Language and Speech*, 23, 199–211.

Scollon, R. (1976), *Conversation with a One Year Old: A case study of the developmental foundation of language*, Honolulu: University Press of Hawaii.

Scribner, S., Cole, M. (1981), *The Psychology of Literacy*, Cambridge, MA: Harvard University Press.

Ségui, J., Kail, M. (1984), 'Le traitement de phrases localement ambigues: l'attribution de la coréférence des pronoms', *in* M. Moscato and G. Piéraut-Le Bonniec (eds), *Le langage: construction et actualisation*, Rouen: Presses Universitaires de Rouen.

Selfe, C. (1985), 'The electronic pen: Computers and the composing process', *in* J. Collins and E. Sommers (eds), *Writing On-Line*, Upper Montclair: Boynton/Cook.

Shanahan, T., Lomax, R.G. (1986), 'An analysis and comparison of theoretical models of the reading–writing relationship', *Journal of Educational Psychology*, 78, 116–23.

Share, D.L., Jorm, A.F., MacLean, R., Matthews, R. (1984), 'Sources of individual differences in reading acquisition', *Journal of Educational Psychology*, 76, 1309–24.

Shatz, M., Gelman, R. (1973), 'The development of communication skills: Modification in the speech of young children as a function of listener', *Monographs of the Society for Research in Child Development*, 38, 1–38.

Shatz, M., Gelman, R. (1977), 'Beyond syntax: The influence of conversation constraints on speech modifications', *in* C. Snow and C.A. Ferguson (eds), *Talking to Children*, London: Cambridge University Press.

Shultz, T.R. (1976), 'A cognitive-developmental analysis of humour', *in* A.J. Chapman and H.C. Foot (eds), *Humour and Laughter: Theory, research, and applications*, Sussex: Wiley.

Shultz, T.R., Robillard, J. (1980), 'The development of linguistic humour in children: Incongruity through rule violation', *in* P. McGhee and A. Chapman (eds), *Children's Humour*, New York: Wiley.

Siegel, L.S. Ryan, E.B. (1988), 'Development of grammatical-sensitivity, phonological, and short-term memory skills in normally achieving and learning disabled children', *Developmental Psychology*, *24*, 28–37.

Siltanen, S.A. (1986), ' "Butterflies are rainbows?": A developmental investigation of metaphor comprehension', *Communication Education*, *35*, 1–12.

Simpson, L., Byrne, B. (1987), 'Phonological awareness in reading-disabled adults: A follow-up and extension', *Australian Journal of Psychology*, *39*, 1–10.

Sinclair, A. (1981), 'Children's judgements of inappropriate "speech acts" ', *International Journal of Psycholinguistics*, *8*, 75–94.

Sinclair, A., Siegrist, F., Sinclair, H. (1983), 'Young children's ideas about the written number system', *in* D. Rogers and J. Sloboda (eds), *The Acquisition of Symbolic Skills*, New York: Plenum.

Sinclair, A., Sinclair, H. (1984), 'Preschool children's interpretation of written numbers', *Human Learning*, *3*, 173–84.

Sinnott, J.A., Ross, B.M. (1976), 'Comparison of aggression and incongruity as factors in children's judgments of humor', *The Journal of Genetic Psychology*, *128*, 241–9.

Slobin, D.I. (1978), 'A case study of early language awareness', *in* A. Sinclair, R.J. Jarvella and W.J.M. Levelt (eds), *The Child's Conception of Language*, Berlin: Springer-Verlag.

Smiley, S., Oakley, D.D., Worthend, D., Campione, J.C., Brown, A.L. (1977), 'Recall of thematically relevant material by adolescent good and poor readers as a function of written versus oral presentation', *Journal of Educational Psychology*, *69*, 381–7.

Smith, C.L., Tager-Flusberg, H. (1982), 'Metalinguistic awareness and language development', *Journal of Experimental Child Psychology*, *34*, 449–68.

Smith, J.W. (1976), 'Children's comprehension of metaphor: A Piagetian interpretation', *Language and Speech*, *19*, 236–43.

Smith, M.E. (1935), 'A study of some factors influencing the development of the sentence in preschool children', *Journal of Genetic Psychology*, *46*, 182–212.

Snyder, A.D. (1914), 'Notes on the talk of a two-and-a-half year old boy', *Pedagogical Seminary*, *21*, 412–24.

Sodian, B. (1988), 'Children's attributions of knowledge to the listener in a referential communication task', *Child Development*, *59*, 378–85.

Sommers, N. (1980), 'Revision strategies of student writers and experienced adult writers', *College Composition and Communication*, *31*, 378–88.

Sonnenschein, S. (1986*a*), 'Developing referential communication: Transfer across novel tasks', *Bulletin of the Psychonomic Society*, *24*, 127–30.

Sonnenschein, S. (1986*b*), 'Development of referential communication: Deciding that a message is uninformative', *Developmental Psychology*, *22*, 164–8.

Sonnenschein, S., Whitehurst, G. (1983), 'Training referential communication: The limits of success', *Journal of Experimental Child Psychology*, *35*, 426–36.

Sonnenschein, S., Whitehurst, G. (1984*a*), 'Developing referential communication: A hierarchy of skills', *Child Development*, *55*, 1936–45.

Sonnenschein, S., Whitehurst, G. (1984*b*), 'Developing referential communication skills: The interaction of role-switching and difference rule training', *Journal of Experimental Child Psychology*, *38*, 191–207.

Spilton, D., Lee, C.L. (1977), 'Some determinants of effective communication in four-year-olds', *Child Development*, *48*, 968–77.

Stanovich, K.E., Cunningham, A.E., Cramer, B.R. (1984), 'Assessing phonological awareness in kindergarten children: Issues of task comparability,' *Journal of Experimental Child Psychology, 38,* 175–90.

Stanovich, K.E., Nathan, R.G., Vala-Rossi, M. (1986), 'Developmental changes in the cognitive correlates of reading ability and the developmental lag hypothesis', *Reading Research Quarterly, 21,* 267–83.

Stanovich, K.E., Nathan, R.G., Zolman, J.E. (1988), 'The developmental lag hypothesis in reading: Longitudinal and matched reading-level comparisons', *Child Development, 59,* 71–86.

Stein, N.L., Policastro, M. (1984), 'The concept of a story: A comparison between children's and teachers' viewpoint', *in* H. Mandl, N.L. Stein and T. Trabasso (eds), *Learning and Comprehension of Text,* Hillsdale, NJ: Erlbaum.

Stenning, K., Michell, L. (1985), 'Learning how to tell a good story: The development of content and language in children's telling of one tale', *Discourse Processes, 8,* 261–79.

Sternberg, R.J. (1986), 'The trickie theory of untouched giftedness', *in* R.J. Sternberg and J.E. Davidson (eds), *Conceptions of Giftedness,* Cambridge: Cambridge University Press.

Streeter, L.A. (1976), 'Language perception of 2-month-old infants shows effects of both innate mechanisms and experience', *Nature, 259,* 39–41.

Stuart-Hamilton, I. (1986), 'The role of phonemic awareness in the reading style of beginning readers', *British Journal of Educational Psychology, 56,* 271–86.

Surian, L., Job, R. (1987), 'Children's use of conversational rules in a referential communication task', *Journal of Psycholinguistic Research, 16,* 369–82.

Sutton-Smith, B. (1976), 'A developmental structural account of riddles', *in* B. Kirschenblatt-Gimblett (ed.), *Speech Play,* Philadelphia: University of Pennsylvania Press.

Swinney, D., Cutler, A. (1979), 'Access and processing of idiomatic expressions', *Journal of Verbal Learning and Verbal Behavior, 18,* 523–34.

Taylor, B.M., Samuels, S.J. (1983), 'Children's use of text structure in the recall of expository material', *American Educational Research Journal, 20,* 517–28.

Taylor, K.K. (1984), 'Can college students summarize?', *Journal of Reading, 26,* 524–8.

Teberosky, A., Ferreiro, E. (1980), 'Genèse et fonctionnement du système d'écriture chez l'enfant', *in* Association Française pour la Lecture (ed.), *Cinq contributions pour comprendre la lecture,* Paris: Editions de l'EFL.

Templeton, S., Spivey, E.M. (1980), 'The concept of word in young children as a function of level of cognitive development', *Research in the Teaching of English, 14,* 265–78.

Tikhomirov, O.K., Klochko, V.E. (1981), 'The detection of a contradiction as the initial stage of problem formation', *in* J. Wertsch (ed.), *The Concept of Activity in Soviet Psychology,* Armonk: Sharpe.

Tinzmann, M., Cox, B., Sulby, Y.E. (1983), 'Children's specification of context in told and dictated story productions', *in* J.A. Niles and L.A. Harris (eds), *Searches for Meaning in Reading, Language Processing, and Instruction,* 'The National Reading Conference', Virginia Polytechnic Institute and State University.

Tolchinsky-Landsmann, L., Levin, I. (1985), 'Writing in preschoolers: An age-related analysis', *Applied Psycholinguistics, 6,* 319–39.

Tolchinsky-Landsmann, L., Levin, I. (1987), 'Writing in four- to six-year-olds: Representation of semantic and phonetic similarities and differences', *Journal of Child Language, 14,* 127–44.

Tornéus, M. (1984), 'Phonological awareness and reading: A chicken and egg problem?', *Journal of Educational Psychology, 76,* 1346–58.

Torrance, N., Olson, D.R. (1984), 'Oral language competence and the acquisition of literacy', *in* A. Pellegrini and T.D. Yawkey (eds), *The Development of Oral and Written Language in Social Contexts,* Norwood, MA: Ablex.

Torrance, N., Olson, D.R. (1987), 'Development of the metalanguage and the acquisition of literacy: A progress report', *Interchange, 18,* 136–46.

Tourangeau, R., Sternberg, R.J. (1982), 'Understanding and appreciating metaphors', *Cognition, 11,* 203–44.

Treiman, R. (1985), 'Onsets and rimes as units of spoken syllables: Evidence from children', *Journal of Experimental Child Psychology, 39,* 161–81.

Treiman, R., Baron, J. (1981), 'Segmental analysis ability: Development and relation to reading ability', *in* G.E. MacKinnon and T.G. Walker (eds), *Reading Research: Advances in theory and practice,* vol. 3, New York: Academic Press.

Tunmer, W.E., Bowey, J.A. (1981), 'The development of word segmentation skills in children', *in* A.R. Nesdale, C. Pratt, R. Grieve, J. Field, D. Illingworth and J. Hogben (eds), *Advances in Child Development: Theory and research,* Perth: NCCD.

Tunmer, W.E., Bowey, J.A. (1984), 'Metalinguistic awareness and reading acquisition', *in* W.E. Tunmer, C. Pratt and M.L. Herriman, (eds), *Metalinguistic Awareness in Children,* Berlin: Springer-Verlag.

Tunmer, W.E., Bowey, J.A., Grieve, R. (1983*a*), 'The development of young children's awareness of the word as a unit of spoken language', *Journal of Psycholinguistic Research, 12,* 567–94.

Tunmer, W.E., Fletcher, C.M. (1981), 'The relationship between conceptual tempo, phonological awareness, and word recognition in beginning readers', *Journal of Reading Behavior, 13,* 173–86.

Tunmer, W.E., Grieve, R. (1984), 'Syntactic awareness in children', *in* W.E. Tunmer, C. Pratt and M.L. Herriman (eds), *Metalinguistic Awareness in Children,* Berlin: Springer-Verlag.

Tunmer, W.E., Herriman, M.L. (1984), 'The development of metalinguistic awareness: A conceptual overview', *in* W.E. Tunmer, C. Pratt and M.L. Herriman (eds), *Metalinguistic Awareness in Children,* Berlin: Springer-Verlag.

Tunmer, W.E., Nesdale, A.R. (1982), 'The effects of disgraphs and pseudo-words on phonemic segmentation in young children', *Journal of Applied Psycholinguistics, 3,* 299–311.

Tunmer, W.E., Nesdale, A.R. (1985), 'Phonemic representation skill and beginning reading', *Journal of Educational Psychology, 77,* 417–27.

Tunmer, W.E., Nesdale, A.R., Pratt, C. (1983*b*), 'The development of young children's awareness of logical inconsistencies', *Journal of Experimental Child Psychology, 36,* 97–108.

Tunmer, W.E., Nesdale, A.R., Wright, A.D. (1987), 'Syntatic awareness and reading acquisition', *British Journal of Developmental Psychology, 5,* 25–34.

Tyler, L.K., Marslen-Wilson, W.D. (1978), 'Some developmental aspects of sentence processing and memory', *Journal of Child Language, 5,* 113–29.

Van Kleeck, A. (1982), 'The emergence of linguistic awareness: A cognitive framework', *Merrill-Palmer Quarterly*, *28*, 237–65.

Van Kleeck, A. (1984), 'Metalinguistic skills: Cutting across spoken and written language and problem-solving abilities', *in* G.P. Wallach and K.G. Butler (eds), *Language Learning Disabilities in School-Age Children*, Baltimore, MD: Williams & Wilkins.

Van Wijk, C.H. (1987), *Speaking, Writing, and Sentence Form: Three psycholinguistic studies*, privately circulated thesis, Nijmegen University, The Netherlands: personal communication.

Vetter, H.J., Volovecky, J., Howell, R.W. (1979), 'Judgments of grammaticalness: A partial replication and extension', *Journal of Psycholinguistic Research*, *8*, 567–83.

Vivier, J. (1988), 'La tâche de l'élève et l'auto-contrôle', *Revue française de Pédagogie*, *82*, 61–4.

Vosniadou, S. (1987), 'Children and metaphors', *Child Development*, *58*, 870–85.

Vosniadou, S., Ortony, A. (1983), 'The emergence of literal-metaphorical-anomalous distinction in young children', *Child Development*, *54*, 154–61.

Vosniadou, S., Ortony, A. (1986), 'Testing the metaphoric competence of the young child: Paraphrase versus enactment', *Human Development*, *29*, 226–30.

Vosniadou, S., Ortony, A., Reynolds, R.E., Wilson, P.T. (1984), 'Sources of difficulty in the young child's understanding of metaphorical language', *Child Development*, *55*, 1588–1606.

Vosniadou, S., Pearson, P.D., Rogers, T. (1988), 'What causes children's failures to detect inconsistencies in text? Representation versus comparison difficulties', *Journal of Educational Psychology*, *80*, 27–39.

Vygotsky, L.S. (1934), *Thought and Language*, English translation: Cambridge, MA: MIT Press, 1962.

Vygotsky, L.S. (1935), 'The prehistory of written language', English translation *in* L.S. Vygotsky, *Mind in Society*, Cambridge, MA: MIT Press, 1978.

Waggoner, J.E., Messe, M.J., Palermo, D.S. (1985), 'Grasping the meaning of metaphor: Story recall and comprehension', *Child Development*, *56*, 1156–66.

Wagner, R.K., Torgesen, J.K. (1987), 'The nature of phonological processing and its causal role in the acquisition of reading skills', *Psychological Bulletin*, *101*, 192–212.

Wales, R.J. (1974), 'Children's sentences make sense of the world', *in* F. Bresson (ed.), *Problèmes actuels en psycholinguistique*, Paris: PUF.

Wallach, L., Wallach, M.A., Dozier, M.G., Kaplan, N.W. (1977), 'Poor children learning to read do not have trouble with auditory discrimination but do have trouble with phoneme recognition', *Journal of Educational Psychology*, *69*, 36–9.

Wallach, M.A., Wallach, L. (1976), *Teaching All Children to Read*, Chicago: University of Chicago Press.

Warden, D. (1976), 'The influence of context on children's uses of identifying expressions and references', *British Journal of Psychology*, *67*, 101–12.

Warren, R.M., (1970), 'Perceptual restoration of missing speech sounds', *Science*, *167*, 392–3.

Warren-Leubecker, A. (1987), 'Competence and performance factors in word order awareness and early reading', *Journal of Experimental Child Psychology*, *43*, 62–80.

Waters, G.S., Seidenberg, M.S., Bruck, M. (1984), 'Children's and adults' use of spelling–sound information in three reading tasks', *Memory and Cognition*, *12*, 293–305.

Watzlawick, P., Beavin, J.H., Jackson, D.D. (1967), *Pragmatics of Human Communication*, New York: Norton.

Weeks, T. (1971), 'Speech registers in young children', *Child Development*, 42, 1119–31.

Weir, R.H. (1962), *Language in the Crib*, The Hague: Mouton.

Weir, R.H. (1966), 'Some questions on the child's learning of phonology', in F. Smith and G.A. Miller (eds), *The Genesit of Language*, Cambridge, MA: MIT Press.

Wellman, H.M., Johnson, C.N. (1979), 'Understanding of mental processes: A developmental study of "remember" and "forget" ', *Child Development*, 50, 79–88.

Wilcox, M.J., Webster, E.J. (1980), 'Early discourse behavior: An analysis of children's response to listener feedback', *Child Development*, 51, 1120–25.

Wilkinson, L.C., Genishi, C.C. (1987), 'Metapragmatic knowledge of school-age Mexican-American children', in S. Goldman and H. Trueba (eds), *Becoming Literate in English as a Second Language*, Norwood, MA: Ablex.

Wilkinson, L.C., Wilkinson, A.C., Spinelli, F., Chi Pang Chiang (1984), 'Metalinguistic knowledge of pragmatic rules in school-age children', *Child Development*, 55, 2130–40.

Williams, J.P. (1980), 'Teaching decoding with an emphasis on phoneme blending', *Journal of Educational Psychology*, 72, 1–15.

Williams, J.P., Taylor, M.B., Ganger, S. (1981), 'Text variations at the level of the individual sentence and the comprehension of simple expository paragraphs', *Journal of Educational Psychology*, 73, 851–65.

Winner, E. (1979), 'New names for old things: The emergence of metaphoric language', *Journal of Child Language*, 6, 469–91.

Winner, E., Engel, M., Gardner, H. (1980), 'Misunderstanding metaphor: What's the problem?', *Journal of Experimental Child Psychology*, 30, 22–32.

Winner, E., McCarthy, M., Kleinman, S., Gardner, H. (1979), 'First metaphors', in H. Gardner and D. Wolf (eds), *Early Symbolization: New directions for child development*, 4, San Francisco: Jossey-Bass.

Winner, E., Rosenstiel, A.K., Gardner, H. (1976), 'The development of metaphoric understanding', *Developmental Psychology*, 12, 289–97.

Winograd, P.N. (1984), 'Strategic difficulties in summarizing texts', *Reading Research Quarterly*, 19, 404–25.

Wise, B., Olson, R., Truman, R. (1990), 'Sub-syllabic units computerized reading instruction: Onset-rime versus post-vowel segmentation', *Journal of Experimental Child Psychology*, 49, 1–19.

Womble, G. (1985), 'Revising and computing', in J. Collins and E. Sommers (eds), *Writing On-line*, Upper Montclair: Boynton/Cook.

Wykes, T. (1981), 'Inference and children's comprehension of pronouns', *Journal of Experimental Child Psychology*, 32, 264–78.

Wykes, T. (1983), 'The role of inferences in children's comprehension of pronouns', *Journal of Experimental Child Psychology*, 35, 180–93.

Yde, P., Spoelders, M. (1985), 'Text cohesion: An exploratory study with beginning writers', *Applied Psycholinguistics*, 6, 407–16.

Zagar, D. (1988), 'L'utilisation du temps d'exposition comme indicateur du temps de traitement pendant la lecture', in J.-P. Caverni, C. Bastien, P. Mendelsohn and G. Tiberghien (eds), *Psychologie cognitive: modèles et méthodes*, Grenoble: Presses Universitaires de Grenoble.

Zhurova, L.Y. (1973), 'The development of analysis of words into their sounds by preschool children', *in* C.A. Ferguson and D.I. Slobin (eds), *Studies of Child Language Development*, New York: Holt, Rinehart & Winston.

Name Index

Subject Index